Issues in Progress

    The Aftermath of Genocide: Psychological Perspectives
    Johanna Vollhardt & Michal Bilewicz
    The Flexibility Stigma
    Joan C. William, Shelly J. Correll, Jennifer Glass, & Jennifer L. Berdahi
    Uncertainty and Extremism
    Michael Hogg, Arie Kruglanski & Kess van den Bos
    Ethnic-racial Stigma and Physical Health Disparities in the United States of America: From Psychological Theory and Evidence to Public Policy Solutions
    Luis M. Rivera & Danielle Beatty

Editorial Advisory Board

    Dominic Abrams, University of Kent at Canterbury, United Kingdom
    Manuela Barreto, University of Exeter, United Kingdom
    Allan B.I. Bernardo, De La Salle University, Philippines
    Chi-yue Chiu, Nanyang Technological University, Singapore
    Jacquelynne Eccles, University of Michigan, United States
    Jennifer E. Graham, The Pennsylvania State University, United States
    Carolin Hagelskamp, New York University, United States
    Nick Haslam, University of Melbourne, Australia
    Ying-yi Hong, Nanyang Technological University, Singapore
    Melanie Killen, University of Maryland, College Park, United States
    Rodolfo Mendoza-Denton, University of California at Berkeley, United States
    Jason Plaks, University of Toronto, Canada
    Luisa Ramirez, Universidad del Rosario, Colombia
    Jennifer Richeson, Northwestern University, United States
    Lisa Rosenthal, Yale University, United States
    Adam Rutland, University of Kent at Canterbury, United Kingdom
    Isis Settles, Michigan State University, United States
    Beth Shinn, Vanderbilt University, United States
    Maykel Verkuyten, Utrecht University, The Netherlands
    Johanna Vollhardt, Clark University, United States

Past JSI Editors
Rick H. Hoyle (2006–2009)
Irene Hanson Frieze (2001–2005)
Phyllis Katz (1997–2000)
Daniel Perlman (1993–1996)
Stuart Oskamp (1988–1992)
George Levinger (1984–1987)
Joseph E. McGrath (1979–1983)
Jacqueline D. Goodchilds (1974–1978)
Bertram H. Raven (1970–1973)
Joshua A. Fishman (1966–1969)
Leonard Solomon (1963)
Robert Chin (1960–1965)
John Harding (1956–1959)
M. Brewster Smith (1951–1955)
Harold H. Kelley (1949)
Ronald Lippitt (1944–1950)

2012 Vol. 68, No. 4

Sustainability in Combining Career and Care

Issue Editors: Marloes L. van Engen, Claartje J. Vinkenburg, and Josje S. E. Dikkers

INTRODUCTION
Sustainability in Combining Career and Care: Challenging Normative
    Beliefs about Parenting   645
    Marloes L. van Engen, Claartje J. Vinkenburg, and Josje S. E. Dikkers

SECTION I: THE WORK-FAMILY INTERFACE
Workload, Work-to-Family Conflict, and Health: Gender Differences
    and the Influence of Private Life Context   665
    Marc J. P. M. van Veldhoven and Susanne E. Beijer
The Association between Work–Family Guilt and Pro- and Anti-Social
    Work Behavior   684
    Whitney Botsford Morgan and Eden B. King

SECTION II: NORMATIVE BELIEFS ABOUT PARENTING
The "Bad Parent" Assumption: How Gender Stereotypes Affect
    Reactions to Working Mothers   704
    Tyler G. Okimoto and Madeline E. Heilman
Bias in Employment Decisions about Mothers and Fathers: The
    (Dis)Advantages of Sharing Care Responsibilities   725
    Claartje J. Vinkenburg, Marloes L. van Engen, Jennifer Coffeng,
    and Josje S. E. Dikkers

**SECTION III: FAMILY-FRIENDLY ARRANGEMENTS
AND INDIVIDUAL CAREER OUTCOMES**
Pursuing Career Success while Sustaining Personal and Family Well-Being:
    A Study of Reduced-Load Professionals over Time   742
    Douglas T. Hall, Mary Dean Lee, Ellen Ernst Kossek,
    and Mireia Las Heras
Entitled to a Sustainable Career? Motherhood in Science, Engineering,
    and Technology   767
    Clem Herman and Suzan Lewis

SECTION IV: THE WORK-FAMILY INTERFACE AND COUPLE- AND FAMILY-RELATED OUTCOMES

Work–Family Conflict in Sri Lanka: Negotiations of Exchange
      Relationships in Family and at Work   790
  Pavithra Kailasapathy and Isabel Metz

The More Things Change, the More They Stay the Same: Gender,
      Culture, and College Students' Views about Work and Family   814
  Wendy A. Goldberg, Erin Kelly, Nicole L. Matthews,
  Hannah Kang, Weilin Li, and Mariya Sumaroka

DISCUSSION

The "Triple-N" Model: Changing Normative Beliefs about Parenting
      and Career Success   838
  Steven Poelmans

Sustainability in Combining Career and Care: Challenging Normative Beliefs about Parenting

Marloes L. van Engen[*]
Tilburg University

Claartje J. Vinkenburg
VU Amsterdam

Josje S. E. Dikkers
University of Applied Sciences Utrecht

In this introduction to the special issue on "Sustainability in Combining Career and Care," we argue that demographic developments such as ageing populations demand attention to the long-term consequences of using family friendly arrangements. In order to create and support sustainability in combining career and care, we address normative beliefs about parenting, behavior or "choices" in combining work and family, and outcomes for individual careers, couples, and children. We provide an integrative framework for combining career and care, thereby incorporating the individual, organizational, and societal level of the work–family interface. In this first paper, the eight empirical contributions to this special issue are introduced, the collective message being that normative beliefs about parenting need to be challenged in order to create change and promote sustainability for working parents.

For working parents, combining work and family or career and care is a source of joy and enrichment but also of conflict and stress. In most industrialized nations, a host of family-friendly arrangements—such as parental leave, part-time work, and flexible hours—are available to help support working parents in their efforts to combine work and care responsibilities. There are few conclusive answers as to what the long-term effects are of the presence and utilization of such arrangements

---

[*]Correspondence concerning this article should be addressed to Marloes L. van Engen, Department of Human Resource Studies, Tilburg University, PO Box 90153, 5000 LE Tilburg, The Netherlands [e-mail: m.l.vengen@tilburguniversity.edu].

on careers, couples, and children, despite ample evidence of the short-term effects of family-friendly arrangements in reducing work–family conflict and promoting work outcomes such as performance and commitment (Kelly et al., 2008).

In the light of current demographic developments common to industrialized nations, such as growing numbers of dual earners and ageing populations, how to create and promote sustainability in combining career and care is an increasingly important social issue. Sustainability or sustainable development refers to meeting present or current needs without compromising the ability to meet future needs (McKenzie-Mohr & Oskamp, 1995; Oskamp, 2000). This responsibility has environmental, economic, and social dimensions, linking planet, profit, and people (Van Marrewijk & Werre, 2003). While the goal of sustainability is not yet commonly applied to Human Resources Management (Ehnert, 2009), this would imply that employers take the present and future well-being and performance of their employees into account. While short-term solutions (e.g., taking up parental leave, working part-time) may sometimes be effective in lessening the daily demands on employees of combining work and family, demographic developments require that we take a long-term perspective. As normative beliefs about parenting (Dikkers, van Engen, & Vinkenburg, 2010) based on gender roles are assumed to underlie work–family behavior and "choices" that parents make in combining career and care, sustainability can only be achieved by critically examining such beliefs and their impact on parents' behavior and outcomes. Ultimately, research showing the long-term benefits of combining career and care for parents and children can be instrumental in challenging traditional notions of (exclusively) caring mothers and working fathers.

This issue of the *Journal of Social Issues* aims to raise awareness of creating and improving sustainability in combining career and care by addressing beliefs, behaviors, and outcomes, and by incorporating the individual, organizational, and societal level of the work–family interface. Because of our interest in long-term rather than short-term consequences of combining work and family we specifically use the term career. When we refer to a career, we mean the evolving sequence of an individual's work experiences over time, following the definition of Arthur, Hall, and Lawrence (1989), and do not mean to imply a career in the sense of hierarchical upward mobility. However, the terms work and career are both used throughout this special issue. While most of the articles in this special issue focus explicitly on working parents and their careers, when we refer to care responsibilities, we also mean to include the responsibility of caring for other dependents and (extended) family members, and do not mean to purposefully exclude nonparents.

The integrative framework for this special issue is depicted in Figure 1, including the individual, organizational, and societal levels which we will address in more detail below. This framework has evident parallels to earlier models of human ecology (e.g., Bronfenbrenner, 1986) and the work–family interface (e.g., Poelmans, 2003), in that it includes multiple levels ranging from macro to micro,

Sustainability in Combining Career and Care

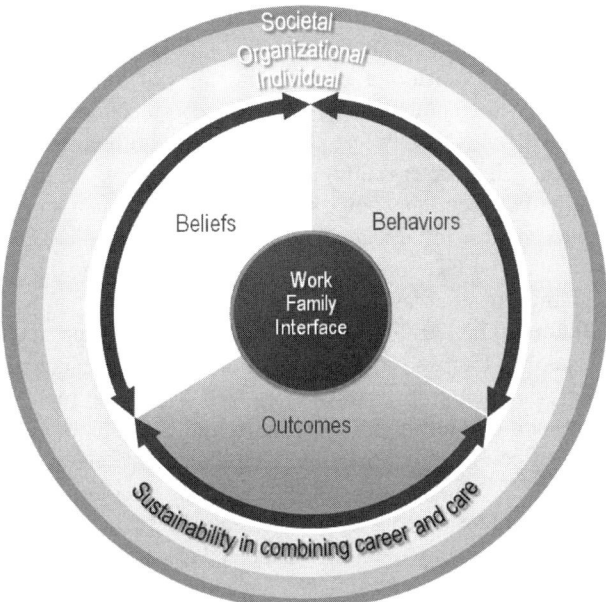

Fig. 1. Conceptual framework *Journal of Social Issues* special issue "Sustainability in Combining Career and Care."

incorporating normative influences on behavior, and taking a process-oriented or developmental rather than "snapshot" perspective. This introduction follows the different layers or levels in our framework. First, we address relevant societal and especially demographic developments related to combining career and care, including societal norms, gender roles, and women's labor force participation. Next, we will look at organizational responses to these demographic developments, by briefly describing family-friendly arrangements currently offered by many employers, organizational factors that influence the utilization of such arrangements, and relevant organizational outcomes of supporting working parents in combining career and care. Finally, we look at individual behavior at the work–family interface, in terms of the individual and couple decision making and behavior involved in the utilization of family-friendly arrangements. We will explain how such behavior is influenced by gender roles and normative beliefs about parenting, and we will look at possible outcomes for careers, couples, and children.

At the *societal* level, several important and interconnected demographic developments can be identified. First, female labor force participation has increased strongly in most industrialized countries over the last few decades, despite large cross-country differences in the timing of the increase and level of female participation (see Jaumotte, 2003 for an overview of this development in countries that belong to the Organisation for Economic Co-operation and Development or OECD). As a consequence, the number of dual earner couples and families has also grown considerably, resulting in new challenges in combining the demands of work and family uncommon to the male breadwinner model (Lewis, 2001). Since the late 20th century, high fertility correlates with high maternal employment, described by Ellingsæter (2009) as the so-called "positive turn" or reversal of the association between labor force participation of women and fertility rates from negative to positive in OECD countries. In spite of this positive turn, total fertility rates among OECD countries have declined dramatically over the past few decades, falling from an average of 2.7 children per woman in 1970 to just over 1.7 in 2009 (OECD, 2011). Postponement of childbearing due to women's wish to first establish themselves in the labor and housing markets is an important reason for this decline in fertility rates well below the replacement level. In combination with low fertility, low mortality rates lead to ageing populations in most developed countries (Christensen, Doblhammer, Rau, & Vaupel, 2009), which implies several challenges for society in terms of not only paying for, but also physically providing care for an increasingly larger part of the population. While many who live longer will also (be expected or even forced to) work longer (OECD, 2006), the main burden of these increasing financial and care responsibilities will lie primarily with younger generations. Postponement of childbearing results in a growing proportion of the population that can be characterized as the "sandwich generation," i.e., mid-life adults who simultaneously raise dependent children and care for elderly parents (Grundy & Henretta, 2006). These demographic developments, common to most industrialized nations, raise the social issue of creating and supporting sustainability in combining demands of work and family. Specifically, if and how social policies can help improve fertility levels and reduce postponement of childbearing has been the subject of much debate for policymakers at the (inter)national level (Bongaarts, 1998). To help resolve the debate, Ellingsæter (2009) calls for comparative studies of the interplay of family-friendly policies with other processes of social change, such as changes on the labor market and changes in gender norms. Indeed, a recent comparison by Daly (2011) of social policy reform across several European countries shows that when norms about work and care remain uncontested reforms typically promote dual earner, gender-specialized family arrangements, resulting in more rather than less complexity and ambiguity for employers and employees. Clearly, national differences in gender roles and government support, laws, and policies for combining work and family (Lewis, Knijn, Martin, & Ostner, 2008) demand a cross-national comparative perspective in studies of combining career and care.

At the *organizational* level, many employers in industrialized nations have adopted family-friendly arrangements (including policies, programs, and benefits), often above and beyond what is legally required. Den Dulk (2001) provides a typology of family-friendly arrangements or organizational work-home policies, distinguishing between flexible work arrangements, leaves, child care arrangements, and supportive arrangements. Part-time work is the flexible work arrangement most frequently offered by employers, and the most prevalent nonstandard employment relationship (Martin & Sinclair, 2007; Plantenga & Remery, 2005). Besides part-time work, other examples of flexible work arrangements are flexible hours (often labeled flextime or flexitime), compressed workweeks (e.g., 4×9 hours), job sharing, and telecommuting (Den Dulk, 2001; Plantenga & Remery, 2005). Telecommuting or teleworking is defined as "an alternative work arrangement in which employees perform tasks elsewhere [typically at home, eds.] that are normally done in a primary or central workplace, for at least some portion of their work schedule, using electronic media to interact with others inside and outside the organization" (Gajendran & Harrison, 2007, p. 1525).

In many cases, however, there appears to be a mismatch between the family-friendly arrangements offered and those actually utilized. Beyond unawareness of the existing arrangements available to them, many working parents fear negative career consequences of utilizing such arrangements (Kossek, Lewis, & Hammer, 2010). The behavior of the direct supervisor, team members, and certain aspects of the organizational culture (e.g., actively discouraging the utilization of a specific arrangement or expecting employees to be continuously available via email or phone) play a crucial role in supporting and/or hindering working parents (e.g., Frye & Braugh, 2004; Major, Fletcher, Davis, & Germano, 2007; Pederson, Minnotte, & Mannon, 2010). Relevant organizational level outcomes of the presence and utilization of family-friendly arrangements are retention, representation of women at different hierarchical levels, and organizational performance (Kelly et al., 2008). Employers often expect that by offering family-friendly arrangements they have an edge in winning the war for talent (Barnett & Hall, 2001), and that they will be perceived in a positive light by important stakeholders (customers as well as future employees) (Casper & Harris, 2007). Indeed, recent research suggests that there may be a positive relationship between family-friendly arrangements and business outcomes, which further strengthens the "business case" for employers (Kelly et al., 2008).

At the *individual* level of the work–family interface (Frone, Yardley, & Markel, 1997), our main concern is the behavior and decision making involved in the utilization of family-friendly arrangements by parents in order to combine career and care. Beyond part-time work, the most prevalent form of family-friendly arrangement as explained above, there is a host of different options for parents to choose from, separately or in combination, as an individual or as a couple. However, the individual decision whether or not to utilize family-friendly arrangements is likely to be influenced by beliefs about parenting and cultural norms about how work and family should be combined. These norms are linked to gender roles (or gender stereotypes; e.g., Eagly & Karau, 2002) and typically differ for fathers and mothers (Crosby, Williams, & Biernat, 2004; Heilman & Okimoto, 2008).

Similarly, the fear of negative career consequences when utilizing family-friendly arrangements is closely linked to notions of the ideal worker (Acker, 1990), who is engaged in full-time paid employment while unencumbered by family demands or other commitments outside the workplace. Individual consequences of the (non) utilization of family-friendly arrangements for careers, couples and children vary widely when we consider different indicators of work-family interaction (e.g., enrichment, harmony, conflict, spillover, guilt, life and marital satisfaction, e.g., Eby, Casper, Lockwood, Bordeaux, & Brinley, 2005; Ford, Heinen, & Langkamer, 2007), objective indicators of career success (e.g., salary growth and career advancement, e.g., Briscoe & Kellogg, 2011), subjective indicators of work and career success (e.g., job and career satisfaction, person–organization fit, engagement or burnout, turnover, e.g., Eby et al., 2005), and children's wellbeing, achievement, and development (e.g., Goldberg, Prause, Lucas-Thompson, & Himsel, 2008). Negative outcomes of combining career and care over time may reinforce traditional (and gendered) notions of the ideal parent and the ideal worker, whereas positive outcomes may challenge and ultimately change such beliefs. Furthermore, not all behaviors will lead to similar outcomes for everyone, which makes it important to consider individual and organizational moderators and mediators of the interplay between beliefs, behaviors, and outcomes at the work–family interface.

The eight contributions within this special issue are categorized in four sections, and will now be discussed in more detail per section. The first section describes the work–family interface, the second section relates to normative beliefs about parenting, the third section presents contributions on the association of family-friendly arrangements with individual career outcomes, and the fourth section focuses on the work–family interface in relation to couple- and family-related outcomes.

Section 1: The Work–Family Interface

In this special issue, the work–family interface is a core concept. The interface between the work and family domain is comprised of all (positive and negative) bi-directional influences between the two domains (Frone et al., 1997). It, therefore, covers both work spilling over—either in an interfering or facilitating manner—into one's family life, and family spilling over into one's work. Traditionally, work–family conflict is defined as "a form of interrole conflict in which the role pressures from the work and family domain are mutually incompatible in some respect." (Greenhaus & Beutell, 1985, p. 77). More recently, Grzywacz and Carlson (2007) conceptualized work–life balance or enrichment as "the accomplishment of role-related expectations that are negotiated and shared between an individual and his/her role-related partners in the work and family domains" (p. 458). Greenhaus and Allen (2011) attempted to capture the holistic nature of the work–family interface by defining it as "an overall appraisal of the extent to which individual's effectiveness and satisfaction in work and family roles are consistent with their life values at a given point in time" (p. 174).

Recent studies have shown that work–family balance can contribute to beneficial outcomes at both the individual employee level and the organizational level (e.g., McMillan, Morris, & Atchley, 2011; Van Steenbergen & Ellemers, 2009). Moreover, recent (Western) societal trends such as technological advancements allowing work to be performed flexibly and new household compositions including the dual-earner family, have led to a growing (academic and organizational) interest in the work–family interface (e.g., Moen & Sweet, 2004; Sullivan & Mainiero, 2007). Because of all these developments, physical and mental borders that have traditionally separated the work and family domains are increasingly becoming blurry, which may seriously challenge current employees and, as a result, affect their employers and society at large (Halpern, 2005; Lyness & Judiesch, 2008; McMillan et al., 2011).

The first section of this special issue deals with the associations of the central constructs depicted in the conceptual framework above (see Figure 1) with the work–family interface at the *individual* level. The two studies comprising this first section test these assumptions and extend our understanding of the work–family interface by examining (i) how different family constellations affect work–family spillover, and (ii) whether work–family guilt is related to pro- or anti-social work behavior. The first contribution in this section by Van Veldhoven and Beijer (*Workload, Work-to-Family Conflict, and Health: Gender Differences and the Influence of Private life Context*) examines gender differences in associations of workload and health with work-to-family conflict across different private life constellations. Van Veldhoven and Beijer argue that previous research on gender differences in work-to-family conflict and its linkages with workload and health has largely neglected the influence of private life context. They hypothesize that gender differences vary across private life contexts. A survey was completed by a representative sample of the Belgian working population ($N = 8,593$) to examine gender differences in six family compositions, based on having a (working) partner, and having children. Women were found to report higher levels of work-to-family conflict than men, but this difference only held in dual-earners with and without children, and in single-earner parents. Gender differences in the strength of the relationships of conflict with workload and health were found in the total sample, but only for specific subgroups. These results suggest that private life context needs attention in future research and policy making aimed at sustainability in career and care.

The second study included in this section by Botsford Morgan and King (*The Association Between Work–Family Guilt and Pro- and Anti-Social Work Behavior*) explores the behavioral outcomes of an understudied emotion, guilt, in the context of the work–family domain. Specifically, the authors propose that work–family guilt—which they define as an emotion that can occur when one's behavior violates the norms of how one believes they should balance the demands of work and family responsibilities and adversely affects an individual—motivates both prosocial (i.e., Organizational Citizenship Behavior) and antisocial (i.e., Counterproductive Work Behavior) behaviors in the workplace. In total, 245 working adults in the Washington D.C. Metropolitan Area completed qualitative and quantitative indicators of behavioral responses to work–family guilt. Results demonstrate that when individuals experience family-to-work guilt, they respond with helping behaviors directed toward individuals. When individuals experience work-to-family guilt, they respond by shirking of work responsibilities. Thus, work–family guilt may be a critical and underexplored determinant of extra role behaviors and an important emotion to manage in order to sustain career and care roles.

Section 2: Normative Beliefs about Parenting

The fear of falling short and feelings of guilt described above appear to be deeply rooted in normative beliefs about parenting. As evidenced by the two experimental studies in this second section, these normative beliefs are connected to societal gender roles and do not merely affect our individual "choices" in combining career and care but also introduce bias in organization-level hiring and promotion decisions. Especially for women, career outcomes may depend on whether their choices reflect societal norms on appropriate behaviors for working mothers.

As argued above, the individual decision whether or not to use family-friendly arrangements is likely to be influenced by normative beliefs about parenting and gender roles (Cuddy, Fiske, & Glick, 2004; Fuegen, Biernat, Haines, & Deaux, 2004; Marks & Houston, 2002). While being a good father is generally not perceived as incompatible with work or a career, earlier research clearly demonstrates ambivalence toward working mothers (e.g., Greenberger, Goldberg, Crawford, & Granger, 1988), the "maternal wall" (Crosby et al., 2004), and motherhood bias (Heilman & Okimoto, 2008; King, 2008). Motherhood, by its implied communality, results in more incongruence between the female gender role and the work role (Eagly & Karau, 2002; Heilman & Okimoto, 2008), and consequently in more negative evaluations and lower compensation at work (Crosby et al., 2004; King, 2008). Beyond gender roles, normative beliefs about the ideal worker (e.g., Acker, 1990) also affect the presence and utilization of family-friendly arrangements (Özbilgin, Beauregard, Tatli, & Bell, 2011). In this special issue, *normative beliefs about parenting* are perceived to be a socio-historical construct, describing what it means to be a good mother or father and prescribing how parenthood should take shape in individual parents' behavior, attitudes, relationships, and identity (Bassin, Honey, & Kaplan, 1994; Van Engen, Dikkers, Vinkenburg, & De Rooy, 2009).

While gender roles and normative beliefs about parenting on the one hand are—to a certain extent—institutionalized in the implementation of family-friendly policies and arrangements, at the individual level they become internalized by choices in work and care that mothers and fathers make. The utilization of family-friendly arrangements is therefore similarly gendered. Countries with comparatively "traditional" views on motherhood are more likely to provide extended maternity leave (e.g., 3 years in Germany) or part-time working options (e.g., the Netherlands) for working mothers. Consequently, German and Dutch mothers may feel a strong need to "choose" to (partly) opt out of a career during the child bearing and rearing years (Den Dulk, 2005; Orloff, 2006). In other words, culturally formed normative beliefs about parenting may affect the family-friendly arrangements that a country (and its companies) offers its working parents and, simultaneously, the gendered use that working mothers and fathers make of these arrangements.

Furthermore, when we talk about normative parenting beliefs, we refer not only to the views held by employees themselves, but also to those expressed by their supervisors, peers or team members, subordinates, family, and friends. While individuals often claim "free will" in making work–family choices, societal norms, work values and peer pressure are likely to form important push or pull factors (Gregory & Milner, 2009; Kossek & van Dyne, 2008; Stephens & Levine, 2011). At the organizational level, parenting beliefs may feed the company's culture and norms regarding the combination of career and caregiving. In a traditional culture, for example, supervisors may offer working mothers more (and other) family-friendly arrangements compared to fathers because this is more in line with their (sub)conscious belief that mothers are and should be the primary caregiver (Brescoll & Uhlmann, 2005). Parents who disregard these (largely unwritten) rules may risk being "punished" for this faux pas by being neglected when opportunities for promotion arise or as reflected in other negative career-related outcomes (Kossek et al., 2010).

The two studies included in this second section shed more light on the effect of individually held normative parenting beliefs on both outcomes at the *individual* level and decisions taken at the *organizational* level by examining the (i) psychological processes underlying the "bad parent" assumption ascribed to working mothers, and (ii) gender bias in evaluative employment recommendations. In the first study, Okimoto and Heilman (*The "Bad Parent" Assumption: How Gender Stereotypes Affect Reactions to Working Mothers*) state that—although balancing work and family commitments may form a significant source of strain for working parents—working mothers in traditionally male positions face additional anxiety due to unfounded assumptions about their competence as employees, assumptions rooted in gender stereotypes. However, stereotype-based assumptions can also bias impressions of these working mothers in family domains, depicting them as bad parents. In all four experimental studies with U.S. volunteers who were recruited for online research participation, participants were told the study investigated first impressions, and were asked to read one short description of a target. The target description varied depending on experimental condition, but all other details were held constant and all targets were described as being parents. The authors found that working mothers were seen as less effective parents than nonworking mothers. Consistent with the argument that gender stereotypes underlie these findings, the bad parent assumption was apparent only for mothers and not fathers (Study 1), only when working in a male sex-typed occupation (Study 2), more intensely when job success was clear (Study 3), and only when working out of personal choice (Study 4). Similar patterns were observed in ratings of interpersonal appeal, suggesting that there also are negative social consequences for working mothers.

In the second contribution within this section, Vinkenburg, Van Engen, Coffeng, and Dikkers (*Bias in Employment Decisions About Mothers and Fathers: The (Dis)Advantages of Sharing Care Responsibilities*) studied whether motherhood bias is attenuated by different ways of dividing work and care in a simulated employment decision for a managerial position. In an experiment, 81 Dutch employees were asked to make employment decisions based on a resume of a candidate for a managerial position. Participants were presented with a job description of a senior marketing manager and a resume of a (mother/father) target job candidate interested in this position. The target candidate's work–home task division was described as either a main provider breadwinner situation or a shared work–home situation. Participants were subsequently asked to rate the anticipated commitment and competence as well as provide a screening recommendation for the target candidate. Results showed that, despite the strong full-time expectancies for managerial roles, mothers who were main providers and worked full-time where seen as less competent and were rated less positively for a managerial position than mothers working part time. In contrast, fathers sharing care responsibilities and work reduced hours were rated less positively with regard to the suitability for a managerial position than full-time working fathers. These findings hint at how normative beliefs about parenting dictate that we applaud mothers— and punish fathers—who combine career and care by working reduced hours.

Section 3: Family-Friendly Arrangements and Individual Career Outcomes

As mentioned above, in order to meet work demands and simultaneously take care of their children, working parents may use family-friendly arrangements offered by their employers. While using such arrangements may offer short-term solutions to day-to-day hassles associated with combining work and family, the two papers in this section address intermediate to long-term career consequences of using family-friendly arrangements and part-time work in particular.

Career outcomes (in terms of objective and/or subjective career success) as well as children's achievements may reinforce (or erode) existing gender roles and normative parenting beliefs thereby reflecting a feedback loop from outcomes to beliefs (see Figure 1). One example of a mother who is successful at her full time job and whose children do not appear to suffer from this arrangement may be viewed as the exception to the rule of the "bad mother" (Heilman and Okimoto, 2008). For most working mothers, not meeting the stereotypical image of the "perfect" or even "good" mother may result in negative evaluations and reduced career success, thereby reinforcing the stereotype (e.g., Wood, Christensen, Hebl, & Rothgerber, 1997). However, one could also argue that a critical mass of working parents who successfully and sustainably combine work and family responsibilities will eventually lead to a change in gender roles and normative beliefs about parenting. Furthermore, not all families are the same and different family structures as well as different work–family choices will affect not only career and family outcomes, but also challenge traditional gender roles.

While the work–family interface and its consequences are issues that employees (in particular those with young children) cope with on a day-to-day basis, (not) using family-friendly arrangements may have long-term career consequences as well. A study of Dutch working parents showed that part-time work not only has absolute but also relative negative effects on salary and career progression, whereas working-from-home and using return policies after an extended leave have positive career consequences (e.g., Van Engen et al., 2009). Bub and McCartney (2004) showed that mothers' use of early childcare for their children predicted later maternal employment: more hours in early childcare were associated with higher maternal wages and more hours of employment when children reached the age of six. The effects of work–home choices on career outcomes can be (partly) explained by the signaling function of parents using such policies as being less (or more) committed, as well as supervisors' beliefs about gender and parenting. Hoobler, Wayne, and Lemmon (2009) showed that bosses' perceptions of family–work conflict and person–organization fit mediated the relation-ships between subordinate sex and bosses' perceptions of performance and promotability. Mothers were perceived as experiencing more conflict, resulting in a lower assessment of fit and of promotability than fathers, regardless of the actual levels of conflict and fit reported by parents themselves. In contrast, Padgett, Harland, and Moser (2009) showed that mothers who return to full time work after having used an alternative (i.e., reduced) work schedule are perceived as having greater advancement motivation, greater advancement capability, and consequently more likely to be recommended for a promotion than mothers who did not change their schedule. These findings can be viewed from the perspective of normative beliefs about parenting; the mother who has worked reduced hours but is now returning to a regular schedule meets the prescriptive norms (Heilman, 2001) of being a good mother but also resembles the ideal worker (Acker, 1990).

The two studies comprising this third section extend the limited (e.g., Eby et al., 2005) research on the effect of family-friendly arrangements offered at the *organizational* level on career-related outcomes at the *individual* level by examining (i) objective and subjective career success among professionals seeking a sustainable way of combining work, personal and family life over time, and (ii) the impact of career breaks and part-time work among mothers working in science, engineering and technology. In the first contribution to this section, Hall, Lee, Kossek, and Las Heras (*Pursuing Career Success While Sustaining Personal and Family Well Being: A Study of Reduced-Load Professionals over Time*) examine the experiences of 73 U.S. managers and high level professionals who reduced their workloads to achieve more sustainable career and family outcomes over a 6-year period. The researchers compared personal, family, and career success outcomes for people who maintained reduced loads over time with those who went back to full time work 6 years later, and found few differences, except for more promotions for the full-timers. To further understand these results, they identified four groups reflecting all possible combinations of extreme levels (either very high or very low) of objective and subjective success. The groups were labeled: Aligned Achievers (scoring high on both success dimensions), Alienated Achievers (scoring high on objective and low on subjective success), Happy Part-timers (scoring low on objective and high on subjective success), and Hard Luck Strivers (scoring low on both success dimensions). Subsequent qualitative analysis of group members' reflections on the meaning of career success as well as the occurrence of significant life events helped explain the variation in their success in sustaining desired career and life arrangements over time. This study shows that reduced load-work arrangements enabled talented professionals to remain in the labor force and sustain career involvement while maintaining the kind of engagement with family life they needed and/or desired. The authors suggest that the use of these arrangements should be studied in terms of their psychological meaning to individuals seeking cross-domain success between work, family and personal life, as they craft lives that work for them.

Herman and Lewis (*Entitled to a Sustainable Career? Motherhood in Science, Engineering and Technology*) explored the challenging issue of sustaining careers and motherhood in the male-dominated Science, Engineering and Technology (SET) sector using a social comparison theory perspective. In this study, the authors draw on semi-structured interviews with 30 mothers (from Italy, France and the Netherlands) and eight fathers (from two French companies) who were all professional engineers and scientists at the time of the interview to explore the lived experiences of parents as they negotiated parenthood in the context of their professional lives as engineers and scientists. They examined how decisions to reduce working hours are influenced by perceived ideological, normative and policy contexts. Despite contextual differences in opportunities and perceived entitlements and supports for family-friendly working hours, the authors found that sense of entitlement to do so without forfeiting career progression is limited across all the contexts. This attests to the enduring power of gendered organizational assumptions about ideal SET careers. Nevertheless, they present examples of three women who achieved senior roles despite working reduced hours and discuss combinations of conditions which may facilitate sustainable careers and caring roles.

Section 4: The Work–Family Interface and Couple- and Family-Related Outcomes

In this final section, we cross over from the organizational level of family-friendly arrangements to the societal level of creating sustainability in career and care. However, the individual working parent is involved in this section as well, by observing couples who are involved in "doing sustainability" in order to resolve issues with regard to their work–family interface, and by associating the individual "choices" that parents have made in terms of combining their career and care responsibilities with the (societally fueled) gender roles and expectations regarding career and care as expressed by their college-aged children.

Following Ellingsæter's (2009) call for comparative studies of the interplay of family policy with other processes of social change, such as labor markets and gender cultures, this special issue aims to provide some answers to the complicated questions of how societal and cultural norms and values affect the work–family interface, with insights from different countries and cultures. Goldberg et al. (2008) have shown that—generally speaking—mothers' employment has positive consequences for children's cognitive development and achievement. Despite these findings, many parents may still hold beliefs that are firmly rooted in the commonly held "maternal deprivation" hypothesis, and mothers may experience guilt when they divide their time between work and care. Tiedje (2004) applies Baldwin's paradox (i.e., acceptance of life as it is, while at the same time never accepting injustice as commonplace) to the mothering role. While most working mothers in her study consistently said they were a "very good parent," almost half of them said they "often feel guilty" about not being a better parent.

The two studies included in this fourth section place the *individual* work–family interface in *societal* context by examining (i) negotiations of exchange relationships in family and work in Sri Lanka couples, and (ii) views about work and family shared by male and female college students. In the first contribution to this final section, Kailasapathy and Metz (*Work–Family Conflict in Sri Lanka: Negotiations of Exchange Relationships in Family and at Work*) aim to understand how partners in dual-earner couples experience and deal with juggling work and family in Sri Lanka. This study was conducted as part of a larger study on work–family conflict which used survey data collected in 2007 among dual-earner heterosexual couples who were employed full-time in Sri Lanka. From the larger sample, 13 couples experiencing high levels of work–family conflict were selected. Subsequently, interviews were conducted to identify if and how couples negotiated within their marital relationships, and between themselves and their supervisors, to reduce or cope with work–family conflict. The interviews indicated that negotiations at home and at work concerned contributions to the exchange relationship and were unlikely to adversely affect the (home or work) exchange relationships. Further, the interviews revealed an influence of spouse's gender role ideology on the success of the negotiation at home. In addition to negotiating with the spouse and/or supervisor, this study found that the extended family serves as a "work–family arrangement" for Sri Lankan dual-earner couples, something not found in most Western cultures. This "work–family" arrangement in combination with gradual negotiations or voluntary contributions (that enable redistributions of domestic labor) facilitate the sustainable combination of career and care for both spouses in an Eastern culture.

In the final contribution to this section and the special issue, Goldberg, Kelly, Matthews, Kang, Li, and Sumaroka (*The More Things Change, the More they Stay the Same: Gender, Culture, and College Students' Views About Work and Family*) let a culturally/ethnically diverse sample of 955 students at a large U.S. university complete online surveys about their parents' division of labor, trajectories of their mothers' employment, gender role ideology, and beliefs about the costs and benefits of maternal employment for children. Differences in these work–care domains were examined by student gender, culture/ethnicity, acculturation status, and own employment. Generational differences in beliefs about maternal employment were also examined. Asian American students, especially male students and those less acculturated, were more likely to endorse gender role segregation and maternal nonemployment when children are young. Own mothers' employment and their own employment status were associated with more positive views about maternal employment. However, students' work–care beliefs were fairly constant since the 1980s. The views of emerging adults about career and care may impinge on their success in attaining work–family goals.

In the final contribution and conclusion to this special issue (*The "Triple-N" Model: Changing Normative Beliefs About Parenting and Career Success*), Poelmans reflects on the eight empirical contributions, deriving an inclusive "Triple N model" incorporating the insights generated by the different authors regarding how to challenge the status quo. Central in the integrative model and future research agenda as offered by Poelmans are normative beliefs about parenting. As Poelmans argues, the first step toward creating and supporting sustainability in career and care is raising awareness about (the dilemma of) normative beliefs (i.e., Nominating Norms). Adopting normative beliefs held by important others is instrumental for being accepted and valued (i.e., Navigating Norms), but change may require challenging the norms openly by not adopting them or even setting a new standard or norm (i.e., creating New No-Nonsense Norms). The way out of this dilemma may be rough, but is crucial to the sustainability challenge.

In sum, in this special issue we bring together scholars from different countries and disciplines that present their research on the association between beliefs, behaviors, and long-term outcomes at the work–family interface, in order to help create and support sustainability in combining career and care. In bringing together these researchers, we meet the call by Kelly et al. (2008) for inter-disciplinary, comparative, and multiple level approaches with regard to the long-term effects of family-friendly arrangements for working parents and their families. Positive career and family consequences and lived experiences of combining career and care, even if only from a small number of trailblazers and early adopters (Ranson, 2010), are likely to challenge and change gender roles and normative beliefs about parenting, thus creating a positive upward spiral.

References

Acker, J. (1990). Hierarchies, jobs, bodies: A theory of gendered organizations. *Gender and Society*, *4*(2), 139–158. doi: 10.1177/089124390004002002.

Arthur, M. B., Hall, D. T., & Lawrence, B. S. (Eds.). (1989). *Handbook of career theory*. Cambridge: Cambridge University Press.

Barnett, R. C., & Hall, D. T. (2001). How to use reduced hours to win the war for talent. *Organizational Dynamics*, *29*(3), 192–210. doi: 10.1016/S0090-2616(01)00024-9.

Bassin, D., Honey, M., & Kaplan, M. M. (1994). *Representations of motherhood*. New Haven, CT: Yale University Press.

Bongaarts, J. (1998). Demographic consequences of declining fertility. *Science*, *282*(5388), 419–420.

Botsford Morgan, W., & King, E. B. (2012). The association between work-family guilt and pro- and anti-social work behavior. *Journal of Social Issues*, *68*(4), 684–703.

Brescoll, V. L., & Uhlmann, E. L. (2005). Attitudes toward traditional and non-traditional parents. *Psychology of Women Quarterly*, *29*(4), 436–445. doi: 0.1111/j.1471-6402.2005.00244.x.

Briscoe, F., & Kellogg, K. C. (2011). The initial assignment effect: Local employer practices and positive career outcomes for work-family program users. *American Sociological Review*, *76*(2), 291–319. doi: 10.1177/0003122411401250.

Bronfenbrenner, U. (1986). Ecology of the family as a context for human development: Research perspectives. *Developmental Psychology*, *22*(6), 723–742. doi: 10.1037//0012-1649.22.6.723.

Bub, K. L., & McCartney, K. (2004). On childcare as a support for maternal employment wages and hours. *Journal of Social Issues*, *60*(4), 819–834. doi: 10.1111/j.0022-4537.2004.00388.x.

Casper, W. J., & Harris, C. M. (2007). Work-life benefits and organizational attachment: Self-interest utility and signaling theory models. *Journal of Vocational Behavior*, *72*(1), 95–109. doi: 10.1016/j.jvb.2007.10.015.

Christensen, K., Doblhammer, G., Rau, R., & Vaupel, J. W. (2009). Ageing populations: The challenges ahead. *The Lancet*, *374*(9696), 1196–1208. doi: 10.1016/s0140-6736(09)61460-4.

Crosby, F. J., Williams, J. C., & Biernat, M. (2004). The maternal wall. *Journal of Social Issues*, *60*(4), 675–682. doi: 10.1111/j.0022-4537.2004.00379.x.

Cuddy, A. J. C., Fiske, S. T., & Glick, P. (2004). When professionals become mothers, warmth doesn't cut the ice. *Journal of Social Issues*, *60*, 701–718. doi: 10.1111/j.0022-4537.2004.00381.x.

Daly, M. (2011). What adult worker model? A critical look at recent social policy reform in Europe from a gender and family perspective. *Social Politics: International Studies in Gender, State & Society*, *18*(1), 1–23. doi: 10.1093/sp/jxr002.

Den Dulk, L. (2001). *Work-family arrangements in organizations. A cross-national study in the Netherlands, Italy, the United Kingdom and Sweden*. PhD thesis, University of Amsterdam. Amsterdam: Rozenburg Publishers.

Den Dulk, L. (2005). Workplace work-family arrangements: A study and explanatory framework of differences between organizational provisions in different welfare states. In S. A. Y. Poelmans (Ed.), *Work and family: An international research perspective* (pp. 211–238). Mahwah, NJ: Lawrence Erlbaum.

Dikkers, J.S.E., Van Engen, M.L. & Vinkenburg, C. J. (2010). Flexible work: Ambitious parents? Recipe for career success in the Netherlands. *Career Development International, 15*(6), 562–582. doi: 10.1108/13620431011084411.

Eagly, A. H., & Karau, S. J. (2002). Role congruity theory of prejudice toward female leaders. *Psychological Review, 109*, 573–598. doi: 10.1037/0033-295X.109.3.573.

Eby, L. T., Casper, W. J., Lockwood, A., Bordeaux, C., & Brinley, A. (2005). Work and family research in IO/OB: Content analysis and review of the literature (1980–2002). *Journal of Vocational behavior, 66*(1), 124–197. doi: 10.1016/j.jvb.2003.11.003.

Ehnert, I. (2009). *Sustainable Human Resource Management: A conceptual and exploratory analysis from a paradox perspective*. Berlin-Heidelberg: Physica-Verlag HD.

Ellingsæter, A. L. (2009). Leave policy in the Nordic welfare states: A 'recipe' for high employment/high fertility?. *Community, Work and Family, 12*(1), 1–19. doi: 10.1080/13668800801890152.

Ford, M. T., Heinen, B. A., & Langkamer, K. L. (2007). Work and family satisfaction and conflict: A meta-analysis of cross-domain relations. *Journal of Applied Psychology, 92*(1), 57–80. doi: 10.1037/0021-9010.92.1.57.

Frone, M. R., Yardley, J. K., & Markel, K. S. (1997). Developing and testing an integrative model of the work-family interface. *Journal of Vocational Behavior, 50*(2), 145–167. doi: 10.1006/jvbe.1996.1577.

Frye, N. K., & Breaugh, J. A. (2004). Family-friendly policies, supervisor support, work-family conflict, family-work conflict, and satisfaction: A test of a conceptual model. *Journal of Business and Psychology, 19*(2), 197–220. doi: 10.1007/s10869-004-0548-4.

Fuegen, K., Biernat, M., Haines, E., & Deaux, K. (2004). Mothers and fathers in the workplace: How gender and parental status influence judgments of job-related competence. *Journal of Social Issues, 60*(4), 737–754. doi: 10.1111/j.0022-4537.2004.00383.x.

Gajendran, R. S., & Harrison, D. A. (2007). The good, the bad, and the unknown about telecommuting: Meta-analysis of psychological mediators and individual consequences. *Journal of Applied Psychology, 92*(6), 1524–1541. doi: 10.1037/0021-9010.92.6.1524.

Goldberg, W. A., Kelly, E., Matthews, N. B., Kang, H., Li, W., & Sumaroka, M. (2012). The more things change, the more they stay the same: Gender, culture, and college students' views about work and family. *Journal of Social Issues, 68*(4), 814–837.

Goldberg, W. A., Prause, J. A., Lucas-Thompson, R., & Himsel, A. J. (2008). Maternal employment and children's achievement in context: A meta-analysis of four decades of research. *Psychological Bulletin, 134*(1), 77–108. doi: 10.1037/0033-2909.134.1.77.

Greenberger, E., Goldberg, W. A., Crawford, T. J., & Granger, J. (1988). Beliefs about the consequences of maternal employment for women. *Psychology of Women Quarterly, 12*, 35–59. doi: 10.1111/j.1471-6402.1988.tb00926.x.

Greenhaus, J. H., & Allen, T. D. (2011). Work-family balance: A review and extension of the literature. In J. C. Quick & L. E. Tetrick (Eds.), *Handbook of occupational health psychology*. Washington, DC: American Psychological Association.

Greenhaus, J. H., & Beutell, N. J. (1985). Sources of conflict between work and family roles. *Academy of Management Review, 10*, 76–88. doi: 10.2307/258214.

Gregory, A., & Milner, S. (2009). Editorial: Work-life balance: A matter of choice? *Gender, Work, & Organization, 16*(1), 1–13. doi: 10.1111/j.1468-0432.2008.00429.x.

Grundy, E., & Henretta, J. C. (2006). Between elderly parents and adult children: A new look at the intergenerational care provided by the 'sandwich generation'. *Ageing & Society, 26*, 707–722. doi: 10.1017/S0144686×06004934.

Grzywacz, J. G., & Carlson, D. S. (2007). Conceptualizing work-family balance: Implications for practice and research. *Advances in Developing Human Resources, 9*(4), 455–471. doi: 10.1177/1523422307305487.

Hall, D. T., Lee, M. D., Kossek, E. E., & Las Heras, M. (2012). Pursuing career success while sustaining personal and family well being: A study of reduced-load professionals over time. *Journal of Social Issues*, 68(4), 742–766.

Halpern, D. F. (2005). Psychology at the intersection of work and family: Recommendations for employers, working families and policymakers. *American Psychologist*, 60(5), 397–409. doi: 10.1037/0003-066X.60.5.397.

Heilman, M. E. (2001). Description and prescription: How gender stereotypes prevent women's ascent up the organizational ladder. *Journal of Social Issues*, 57(4), 657–674. doi: 10.1111/0022-4537.00234.

Heilman, M. E., & Okimoto, T. G. (2008). Motherhood: A potential source of bias in employment decisions. *Journal of Applied Psychology*, 93(1), 189–198. doi: 10.1037/0021-9010.93.1.189.

Herman, C., & Lewis, S. (2012). Entitled to a sustainable career? Motherhood in science, engineering and technology. *Journal of Social Issues*, 68(4), 767–789.

Hoobler, J. M., Wayne, S. J., & Lemmon, G. (2009). Bosses' perceptions of family-work conflict and women's promotability: Glass ceiling effects. *Academy of Management Journal*, 52(5), 939–957. doi: 10.5465/AMJ.2009.44633700.

Jaumotte, F. (2003). *Female labour force participation – Past trends and main determinants in OECD countries*. Organisation for Economic Co-operation and Development (OECD) Economics Department Working Papers No. 376. doi: 10.1787/082872464507.

Kailasapathy, P., & Metz, I. (2012). Work-family conflict in Sri Lanka: Negotiations of exchange relationships in family and at work. *Journal of Social Issues*, 68(4), 790–813.

Kelly, E. L., Kossek, E., Hammer, L. B., Durham, M., Bray, J., Chermack, K., Murphy, L. A., & Kaskubar, D. (2008). Getting there from here: Research on the effects of work-family initiatives on work-family conflict and business outcomes. *The Academy of Management Annals*, 2(1), 305–349. doi: 10.1080/19416520802211610.

King, E. B. (2008). The effect of bias on the advancement of working mothers: Disentangling legitimate concerns from inaccurate stereotypes as predictors of advancement in academe. *Human Relations*, 61(12), 1677–1711. doi: 10.1177/0018726708098082.

Kossek, E. E., & Van Dyne, L. (2008). Face-time matters: A cross level model of how work-life flexibility influences work performance of individuals and groups. In K. Korabik, D. S. Lero, & D. L. Whitehead (Eds.), *Handbook of work-family integration: Research, theory, and best practices* (pp. 305–330). San Diego, CA: Elsevier.

Kossek, E. E., Lewis, S., & Hammer, L. B. (2010). Work-life initiatives and organizational change: Overcoming mixed messages to move from the margin to the mainstream. *Human Relations*, 63(1), 3–19. doi: 10.1177/0018726709352385.

Lewis, J. (2001). The decline of the male breadwinner model: Implications for work and care. *Social Politics: International Studies in Gender, State & Society*, 8(2), 152–169. doi: 10.1093/sp/8.2.152.

Lewis, J., Knijn, T., Martin, C., & Ostner, I. (2008). Patterns of development in work/family reconciliation policies for parents in France, Germany, the Netherlands, and the UK in the 2000s. *Social Politics: International Studies in Gender, State & Society*, 15(3), 261–286. doi: 10.1093/sp/jxn016.

Lyness, K. S., & Judiesch, M. K. (2008). Can a manager have a life and career? International and multisource perspectives on work-life balance and career advancement potential. *Journal of Applied Psychology*, 93(4), 789–805. doi: 10.1037/0021-9010.93.4.789.

Major, D. B., Fletcher, T. D., Davis, D. D., & Germano, L. M. (2007). The influence of work-family culture and workplace relations on work interference with family: A multilevel model. *Journal of Organizational Behavior*, 29(7), 881–897. doi: 10.1002./job.502.

Marks, G., & Houston, D. M. (2002). Attitudes towards work and motherhood held by working and non-working mothers. *Work Employments Society*, 16(3), 523–536. doi: 10.1177/095001702762217470.

Martin, J. E., & Sinclair, R. R. (2007). A typology of the part-time workforce: Differences on job attitudes and turnover. *Journal of Occupational and Organizational Psychology*, 80, 301–319. doi: 10.1348/096317906×113833.

McKenzie-Mohr, D., & Oskamp, S. (1995). Psychology and sustainability: An introduction. *Journal of Social Issues, 51*(4), 1–14. doi: 10.1111/j.1540-4560.1995.tb01345.x.

McMillan, H. S., Morris, M. L., & Atchley, E. K. (2011). Constructs of the work/life interface: A synthesis of the literature and introduction of the concept of work/life harmony. *Human Resource Development Review, 10*(1), 6–25. doi: 10.1177/1534484310384958.

Moen, P., & Sweet, S. (2004). From 'work-family' to 'flexible careers'. A life course reframing. *Community, Work & Family, 7*(2), 209–226. doi: 10.1080/1366880042000245489.

OECD (2006). *Live longer, work longer*. Organisation for Economic Co-operation and Development. Paris: OECD Publishing. doi: 10.1787/9789264035881-en.

OECD (2011). *Doing better for families*. Organisation for Economic Co-operation and Development. Paris: OECD Publishing. doi: 10.1787/9789264098732-en.

Okimoto, T. G., & Heilman, M. E. (2012). The "bad parent" assumption: How gender stereotypes affect reactions to working mothers. *Journal of Social Issues, 68*(4), 704–724.

Orloff, A. S. (2006). From maternalism to "employment for all": State policies to promote women's employment across the affluent democracies. In J. D. Levy (Ed.), *The State after Statism: New State Activities in the Age of Liberalization* (pp. 230–268). Cambridge, MA: Harvard University Press.

Oskamp, S. (2000). Psychology of promoting environmentalism: Psychological contributions to achieving an ecologically sustainable future for humanity. *Journal of Social Issues, 56*(3), 373–390. doi: 10.1111/0022-4537.00173.

Özbilgin, M. F., Beauregard, T. A., Tatli, A., & Bell, M. P. (2011). Work–life, diversity and intersectionality: A critical review and research agenda. *International Journal of Management Reviews, 13*(2), 177–198. doi: 10.1111/j.1468-2370.2010.00291.x.

Padgett, M., Harland, L., & Moser, S. B. (2009). The bad news and the good news: The long-term consequences of having used an alternative work schedule. *Journal of Leadership & Organizational Studies, 16*(1), 73–84. doi: 10.1177/1548051809333241.

Pederson, D. E., Minnotte, K. L., & Mannon, S. E. (2010). Getting by with a little help from workplace friends: Workplace culture, social support and family cohesion. *Marriage & Family Review, 46*(6–7), 400–419. doi: 10.1080/01494929.2010.528322.

Plantenga, J., & Remery, C. (2005). *Reconciliation of work and private life: A comparative review of thirty European countries*. EGGSIE report for the European Commission. Retrieved September 27, 2007, from http://www.mbs.ac.uk/research/europeanemployment/projects/gendersocial/publications.aspx.

Poelmans, S. (2003). Editorial. The multi-level "fit" model of work and family. *International Journal of Cross-Cultural Management, 3*(3), 267–274. doi: 10.1177/1470595803003003001.

Poelmans, S. (2012). The "Triple-N" model: Changing normative beliefs about parenting and career success. *Journal of Social Issues, 68*(4), 838–847.

Ranson, G. (2010). *Against the grain: Couples, gender and the reframing of parenting*. Canada: University of Toronto Press.

Stephens, N. M., & Levine, C. S. (2011). Opting out or denying discrimination? How the framework of free choice in American society influences perceptions of gender inequality. *Psychological Science, 22*(10), 1231–1236. doi: 10.1177/0956797611417260.

Sullivan, S. E., & Mainiero, L. A. (2007). The changing nature of gender roles, alpha/beta careers and work-life issues. Theory-driven implications for human resource management. *Career Development International, 12*(3), 238–263. doi: 10.1108/13620430710745881.

Tiedje, L. B. (2004). Processes of change in work/home incompatibilities: Employed mothers 1986–1999. *Journal of Social Issues, 60*(4), 787–800. doi: 10.1111/j.0022-4537.2004.00386.x.

Van Engen, M. L., Dikkers, E. J., Vinkenburg, C. J., & Rooy, de, E. (2009). Carrièresucces van vaders en moeders: de rol van moederschapsideologie, werk-thuis-cultuur en werk-thuis-arrangementen. *Gedrag en Organisatie, 22*(2), 146–171.

Van Marrewijk, M., & Werre, M. (2003). Multiple levels of corporate sustainability. *Journal of Business Ethics, 44*(2), 107–119. doi: 10.1023/a:1023383229086.

Van Steenbergen, E. F., & Ellemers, N. (2009). Is managing the work-family interface worthwhile? Benefits for employee health and performance. *Journal of Organizational Behavior, 30*, 617–642. doi: 10.1002/job.569.

Van Veldhoven, M. J. P. M., & Beijer, S. E. (2012). Workload, work-to-family conflict, and health: Gender differences and the influence of private life context. *Journal of Social Issues*, *68*(4), 665–683.

Vinkenburg, C. J., Van Engen, M. L., Coffeng, J., & Dikkers, J. S. E. (2012). Bias in employment decisions about mothers and fathers: The (dis)advantages of sharing care responsibilities. *Journal of Social Issues*, *68*(4), 725–741.

Wood, W., Christensen, P. N., Hebl, M. R., & Rothgerber, H. (1997). Conformity to sex-typed norms, affect, and the self-concept. *Journal of Personality and Social Psychology*, *73*(3), 523–535. doi: 10.1037//0022-3514.73.3.523.

MARLOES L. VAN ENGEN is Assistant Professor at the Department of Human Resource Studies, Tilburg School of Social and Behavioral Sciences at Tilburg University where she lectures in Diversity in Organizations and Human Resource Studies. She studied social psychology with a minor in the psychology of culture and religion at the Radboud University in Nijmegen. She lectured at Communication Sciences before she moved to Tilburg University. Her research interests are in the area of gender in organizations, gender and careers, work-family issues in organizations, diversity in teams and organizations, effectiveness of diversity practices and policies and methodology such as meta-analysis, multi-level analysis, qualitative research and intervention studies. She earned her PhD in 2001 on gender and leadership. She was a visiting academic at Northwestern University (USA), the University of Queensland (Australia), and Monash University (Australia). She has published in *Psychological Bulletin*, the *Journal of Organizational and Occupational Psychology*, *Organizational Behavior and Human Decision Processes*, and *Leadership Quarterly*.

CLAARTJE J. VINKENBURG is Associate Professor of organizational behavior and development at the VU University Amsterdam. She studied social psychology at the University of Groningen, and earned her PhD in Business Administration in 1997 at the VU University Amsterdam on gender differences in managerial behavior and effectiveness. From 1997 to 2001 she worked as a management consultant (at Berenschot and independently) and a visiting scholar and adjunct lecturer at Northwestern University (USA). As managing director of the Amsterdam Center for Career Research (www.accr.nl), Claartje's research focuses on gender, leadership, and career advancement, including the effects of normative beliefs about parenting on women's career patterns and outcomes, with Josje Dikkers (VU) and Marloes van Engen (UvT). She has published several book chapters and articles (e.g., *Journal of Vocational Behavior* and the *Journal of Occupational and Organizational Psychology*, *Leadership Quarterly*) on her research, as well as edited a book on "Top potentials" for the Dutch Foundation of Management Development.

JOSJE S. E. DIKKERS works at the Department of Human Resource Management, University of Applied Sciences Utrecht. She studied Work- & Organizational

Psychology at Tilburg University and completed this study with honors (Cum Laude). In 2008, she earned her PhD on "Work–home interference in relation to work, organizational, and home characteristics" at the Department of Work- & Organizational Psychology of the Radboud University Nijmegen. From 2006 to 2012, she worked at VU University Amsterdam within the Department of Management & Organization Studies. Josje Dikkers has published several (inter)national articles and book chapters based on her research. Since 2004 she has also worked part time at Qidos as a research consultant. Her research interests primarily focus on the interaction between people's work and private lives and work–home culture.

Workload, Work-to-Family Conflict, and Health: Gender Differences and the Influence of Private Life Context

Marc J. P. M. van Veldhoven* and Susanne E. Beijer

Tilburg University

Previous research on gender differences in work-to-family conflict, and the latter's linkages with workload and health, has largely ignored the influence of private life context. Here, it is hypothesized that gender differences vary across private life contexts. A multiple-group analysis (SEM) is performed on a representative sample (N = 8,593) of the working population in Flanders (Belgium) to examine gender differences in six family configurations, based on having (or not) a partner (working or not), and having children. Women were found to report higher levels of work-to-family conflict than men, but this difference only holds when both partners are earning (with and without children), and in single-income families with children. Gender differences in the strength of the relationships between conflict and both workload and health were found in the overall sample, but were only reflected in specific subgroups. Our results suggest that private life context should receive attention in future research and policymaking aimed at achieving sustainable careers and caring.

Introduction

Nowadays, more and more people combine work and family roles. Demands placed in one role can spillover and affect another role (Netemeyer, Boles, & Murrian, 1996). This spillover is defined as work-to-family conflict where work

---

*Correspondence concerning this article should be addressed to Marc van Veldhoven, Department of Human Resource Studies, Tilburg University, PO Box 90153, 5000 LE Tilburg, The Netherlands [e-mail: m.j.p.m.vanveldhoven@tilburguniversity.edu].

This study used data gathered by the Flanders Social and Economic Council (SERV). The interpretation of these data in this article reflects the views of the authors alone. The authors would like to thank the guest editors for their constructive suggestions in preparing this article.

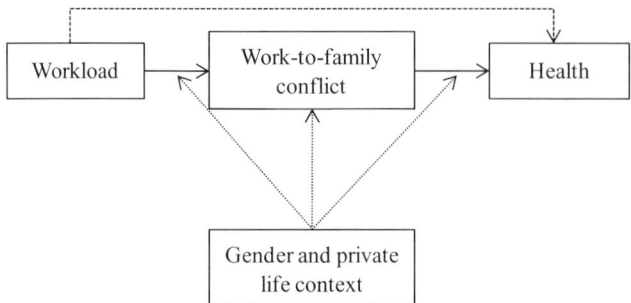

Fig. 1. Conceptual model.

negatively affects the family life of an employee (Frone, Russell, & Cooper, 1992a; 1992b). Work-to-family conflict is an important issue in the context of the sustainability of careers and caring (Van Engen, Vinkenburg, & Dikkers, 2012), and constitutes the focal point of this article.

Experiencing work-to-family conflict has been found to have a negative impact on employee health (Allen, Herst, Bruck, & Sutton, 2000; Eby, Casper, Lockwood, Bordeaux, & Brinley, 2005). The overall causal model that we use as our starting point for the analysis is the "work-home spillover chain" (Frone et al., 1992a; 1992b), and is represented in Figure 1. We follow Geurts, Kompier, Roxburgh, and Houtman's (2003) work, and further investigate the mediating role of work-to-family conflict in the relationship between workload and health. In this model, work-to-family conflict is predicted by *workload,* as such a conflict is more likely to occur when one has too much work to do and not enough time to do it in (Geurts et al., 2003). The central variable in the chain is w*ork-to-family conflict* which refers to a situation where work interferes with family life (Frone et al., 1992a; 1992b). Work-to-family conflict is, in turn, expected to influence *health,* both physically and psychologically (Greenhaus, Allen, & Spector, 2006). Ultimately, health has implications for career and family outcomes, as it influences the amount of effort and time a person can invest in achieving desired outcomes. This "state-of-the-art" model has previously been supported in a number of studies (e.g., Geurts et al., 2003; Geurts, Taris, Kompier, Dikkers, van Hooff, & Kinnunen, 2005; Sonnentag, 2001).

Previous research on gender differences in work–family conflict and in its antecedents and consequences shows mixed findings (Byron, 2005). One possible explanation could be that previous studies have examined gender differences separately from other relevant personal characteristics such as the presence of a partner (working or not), or having children (Allen et al., 2000). Ignoring such characteristics of the private life context is common: only 36% of all studies in this area report any information on the family configuration of respondents

(Casper, Bordeaux, Eby, & Lockwood, 2007). Only a few studies have examined private life characteristics simultaneously, a notable example being that of Erickson, Martinengo, and Hill (2011) which examines work–family conflict among individuals in different family life stages, although this study does not focus on gender differences within these groups. A second explanation for the mixed findings is that the majority of studies on work–family conflict have, despite the growing diversity in family composition, focused on employed individuals with a partner and/or children (Byron, 2005). As a result, important groups within the contemporary workforce such as single-earner parents and childless employees have been omitted from much of the research (Casper et al., 2007; Parasuraman & Greenhaus, 2002). We argue that, in order to fully understand work-to-family conflict and its associations with workload and health, greater knowledge is required on the influence of the various family configurations in which individuals today live.

Role of the Private Life Context

We are interested in the role of private life context in gender differences in the *levels* of work-to-family conflict, and on the *strength of relationships* of such a conflict with workload and health. We build on a small number of studies that compare such variables and relationships for various private life contexts, albeit focusing on only one characteristic of this context at a time. Our study is based on a large heterogeneous sample such that nontraditional family configurations are also included. Rather than examining homogeneous populations, as in many of the previous studies (Casper et al., 2007; Kossek & Ozeki, 1998), this sample allows us to investigate the generalizability of the findings on gender differences in work-to-family conflict across subgroups of the population.

We use a typology of private life context (Schneer & Reitman, 1993; Tharenou, 1999) based on three variables: having a partner, whether the partner is employed, and providing care for children. By simultaneously taking these three characteristics of the private life context into account, six unique groups are distinguished. Further, for each group, we further subdivide into men and women, resulting in a total of 12 subgroups. The first paired groups are families with children where both parents work, or "dual-earner parents" (with dual-earner fathers referred to as group 1 and dual-earner mothers referred to as group 7). The next pairing are again couples who both work but this time without children (groups 2: dual-earner men and 8: dual-earner women). Next, we have couples with children where only one parent works (groups 3: single-earner fathers and 9: single-earner mothers); followed by single-income couples without children (groups 4: single-earner men and 10: single-earner women). Finally we have single adults: first with children (group 5: single fathers and group 11: single mothers), and then without children (groups 6: single men and 12: single women). By analyzing and comparing these 12 groups, we will cover the possibility that the results cannot be reduced to interactions of the three constituting factors (having a partner, having a working partner, and having children) and explore the possibility that gender differences within a specific private life context, for example, single fathers versus single mothers, lead to different results.

Below, hypotheses are developed concerning gender differences and the role of private life context, more specifically on (a) the level of work-to-family conflict, (b) the relationship between workload and work-to-family conflict, and (c) the relationship between work-to-family conflict and health. Since only a few studies have previously examined combinations of characteristics of the private life context, and more research has been urged (Allen et al., 2000; Eby et al., 2005), our specific hypotheses will only refer to the subgroups where children are present. For the three remaining contexts (i.e., those without children) our analysis will be explorative, as there is an insufficient basis on which to justify explicit subgroup hypotheses.

Gender Differences in the Level of Work-to-Family Conflict

Several theories can be used to ground our hypotheses as to gender differences in the level of work-to-family conflict. Using Conservation of Resources (COR) theory as a starting point, Grandey and Cropanzano (1999) expected women to report higher levels of work-to-family conflict than men. Research shows that women are more likely to have jobs which contain high levels of job stressors, which will threaten their personal resources to a larger extent. At the same time, the resources available in women's jobs tend to be lower than in men's. This makes it more difficult for women to cope given the same workload, with a higher level of spillover from work to home as a likely result.

In terms of parenting, it is expected, based on traditional gender roles (Gutek, Nakamura, & Nieva, 1981), that mothers will take more responsibility for satisfying family demands than fathers. As a consequence, mothers will experience higher levels of work-to-family conflict than fathers. However, single fathers are expected to have the same responsibility for meeting family demands as single mothers given the absence of a partner with whom to share responsibilities. Here, the conflict levels are expected to be similar.

Private life context is also expected to indirectly affect the level of work-to-family conflict through descriptive and injunctive norms (Eagly & Karau, 2002) held by individuals themselves, or by others in the work environment, on what a good parent—and especially a good mother—is or should be like (Heilman & Okimoto, 2008; Okimoto & Heilman, 2012; van Engen, Dikkers, Vinkenburg, & de Rooy, 2009; Van Engen et al., 2012). These norms can be expected to increase the level of conflict when one's private life context fails to match the prescribed role. For example, whereas a single-earner father working overtime might be viewed as complying with the traditional gender role as breadwinner, a mother who is part of a dual-earner or single-earner couple might be seen as going against what is expected according to her gender-role, and this could lead to a so-called "maternal wall" (Crosby, Williams, & Biernat, 2004). Consequently, this mother might have to defend the choices she made to others and/or to herself in order to maintain a positive identity (Burke, 1991).

Gender differences in the level of work-to-family conflict have been reported in empirical studies, but only when considering single characteristics of the private life context rather than the overall private life configuration. A meta-analysis of 61 studies examined, with respect to gender differences and parental status, whether differences in sample composition moderated the relationships between antecedents and work–family conflict (Byron, 2005). It was shown that, when samples include a higher proportion of parents, the effect of gender on work–family conflict is stronger because mothers experience higher levels of conflict than fathers (Byron, 2005). Previous research on the effect of marital status on work–family conflict showed that being married is associated with greater conflict for men, while this relationship is near zero for women (Byron, 2005). Dual employment is argued to be more important for women than men since the hours spent at work by partners are associated with more work–family role strain for women than for men (Keith & Schafer, 1980). Based on the above, we formulate our first hypothesis. In brackets, we refer to the specific groups involved in a particular comparison, using the group numbers introduced earlier.

Hypothesis 1: In general, the level of work-to-family conflict is higher for women than men. More specifically, the level of work-to-family conflict is higher for dual- and single-earner mothers than for dual- and single-earner fathers (groups 7 vs. 1, and 9 vs. 3), but the same for single mothers and single fathers, where we do not expect gender differences (group 5 vs. group 11).

Gender Differences in the Relationship between Workload and Work-to-Family Conflict

Given that few empirical studies have examined gender differences in the strength of the relationships between workload, conflict, and health within private life configurations, we base Hypotheses 2 and 3 on theoretical arguments as presented below.

The main thrust of the COR model is that people are motivated by the desire to protect and/or build their resources (of various kinds), as was first outlined by Hobfoll (1989). This is relevant to work-to-family conflict in that high workloads may act as a stressor by threatening the personal and family resources of the individual.

Based on traditional gender roles (Gutek et al., 1981) and norms on what men "should be like" (Eagly & Karau, 2002), men are expected to give priority to the work role over the family role, devoting more energy and other resources to work than to the family. This implies that, if work intensifies, for example, through extended working time, the already limited resources that can be invested in the family are easily threatened. In this view, men have smaller reserves of resources available for family role tasks, and fewer obligations than women, resulting in the expectation of a stronger relationship between workload and work-to-family conflict for men than for women.

In one-parent families, men are expected to attach as much priority to the family role as women. Due to the lack of a partner to share responsibilities with, men are not expected to prioritize work over family and, as a result, no gender differences in the relationship between workload and conflict are expected in this context.

Hypothesis 2: In general, we expect the positive relationship between workload and work-to-family conflict to be stronger for men than women. More specifically, the relationships between workload and work-to-family conflict for dual- and single-earner fathers are stronger than those for dual- and single-earner mothers (1 vs. 7, and 3 vs. 9), but not for single fathers relative to single mothers, where gender differences are not expected (5 vs. 11).

Gender Differences in the Relationship between Work-to-Family Conflict and Health

Resources invested by employees specifically in managing their work–family balance may pose an additional threat to their health (Grandey & Cropanzano, 1999; Jansen, Kant, Kristensen, & Nijhuis, 2003; Moreno-Jiménez, Mayo, Sanz-Vergel, Geurts, Rodríguez-Muñoz, & Garrosa, 2009). Such balancing requires additional personal resources on top of those needed to perform work- and family-related tasks as such (they constitute what Hochschild (1997) calls the "third shift"). This may therefore exacerbate conflict, with possible negative implications for health.

In terms of gender differences, one could expect the relationship between work-to-family conflict and health to be stronger for women than for men since—according to identity theory—work-to-family conflict impedes achieving a positive family identity (Frone, Russell, & Barnes, 1996). According to traditional gender roles (Eagly & Karau, 2002; Frone et al., 1996) and normative beliefs about parenting (Van Engen et al., 2012), family identity is more highly valued by women. Women are expected, based on existing descriptive and injunctive norms, to value family over work. This is, for example, illustrated in the concept of motherhood ideology. Identity theory predicts that impediments to forming a positive family self-identity are associated with experiencing strain (Frone et al., 1996). As women are expected to experience these impediments more strongly than men, this, in turn, is expected to result in a stronger relationship between conflict and health for women.

The gender difference argued for above applies to dual- and single-earner mothers and also to single mothers. Although in Hypotheses 1 and 2 we expected single mothers and fathers (groups 5 and 11) not to differ, we do expect a difference in the work-to-family conflict–health linkage. This is because, unlike in a time-related argument where we expect no differences between single mothers and single fathers, the *identity* argument presented above is expected to be stronger for single mothers than for single fathers. Thus, we present our third hypothesis as:

> *Hypothesis 3:* In general, the positive relationship between work-to-family conflict and health complaints is stronger for women than for men. More specifically, the relationship between work-to-family conflict and health is stronger for dual- and single-earner mothers, and for single mothers compared to dual- and single-earner fathers, and single fathers, respectively (7 vs. 1, 9 vs. 3, and 11 vs. 5).

Method

Participants and Procedure

This study used data gathered through the 2004 Flemish "Workability monitor." This survey was commissioned in order to examine the quality of labor and employee wellbeing in Flanders (the Dutch-speaking part of Belgium) by the national government, and was performed on a representative sample of the working population. The survey was focused on a multitude of labor issues, of which work-to-family conflict was one. A random sample was drawn from the total working population of 2,081,969 individuals at the time (Bourdeaud'hui, Janssens, & Vanderhaege, 2004). The survey organizers sent the questionnaires to the potential respondents by mail. The data are not nested in that both partners in a working couple are included as individuals in the dataset, and the likelihood of having included a couple by chance in the sample is extremely small. The representativeness of the sample was examined by comparing the sample to statistics for the entire working population for gender, sector, and age. No deviations were found from the total working population in Flanders. A nonresponse analysis was performed, which showed that only very small deviations from the sample population were found, namely slightly fewer males and individuals younger than 25 were included in the dataset than might be expected. Based on the above, it was concluded that the final sample was representative of the total working population in Flanders (Bourdeaud'hui et al., 2004). The representation of ethnicities in this sample can be expected to be similar to the total Flemish working population, with 92.2% of all workers being born in Belgium, 3.8% in another EU country, and 4.0% in a non-EU country (Flemish Service for Employment, 2009).

After removing nonusable questionnaires (a listwise deletion of cases with missing data was performed), our dataset contains a total of 8,593 respondents. In the sample, 46.3% of the respondents were women and the mean age was 38.9 ($SD = 9.9$). The average tenure (period in current employment) was 12.8 years ($SD = 10.1$). Just over three quarters, 76.3%, of the respondents were working full-time, 14.4% part-time but equivalent to more than 60% of full-time (i.e., at least 3 days a week, or equivalent), and 9.3% of the respondents worked less than 60% of full-time. 56.7% of the respondents had children living at home. 77.5% of the respondents lived with a partner and, of these partners, 84.7% were currently working. With regard to educational level, 5.5% of the respondents were not educated or had received only primary education, 19.1% had completed lower secondary education before leaving school, 33.9% higher secondary education, 27.4% higher education (2–3 years), and 14.1% had completed higher education (for more than 3 years) or university level education. 5.4% of the respondents held a management position, 14.2% a professional position, 16.5% a position involving caring or teaching, 29.5% had an applied job, 20.5% were skilled workers or technicians, and 13.9% were untrained.

Measures

Health was assessed using a 14-item *health complaints* scale and this measure examined, in line with Greenhaus et al. (2006), physical as well as psychological aspects of health. The items were drawn from two sources. Physical health was assessed with a measure of psychosomatic complaints consisting of nine items developed by Bourdeaud'hui et al. (2004). These items questioned whether the respondent had experienced any of the following complaints in the last 2 weeks: backache, stomachache, headache, neck or shoulder pain, sleeping difficulties, muscle pain, fatigue, restless sleep, and emotional problems. Psychological health was assessed using five selected items from the measure of need for recovery after work developed by Van Veldhoven and Meijman (1994). A sample item being: "by the end of the working day, I feel really worn out." All 14 items about health were dichotomous (*yes/no*), with a higher score indicating suffering from more health complaints. A confirmatory factor analysis was performed on the 14 items which showed that a two-factor model (with three pairs of correlated errors) fitted the data well ($\chi^2 = 1,716.65$, $df = 73$, $p < .00$, RMSEA $= .05$, AGFI $= .96$, TLI $= .94$). The fact that the two factors were highly correlated ($r = .78$) is indicative of a large overlap between the two health dimensions. For reasons of parsimony we therefore decided to combine the two sets of items in a single scale score. The

Cronbach's Alphas of the total scale were .83 for the group of all men, and .83 for the group of all women. The subgroup Alpha values varied from .81 in group 5 (single fathers) to .87 in group 9 (single-earner mothers).

Workload was assessed using an 11-item scale that is part of the Questionnaire on the Experience and Evaluation of Work (VBBA, Van Veldhoven & Meijman, 1994). This specific scale examines quantitative work demands in terms of volume and speed. An example item is: "do you work under time pressure?" Respondents reported their experience of specified job demands on a four-point scale ranging from 0 (*never*) to 3 (*always*). An average score was calculated by dividing the summed scores by the number of items. Cronbach's Alphas were .89 for the group of all men, and .90 for the group of all women. The Alpha values for the specific subgroups varied from .88 for groups 4 (single-earner men) and 6 (single men) to .91 for group 9 (single-earner mothers).

Work-to-family conflict was measured using three items from the Survey Work–Home Interaction Nijmegen (SWING, Geurts et al., 2005). A sample item was: "how often does it happen that you find it difficult to fulfill your domestic obligations because you are constantly thinking about your work?" Items included in the questionnaire relating to strain or fatigue-related content were excluded to avoid item overlap with the scale used in this study for measuring health. Respondents reported their experience of work-to-family conflict on a four-point scale ranging from 0 (*never*) to 3 (*always*). Cronbach's Alpha for this scale was .77 for the group of all men, and .70 for the group of all women. The values ranged from .60 for group 5 (single fathers) to .78 for group 1 (dual-earner fathers).

Analyses

Analyses were performed on the 12 subgroups. The average subgroup size was 716 and varied from 89 respondents for group 9 (single-earner mothers) to 2016 for group 7 (dual-earner mothers). All the subgroup sizes are reported in Table 2. In addition to the twelve subgroups, two general groups were analyzed which comprised all the men ($n = 4{,}617$) and all women ($n = 3{,}976$), respectively. First, the mean scores were compared for the all men and the all women groups, such that gender differences were effectively assessed without taking private life context into account. Next, equivalent groups were compared to examine whether the level of conflict differs significantly between men and women in specific private life contexts.

Gender Differences in the Level of Work-to-Family Conflict versus in the Strength of the Hypothesized Relationships

Mean differences in the levels of work-to-family conflict were examined by performing *t*-tests. Further, to assess gender differences in the hypothesized

Table 1. Descriptives and Correlations

	M	SD	1.	2.	3.	4.	5.
1. Workload	1.36/1.32	0.52/0.52	(.89/.90)	.50***	.52***	.07***	.07***
2. Work-to-family conflict	0.81/0.86	0.66/0.64	.47***	(.77/.70)	.51***	.07***	.09***
3. Health complaints	0.34/0.41	0.26/0.27	.50***	.53***	(.83/.83)	.03*	.03*
4. Partner[a]	1.78/1.78	0.42/0.42	.04*	.07***	−.01		.48***
5. Children[b]	1.56/1.60		.01	.09***	−.03	.33***	

Note. Correlations indicated above the diagonal are for men, below for women.
M, SD, and Cronbach's Alpha (diagonal) are indicated as follows: men/women.
[a] 0 = not living together with a partner, 1 = living together with a partner.
[b] 0 = no children living at home, 1 = children living at home.
*$p < .05$, **$p < .01$, ***$p < .001$.

relationships, multiple group analyses were performed using AMOS 18. An alternative approach, using moderated regression, would have involved, in our situation, four-way interactions in the regression equation. We considered this a less preferable option because of the notoriously low statistical power of the latter technique, the associated high Type II error rates (Aguinis, 2002), as well as the difficulties associated with interpreting any interaction effects found. Multiple group analysis, on the other hand, enables one to estimate a model for each of the different private life contexts and compare the regression coefficients between subgroups (Kline, 2004). By imposing equal estimates on equivalent groups (i.e., groups that vary by gender of the respondent but are equal in terms of the private life context) one can assess, through a χ^2 difference test, whether the fit of the work–home spillover chain model is changed significantly by imposing this equality constraint. A significant decrease in model fit when the constraint is imposed is indicative of significant gender differences between otherwise equivalent groups.

All the analyses were performed both with and without the following three control variables: age, education level, and an indicator for part-time or full-time work. Including these control variables did not affect the fit of the models, the significance of χ^2 difference tests, or the direction of the gender differences found and, consequently, only the results of the analyses without these control variables are reported here.

Results

Descriptive statistics of the three scales are reported for all men and all women in Table 1. Moderate to strong correlations were found between the three survey measures. Having a partner and having children is positively correlated with work-to-family conflict for both men and women. Partner employment is not included in this table since this variable only applies to part of the sample (those employees with a partner).

We now present gender differences in the level of work-to-family conflict. Subsequently, results on gender differences in the strengths of the relationships in the work-home spillover chain are presented.

Gender Differences in the Level of Work-to-Family Conflict

In Table 2, the levels of work-to-family conflict are reported for each of the 12 groups. Before we examine the gender differences between equivalent groups, we comment briefly on the subgroups which reported relatively high levels of conflict. First, both men and women who are part of dual-earner families with children report relatively high levels of conflict compared to men and women in general. Dual-earner fathers report higher levels of such conflict ($M = .88$; $SD = .68$) than men in general ($M = .81$; $SD = .66$); $t(1,894) = 4.35, p < .00$; and dual-earner mothers score higher ($M = .91$; $SD = .63$) than women in general ($M = .86$; $SD = .64$); $t(2,015) = 3.77, p < .00$. Single fathers also report significantly higher levels of conflict than men in general ($M = .94$; $SD = .60$ vs. $M = .81$; $SD = .66$); $t(110) = 2.27, p = .03$. Both single childless men and women report relatively low levels of conflict compared to men and women in general (men: $M = .70$ ($SD = .65$) vs. $M = .81$ ($SD = .66$); $t(944) = -5.37, p < .00$; women: $M = .74$ ($SD = .62$) vs. $M = .86$ ($SD = .64$); $t(620) = -4.88, p < .00$). Among women, dual-earner mothers (group 7) report the highest levels of work-to-family conflict. Among men, single fathers report the highest levels (group 5). Across all twelve groups, the highest value ($M = .94$) is found in single fathers (group 5), the lowest ($M = .70$) in single men without children (group 6).

With respect to gender differences in equivalent groups, we found evidence to support the consensual view that women in general report significantly higher levels of work-to-family conflict than men ($M = .86$ ($SD = .64$) vs. $M = .81$ ($SD = .66$); $t(8,591) = 3.77, p < .00$), thus confirming our first hypothesis. However, when taking private life context into account, only a few significant differences in the level of work-to-family conflict were found between the gender subgroups. Women who are dual-earners with children report higher levels of conflict than men in a similar position ($M = .91$ ($SD = .63$) vs. $M = .88$ ($SD = .68$); $t(3,909) = 1.81, p = .07$ for groups 7 and 1). The gender difference for single-earner parents is not significant although the pattern of results is in line with H1 since the level of work-to-family conflict is higher for women than men ($M = .88$ ($SD = .68$) vs. $M = .81$ ($SD = .65$); $t(598) = 1.04, p = .30$ for groups 9 and 3). In line with H1, no gender differences were found for single parents (groups 5 and 11).

With respect to the groups not explicitly included in H1, dual-earner women without children also seem to experience higher levels of conflict than men in this context, although this is only significant at the $p < .10$ level ($M = .84$ ($SD = .64$) vs. $M = .78$ ($SD = .62$); $t(1,738) = 1.76, p = .08$ for groups 8 and 2). No gender

Table 2. Gender Differences in Levels and Strength of Relationships

Group number	Group label	Group size Men/Women	Level Work-to-family conflict Men/Women	Relationship Workload → Work-to-family conflict Men/Women	Relationship Work-to-family conflict → Health complaints Men/Women
Group 1–6/7–12	All men/women	4,617/3,976	.81/.86 $t(8,591) = 3.77, p < .00$	50/.47	35/.38
Group 1/7	Dual-earner parents	1,895/2,016	.88/.91 $t(3,909) = 1.81, p = .07$	53/.46	35/.40
Group 2/8	Dual-earners without children	866/874	.78/.84 $t(1,738) = 1.76, p = .08$		
Group 3/9	Single-earner parents	511/89	.81/.88 $t(598) = 1.04, p = .30$		
Group 4/10	Single-earners without children	289/121	.77/.75 $t(408) = -0.22, p = .83$		
Group 5/11	Single parents	111/255	.94/.87 $t(364) = -0.92, p = .36$		.24/.39
Group 6/12	Singles without children	945/621	.70/.74 $t(1,564) = 1.37, p = .17$		

Note. All regression weights are significant at the .001 level.

differences exist in the conflict levels of single men and women without children (groups 6 and 12) and single-earners without children (groups 4 and 10).

Gender Differences in the Relationship between Workload and Work-to-Family Conflict

In line with our second hypothesis, we found that the effect of workload on work-to-family conflict is stronger for dual-earner men with children than women in the same situation ($\beta = .53$ vs. $\beta = .46$ for groups 1 and 7, respectively [$\Delta \chi^2 (1) = 10.93$, $p = .001$]). The expectation that no gender differences would exist for single parents (groups 5 and 11) is also confirmed. Although it was hypothesized that the relationship between workload and work-to-family conflict would be stronger for single-earner fathers than single-earner mothers, no gender differences were found between these groups (groups 3 and 9).

No gender differences were detected for any of the groups not explicitly included in our hypotheses, namely dual-earners without children (groups 2 and 8), single-earners without children (groups 4 and 10), and singles without children (groups 6 and 12).

Gender Differences in the Relationship between Work-to-Family Conflict and Health

In line with our third hypothesis, we found that the relationship between work-to-family conflict and health complaints is significantly stronger for women than for men in dual-earner families with children ($\beta = .40$ vs. $\beta = .35$ in groups 7 and 1, respectively [$\Delta \chi^2 (1) = 5.70$, $p = .017$]). This is also true for single parents, with the relationship between conflict and health complaints significantly stronger for women than for men ($\beta = .39$ vs. $\beta = .24$ in groups 11 and 5, respectively [$\Delta \chi^2 (1) = 4.33$, $p = .037$]). Contrary to H3, however, no gender differences were found in the strength of the effect for single-earner parents (groups 3 and 9).

For the other groups (dual-earners without children, single-earners without children, and singles without children) no gender differences were found in the strengths of the effects of work-to-family conflict on health complaints.

Discussion

Overall, the findings of this study illustrate that gender differences can be found between men and women in the overall sample, but that these are really only reflected in specific private life contexts. On average, women report higher levels of work-to-family conflict than men, but this difference stems from dual-earners with and without children and from single-earner parents. This general pattern is not seen with single parents, with single fathers reporting the highest level of work-to-family conflict across all twelve subgroups investigated, albeit at a level not significantly different to that for single mothers. Gender differences in the strength of the relationships between work-to-family conflict and both workload and health are even more limited to certain subgroups in the workforce. Gender differences in the relationship between workload and work-to-family conflict are only seen for dual-earners with children, with men showing a stronger relationship. Gender differences in the relationship between work-to-family conflict and health were only found for dual-earner parents and single parents, with women showing a stronger relationship in both situations. Overall our results indicate that considering only gender can result in overestimating gender differences for a considerable component of the workforce.

Our hypotheses on general gender differences in the levels of conflict and in the strength of the relationships are all confirmed. Furthermore, for dual-earners with children, the expected gender differences, as predicted in our three hypotheses, are also all confirmed. These findings are in line with gender role theory as well as with identity theory and underline the relevance of established work-home spillover patterns to dual-earners with children.

Our findings for single parents are also in line with expectations, in that gender differences were not found in the level of work-to-family conflict or in the strength of the relationship between workload and work-to-family conflict. This is in line with role theory, which argues that, as men have the same amount of responsibility as women for satisfying family demands in this context, no gender differences will be found. Also in line with our prediction, we found that, with single parents, the relationship between work-to-family conflict and health complaints is stronger for women than men. This we had argued based on identity theory rather than role theory. This latter finding contradicts earlier findings by Frone, Russell, and Cooper (1993) and Frone et al. (1996) that gender differences did not exist in the effect of work-to-family conflict on depression, poor physical health, and heavy alcohol use. A possible explanation is that Frone et al. (1993; 1996) combined individuals currently married, living as married, and/or with children living at home, in one group, thereby possibly masking gender differences in the relatively few single parents contained within the group.

Contrary to our hypotheses, no gender differences were found for single-earner parents in either the level of work-to-family conflict or the strength of the relationships of work-to-family conflict with both workload and health. This is somewhat surprising, and we have considered possible explanations. Baxter, Hewitt, and Western (2005) have shown that women spend more time on household tasks and childcare than men in general, and also that this difference continues when men are unemployed and women are employed. The women in these groups are not only responsible for providing for their family financially but also, it is argued, for managing household and childcare. The pressure to fulfill societal expectations associated with their own gender role, as well as expectations from the family to fulfill the traditionally male role (in terms of providing financially) might certainly lead one to expect high levels of work-to-family conflict in single-earner mothers. Although this was to an extent supported (the score was above the average for all women), it was not statistically significant. This lack of significance could be due to this being a relatively small subgroup of the working population, and indeed the smallest subsample in this study. Sample size may also have played a role in not finding the hypothesized pattern in the linkages between work-to-family conflict, workload, and health for this group. More research is needed on the negotiations between partners regarding the division of work and family responsibilities (see Kailasapathy & Metz, 2012) in the context of single-income families, especially when the women provided the income.

We concluded from our literature review that, for the subgroups without children, the literature was too preliminary to put forward any specific hypotheses. Further, our exploration failed to find any gender differences in the comparisons made for childless dual-earners, single-earners, and singles. From this, we infer that, in terms of gender roles and identities influencing gender differences in work-to-family conflict and its linkages, taking care of children is the major impact factor. Having a partner, and whether the partner works, appears to be less influential. We found only one exception to this general observation, and this was only weakly significant at the $p < .10$ level. This concerned dual-earners without children, where women were found to have higher levels of work-to-family conflict.

Limitations

With regard to the methodology used in this study, the multiple group analysis used to examine differences between overall and subgroup linkages has important advantages over a moderated regression technique. Both techniques do however share a drawback in that the power of the statistical test, used to examine whether differences between groups are significant, depends on group size and reliability fluctuations in the measurement scales between groups. As a result, our procedure will be less sensitive to differences between small groups and/or groups with lower scale reliabilities. As already commented, this could especially have influenced our comparisons between the male and female single-earner parents.

As our study is based on cross-sectional data, no firm conclusions can be drawn on causality or temporal ordering. The work-home spillover chain is however strongly grounded in theory as well as empirics and, therefore, studying gender differences in the proposed chain while considering the private life context can produce valuable results, even with cross-sectional data. The drawback of not having longitudinal data is balanced, we believe, by the fact that we have been able to use a large, representative sample of the working population of Flanders (Belgium). This heterogeneous sample includes nontraditional family configurations, and these have generally been omitted in previous studies or not singled out (Casper et al., 2007; Kossek & Ozeki, 1998). A possible limitation of this sample concerns the generalizability of the findings beyond Flanders. Based on the cultural dimensions by Hofstede (1983), Belgium can be characterized by a moderate level of masculinity, comparable with a number of Latin, and a cluster of Anglo-Saxon, countries. This cultural characteristic may partly explain the gender differences found in our study. More specifically, the extent to which a society has a sharp gender-role division is expected to increase the level of work-to-family conflict experienced by employed women since they face the dual burden of having work and family-related responsibilities. As Belgium is characterized by a moderate level of masculinity, the generalizability of our findings may not extend to countries with a strong gender-role division (such as Japan or Austria) or to countries with a weak gender-role division (including the Scandinavian countries and the Netherlands).

A further limitation of this study relates to the way in which inferences are drawn about the level of care responsibilities based on the presence of a partner and children. It is possible that these characteristics are inadequate for qualifying the level of care responsibilities for individuals who have separated from their partner. Similarly, a number of other factors that could be expected to strongly influence the intensity of private-life demands are not considered in our study. These include the number of children, the age of children, the level of family income [which could determine possibilities for outsourcing household and care responsibilities (Bittman, Matheson, & Meagher, 1999)], the crossover of conflict levels between spouses (Song, Foo, Uy, & Sun, 2011), and additional responsibilities for caring for elderly relatives (Chapman, Ingersoll-Dayton, & Neal, 1994). However, with respect to the final aspect, it should be noted that nuclear families are more common than extended families in Belgium, partly due to highly developed institutional care for the elderly (Anttonen & Sipilä, 1996), resulting in a relatively limited amount of time spent on caring for elderly relatives compared to children (Parent-Thirion, Macías, Hurley, & Vermeylen, 2007). Furthermore, while the choices parents make in combining careers and caring are argued to play a significant role, these "choices" themselves might be influenced by normative beliefs about parenting (Van Engen et al., 2012). Overall, we believe that this study takes an important first step by investigating the effects of private life context and considering three important variables simultaneously. Nevertheless, the specification of private life context could certainly be further refined in future research.

Implications

The results of our study indicate that taking into account three aspects of the private life context (children, partner, partner's employment) can add to our understanding of gender differences in work-to-family conflict. It was shown that ignoring the private life context can result in the identification of gender differences that are seen as applying to the entire population. However, on closer analysis, these differences only apply to certain subgroups of men and women. Based on this study, our suspicion is that a considerable amount of the previous research on work–family conflicts has been strongly influenced by patterns that are common among dual-earner parents. This specific subgroup makes up half of our total sample, and therefore has a large effect on the findings for the overall group.

The insights from our study into gender differences in work-to-family conflict have implications for developing effective policies to facilitate sustainable careers and caring. It can be argued that policies should be more differentiated based on specific private life contexts since the work-home spillover chain functions differently for specific contexts. Our study shows that dual-earner parents and single parents experience particular difficulties in balancing work and family roles. More attention could be paid to employees in these specific contexts by optimizing the availability of family-friendly human resource practices. Further, the actual use of family-friendly arrangements warrants further examination as this could be affected by normative parenting beliefs and gender roles (Van Engen et al., 2012). It is possible that providing additional support to certain groups of employees could result in negative reactions by employees belonging to other groups not receiving such specific support. It might therefore be necessary to consider family-related care responsibilities in the widest possible sense when providing additional support to employees. Supporting employees in such ways to achieve a better balance between work and private life, and create more sustainable careers and caring, could significantly enhance employee wellbeing and, along with that, career and family outcomes.

References

Aguinis, H. (2002). Estimation of interaction effects in organization studies. *Organizational Research Methods, 5*(3), 207–211. doi: 10.1177/1094428102005003001

Allen, T.D., Herst, D.E.L., Bruck, C.S., & Sutton, M. (2000). Consequences associated with work-to-family conflict: A review and agenda for future research. *Journal of Occupational Health Psychology, 5*(2), 278–308. doi: 10.1037/1076-8998.5.2.278

Anttonen, A., & Sipilä, J. (1996). European social care services: Is it possible to identify models? *Journal of European Social Policy, 6*(2), 87–100. doi: 10.1177/095892879600600201

Baxter, J., Hewitt, B., & Western, M. (2005). Post-familial families and the domestic division of labour. *Journal of Comparative Family Studies, 36*(4), 583–600.

Bittman, M., Matheson, G., & Meagher, G. (1999). The changing boundary between home and market: Australian trends in outsourcing domestic labour. *Work Employment & Society, 13*(2), 249–273. doi: 10.1177/09500179922117935

Bourdeaud'hui, R., Janssens, F., & Vanderhaege, S. (2004). *Informatiedossier nulmeting Vlaamse werkbaarheidsmonitor. Indicatoren voor de kwaliteit van de arbeid op de Vlaamse arbeidsmarkt 2004*. Brussel: Sociaal-Economische Raad–STV-Innovatie & Arbeid.

Burke, P.J. (1991). Identity processes and social stress. *American Sociological Review, 56*(6), 836–849. doi: 10.2307/2096259

Byron, K. (2005). A meta-analytic review of work-family conflict and its antecedents. *Journal of Vocational Behavior, 67*(2), 169–198. doi: 10.1016/j.jvb.2004.08.009

Casper, W.J., Bordeaux, C., Eby, L.T., & Lockwood, A. (2007). A review of methods in IO/OB work-family research. *Journal of Applied Psychology, 92*(1), 28–43. doi: 10.1037/0021-9010.92.1.28

Chapman, N. J., Ingersoll-Dayton, B., & Neal, M. B. (1994). Balancing the multiple roles of work and caregiving for children, adults, and elders. In C. P. Keita & J. J. Hurrel, Jr. (Eds.), *Job stress in a changing workforce* (pp. 283–300). Washington, DC: American Psychological Association.

Crosby, F. J., Williams, J. C., & Biernat, M. (2004). The maternal wall. *Journal of Social Issues*, *60*(4), 675–682. doi: 10.1111/j.0022-4537.2004.00379.x

Eagly, A. H., & Karau, S. J. (2002). Role congruity theory of prejudice toward female leaders. *Psychological Review*, *109*(3), 573–598. doi: 10.1037//0033-295X.109.3.573

Eby, L. T., Casper, W. J., Lockwood, A., Bordeaux, C., & Brinley, A. (2005). Work and family research in IO/OB: Content analysis and review of the literature (1980–2002). *Journal of Vocational Behavior*, *66*(1), 124–197. doi: 10.1016/j.jvb.2003.11.003

Erickson, J. J., Martinengo, G., & Hill, E. J. (2011). Putting work and family experiences in context: Differences by family life stage. *Human Relations*, *63*(7), 955–979. doi: 10.1177/0018726709353138

Flemish Service for Employment (2009). Kansengroepen in Kaart [Disadvantaged groups mapped]. Retrieved February 22, 2011, from http://vdab.be/trends/kik/

Frone, M. R., Russell, M., & Barnes, G. M. (1996). Work-family conflict, gender, and health related outcomes: A study of employed parents in two community samples. *Journal of Occupational Health Psychology*, *1*(1), 57–69. doi: 10.1037/1076-8998.1.1.57

Frone, M. R., Russell, M., & Cooper, M. L. (1992a). Prevalence of work-family conflict: Are work and family boundaries asymmetrically permeable? *Journal of Organizational Behavior*, *13*(7), 723–729. doi: 10.1002/job.4030130708

Frone, M. R., Russell, M., & Cooper, M. L. (1992b). Antecedents and outcomes of work family conflict: Testing a model of the work-family interface. *Journal of Applied Psychology*, *77*(1), 65–78. doi: 10.1037/0021-9010.77.1.65

Frone, M. R., Russell, M., & Cooper, M. L. (1993). Relationship of work-family conflict, gender, and alcohol expectancies to alcohol use/abuse. *Journal of Organizational Behavior*, *14*(6), 545–558. doi: 10.1002/job.4030140604

Geurts, S. A. E., Kompier, M. A. J., Roxburgh, S., & Houtman, I. L. D. (2003). Does work home interference mediate the relationship between workload and well-being? *Journal of Vocational Behavior*, *63*(3), 532–559. doi: 10.1016/S0001-8791(02)00025–8

Geurts, S. A. E., Taris, T. W., Kompier, M. A. J., Dikkers, J. S. E., van Hooff, M. L. M., & Kinnunen, U. M. (2005). Work-home interaction from a work psychological perspective: Development and validation of a new questionnaire, the SWING. *Work & Stress*, *19*(4), 319–339. doi: 10.1080/02678370500410208

Grandey, A. A., & Cropanzano, R. (1999). The conservation of resources model applied to work-family conflict and strain. *Journal of Vocational Behavior*, *54*, 350–370 doi: 10.1006/jvbe.1998.1666

Greenhaus, J. H., Allen, T. D., & Spector, P. E. (2006). Health consequences of work-family conflict: The dark site of the work-family interface. In P. L. Perrewe & D. C. Ganster (Eds.), *Employee health, coping and methodologies* (pp. 61–99). Research in occupational stress and well being, 5. Bingley, UK: JAI Press.

Gutek, B. A., Nakamura, C. Y., & Nieva, V. F. (1981). The independence of work and family roles. *Journal of Occupational Behaviour*, *2*(1), 1–16. doi: 10.1002/job.4030020102

Heilman, M. E., & Okimoto, T. G. (2008). Motherhood: A potential source of bias in employment decisions. *Journal of Applied Psychology*, *93*(1), 189–198. doi: 10.1037/0021-9010.93.1.189

Hobfoll, S. E. (1989). Conservation of resources. A new attempt at conceptualizing stress. *American Psychologist*, *44*(3), 513–524. doi: 10.1037/0003-066X.44.3.513

Hochschild, A. R. (1997). *The time bind: When work becomes home and home becomes work*. New York: Metropolitan/Holt.

Hofstede, G. (1983). The cultural relativity of organizational practices and theories. *Journal of International Business Studies*, *14*(2), 75–89. doi: 10.1057/palgrave.jibs.8490867

Jansen, N. W. H., Kant, I. J., Kristensen, T. S., & Nijhuis, F. J. N. (2003). Antecedents and consequences of work-family conflict: A prospective cohort study. *Journal of Occupational and Environmental Medicine*, *45*(5), 479–491.

Kailasapathy, P., & Metz, I. (2012). Work-family conflict in Sri Lanka: Negotiations of exchange relationships in family and at work. *Journal of Social Issues*, *68*(4), 790–813.

Keith, P. M., & Schafer, R. B. (1980). Role strain and depression in two-job families. *Family Relations*, *29*(4), 483–488.

Kline, R. B. (2004). *Principles and practice of structural equation modeling* (2nd ed.). New York: Guilford Publications.

Kossek, E. E., & Ozeki, C. (1998). Work family conflict, policies, and the job-life satisfaction relationship: A review and directions for organizational behavior-human resource research. *Journal of Applied Psychology*, *83*(2), 139–149. doi: 10.1037/0021 9010.83.2.139

Moreno-Jiménez, B., Mayo, M., Sanz-Vergel A. I., Geurts, S., Rodríguez-Muñoz, A., & Garrosa, E. (2009). Effects of work-family conflict on employees' well-being: The moderating role of recovery strategies. *Journal of Occupational Health Psychology*, *14*(4), 427–440. doi: 10.1037/a0016739

Netemeyer, R. G., Boles, J. S., & Murrian, R. (1996). Development and validation of work family conflict and family-work conflict scales. *Journal of Applied Psychology*, *81*(4), 400–410. doi: 10.1037/0021-9010.81.4.400

Okimoto, T. G., & Heilman, M. E. (2012). The "bad parent" assumption: How gender stereotypes affect reactions to working mothers. *Journal of Social Issues*, *68*(4), 704–724.

Parasuraman, S., & Greenhaus, J. H. (2002). Toward reducing some critical gaps in work family research. *Human Resource Management Review*, *12*(3), 299–312. doi: 0.1016/S1053-4822(02)00062-1

Parent-Thirion, A., Macías, E. F., Hurley, J., & Vermeylen, G. (2007). *European Foundation or the Improvement of Living and Working Conditions. Fourth European working conditions survey*. Luxembourg: Office for Official Publications of the European Communities.

Schneer, J. A., & Reitman, F. (1993). Effects of alternate family structures on managerial career paths. *The Academy of Management Journal*, *36*(4), 830–843. doi: 10.2307/256760

Song, Z., Foo, M.-D., Uy, M. A., & Sun, S. (2011). Unraveling the daily stress crossover between unemployed individuals and their employed spouses. *Journal of Applied Psychology*, *96*(1), 151–168. doi: 10.1037/a0021035

Sonnentag, S. (2001). Work, recovery activities, and individual well-being: A diary study. *Journal of Occupational Health Psychology*, *6*(3), 196–210. doi: 10.1037/1076 8998.6.3.196

Tharenou, P. (1999). Is there a link between family structures and women's and men's managerial career advancement. *Journal of Organizational Behavior*, *20*(6), 837–863. doi: 10.1002/(SICI)1099-1379(199911)20:6<837::AID-JOB978>3.0.CO;2-W

Van Engen, M. L., Dikkers, J. S. E., Vinkenburg, C. J., & de Rooy, E. (2009). Carrieresucces Van vaders en moeders: De rol van moederschapsideologie, werk-thuis-cultuur en werk thuis-arrangementen. [Career success of fathers and mothers: the impact of motherhood ideology, work-home culture, and work-home arrangements]. *Gedrag en Organisatie*, *22*(2), 146–171.

Van Engen, M. L., Vinkenburg, C. J., & Dikkers, J. S. E. (2012). Sustainability in combining career and care: Challenging normative beliefs about parenting. *Journal of Social Issues*, *68*(4), 645–664.

Van Veldhoven, M., & Meijman, T. F. (1994). *Het meten van psychosociale arbeidsbelasting met een vragenlijst: de vragenlijst beleving en beoordeling van de arbeid (VBBA)*. [The measurement of psychosocial job demands with a questionnaire: The questionnaire on the experience and evaluation of work (QEEW)]. Amsterdam: Nederlands Instituut voor Arbeidsomstandigheden.

MARC J.P.M. VAN VELDHOVEN (PhD, Groningen University, 1996) worked as a practitioner in occupational health psychology for 15 years. He returned to academia in 2002, and is currently a full professor in the Department of Human Resource Studies at Tilburg University. His main interest is in building bridges between research on occupational health psychology and HRM. He is an associate editor for the *Journal of Occupational and Organizational Psychology*.

SUSANNE E. BEIJER is a PhD candidate in the Department of Human Resource Studies at Tilburg University. Susanne's research interests and PhD project both focus on the concept of HR practices and their relationship with employee wellbeing (including health) and organizational outcomes.

The Association between Work–Family Guilt and Pro- and Anti-Social Work Behavior

Whitney Botsford Morgan*
University of Houston Downtown

Eden B. King
George Mason University

This article explores the behavioral outcomes of an understudied emotion, guilt, in the context of the work–family domain. Specifically, we propose that work–family guilt motivates both pro- and anti-social behaviors in the workplace. Working undergraduate students in the United States completed qualitative and quantitative indicators of behavioral responses to work–family guilt. Results demonstrated that when individuals experienced family-to-work guilt, they responded with helping behaviors directed toward individuals. When individuals experienced work-to-family guilt, they responded by shirking of work responsibilities. Thus, work–family guilt may be a critical and underexplored determinant of extrarole behaviors and an important emotion to manage in order to sustain career and care roles.

The study of emotion and emotions at work has experienced resurgence in the organizational psychology literature. Affective events theory (Weiss & Cropanzano, 1996) was a driving force in this renewed interest, as it identified the role of emotion among workplace experiences (attitudes and behaviors). Affective events theory specifically proposed that affective reactions to work events led directly to job-related behavior, thereby establishing the motivational link between emotion and behavioral outcomes (e.g., Rodell & Judge, 2009). One area where the role of emotion has been relatively, at least explicitly, unexplored is the work–family interface (Friede & Ryan, 2005). Given the centrality of work and family to adults' lives (Barnett & Hyde, 2001), it is important to recognize that work–family conflict may produce not only cognitive, but also emotional experiences

---

*Correspondence concerning this article should be addressed to Whitney Botsford Morgan, Department of Management, Marketing, and Business Administration, University of Houston-Downtown, One Main Street B-466, Houston, TX 77004 [e-mail: morganw@uhd.edu].

(MacDermind, Seery, & Weiss, 2002) that may, in turn, affect work and career outcomes.

Although theoretical work (Baumeister, Stillwell, & Heatherton, 1994) highlights the motivational tendencies of guilt (such as desire for punishment, pro-social effects, and anti-social effects), there has been little empirical exploration of its influence as a motivator of behavior in the workplace. The purpose of the current article is to empirically test the behavioral outcomes of an understudied emotion, guilt, in the context of the work–family domain in the United States. In so doing, we contribute to an understanding of experiences that make sustaining work and family roles challenging. First, we explore the nature and prevalence of guilt related to the work–family interface. Second, we propose that family-to-work guilt is a motivator of pro-social behavior, as people enact compensatory behaviors to make amends for perceived transgressions. Finally, we also propose that work-to-family guilt is a motivator of antisocial behavior, as people attempt to redress perceived inequity in their work-life.

Common Conceptions of the Work–Family Interface

The work–family interface is typically characterized by concepts such as work–family conflict, spillover, and balance (MacDermind et al., 2002). The most prominent of these notions, work–family conflict, can be defined as inter-role conflict that emerges when the demands in one domain are incompatible with the demands in another domain (family or work) (Greenhaus & Beutell, 1985). The work–family interface is classified as bidirectional in nature; elements of the family domain can influence the work domain and elements of the work domain can influence the family domain (Gutek, Searle, & Klepa, 1991). Both aspects of work–family conflict have been linked with important job outcomes, including stress and well-being (Frone, Russell, & Cooper, 1992), and performance (Kahn & Byosiere, 1992).

It is important to note that given changing definitions of families (U.S. Census Bureau, 2008) we take an intentionally broad approach (e.g., spouses, siblings, children) when considering family throughout our research. With the rise in dual earner couples, more and more families are juggling both work and family responsibilities (Hochschild & Machung, 2003; Tiedje, 2004) and perhaps prone to situations or experiences that produce emotions. Furthermore, in today's contemporary workforce employees are likely to have multiple roles that may give rise to emotional responses. For example, a worker is juggling school and sick parent. Researchers have focused on work–family conflict as the primary affective experience associated with involvement in work and family roles (Geenhaus & Beutell, 1985). Indeed, a major dimension of most typologies of work–family conflict reflects the affective experience of conflict (see Eby, Casper, Lockwood, Bordeaux, & Brinley, 2005) including feeling tension, anxiety, fatigue, depression, apathy, and irritability (Greenhaus & Beutell, 1985). Several recent models emphasize the linkages between work–family conflict and a wide range of emotions (e.g., Judge, Ilies, & Scott, 2006). However, recent media reports and preliminary evidence suggest that the affective experiences of working parents may best be captured by the emotion of guilt (Guendouzi, 2004). We propose employees experiencing such emotional discomfort (i.e., guilt) seek to restore balance in an effort to sustain multiple roles, however, these attempts to create balance may or may not facilitate a truly sustainable lifestyle.

Work–Family Guilt

Guilt is defined as "an aroused form of emotional distress...based on the possibility that one may be in the wrong or that others may have such a perception" (Baumeister et al., 1994, p. 245). The key to this definition is the subjective state that is driven by actual or perceived wrongdoing. Individuals independently evaluate their transgressions based upon perceived norms of the situation. The concept of wrongdoing based upon norms regarding parenthood is exemplified in Okimoto and Heilman's (2012) contribution to this special issue on "bad mothers." This idea is also explored in Fuegen, Biernat, Haines, and Deaux's (2004) work that demonstrated that gender and parental status influenced judgments of competence. Specifically, people rated parents as less agentic and less committed to employment than nonparents. Such judgments likely lead to normative expectations for parents. Importantly, researchers typically conceptualize guilt as an emotion, or affective state, and therefore view guilt as a response to a specific event (Oatley & Jenkins, 1992). Judge et al. (2006) stated that studying discrete emotional states is the most effective approach to understanding the emotional outcomes of work–family conflict. We conceptualize *work–family guilt* as an emotion that can occur when one's behavior violates the norms of how one believes they should balance the demands of work and family responsibilities and adversely affects an individual. In effect, people independently evaluate themselves based upon their perceptions of how an individual *should* manage work and family.

In the only published empirical study of guilt related to work and family, Livingston and Judge (2008) demonstrated that family-to-work conflict predicted guilt, and that the relationship between both family-to-work conflict and work-to-family conflict and guilt was moderated by gender-role orientation. Using multiple daily surveys, a sample of working adults completed measures of gender-role orientation, daily work–family conflict, and daily guilt. The results of Livingston and Judge's (2008) study imply that the role of emotion in the work–family interface likely depends on episodes wherein cross-domain effects come into play (MacDermind et al., 2002). For example, an emotion-generating event can lead to an appraisal and reaction in the domain in which the event occurred, or in the opposite domain. In addition, emotional responses and affect-driven behaviors are argued to emerge in both work and family domains. Thus, emotion-based events can produce behaviors in both work and family domains. For the purpose of this article we explore the experiences of guilt in both work and family domains, but we intentionally study the behavioral responses to guilt only within the work domain.

Pro- and Anti-Social Work Behaviors

Researchers have acknowledged that employee behavior includes not only behaviors directly related to the task at hand (i.e., task performance), but also organizational citizenship behavior (OCB) and counterproductive work behavior (CWB) (Rotundo & Sackett, 2002). We contend that work–family guilt can motivate both OCB and CWB. Consonant with affective events theory (Weiss & Cropanzano, 1996), we propose the outcomes of affective experiences (work–family guilt) are both attitudinal and behavioral. Affective experiences lead to affect driven behaviors, as well as judgment-driven behaviors where work attitudes, or evaluation of one's situation, influence the behavioral outcomes. Drawing upon social exchange and equity frameworks (see Adams, 1965; Blau, 1964) that emphasize balance we propose that an individual evaluates the situation and attempts to restore balance. Exchange-based equity perspectives suggest that individuals engage in behaviors (e.g., OCB; Konovsky, Organ, & Dennis, 1996; CWB; Weiss, Suckow, & Cropanzano, 1999) when they perceive inequity in an effort to restore balance. In effect, the evaluation of the event drives a behavioral response, and consideration of variability in evaluations surrounding the experience may clarify the conditions under which guilt may give rise to seemingly opposing behaviors. The following discussion reviews the behavioral responses of interest. We first discuss pro-social work behavior and then discuss anti-social work behavior.

Pro-Social Work Behavior

Organizational citizenship behavior can be defined as discretionary behavior that positively contributes to the organization (Organ, 1997). Podsakoff, MacKenzie, Moorman, and Fetter (1990) identified five factors of OCBs including altruism, conscientiousness, sportsmanship, courtesy, and civic virtue. These dimensions were further categorized into two separate dimensions: individual and organizational (Williams & Anderson, 1991). The former, OCB-Individual, refers to the dimensions directed toward the individual (including altruism and courtesy). The latter, OCB-Organizational, refers to the dimensions directed toward the organization (including sportsmanship, conscientiousness, and civic virtue). Because both OCB-Individual and OCB-Organizational contribute to organizational goals, researchers and practitioners have endeavored to identify their determinants.

There are differing perspectives that attempt to explain the performance of OCBs. One perspective is rooted in theories of social exchange and the norm of reciprocity (see Blau, 1964) which suggest that a series of reciprocal, positive exchanges with an organization or individual within an organization can lead to a general desire to perform OCBs toward the organization or toward the individual. A complementary explanation for the enactment of OCBs rests in equity theory or perceptions of fairness. This suggests that an individual must attend to the inputs and outputs and act accordingly to maintain balance (Adams, 1965). Therefore, the higher a person's perceived equity the more likely a person is to perform OCBs in order to maintain this positive, equitable relationship (e.g., Konovsky, Organ, & Dennis, 1996). Although these explanations have emerged in a somewhat disconnected manner, they are not necessarily competing models. Indeed, it is likely that exchange, reciprocity, equity, and individual differences work together to influence OCB. Arguably of more immediate importance are the proximal predictors of such extrarole behaviors; that is, the affective and motivational processes that are influenced by the nature of the situation and that give rise to behavior directly. This is consistent with previous work (e.g., Lee & Allen, 2002; Miles, Borman, & Spector, 2002) that has demonstrated a link between affect and OCB, supporting affect as a proximal predictor of extrarole behavior. Therefore, we focus on the experience of guilt as a proximal motivator of behavior.

The Role of Work–Family Guilt in Pro-Social Work Behavior

When individuals behave in a manner that they believe to be inconsistent with their values or norms (i.e., experience guilt), they are motivated to reconcile, repair, or compensate for their actions (Baumeister et al., 1994; Sommer & Baumeister, 1997; Tangney, 1995). Specifically, in a review of research on the experience of guilt, Baumeister et al. (1994) concluded that guilt motivates three types of behavior: desire for punishment, pro-social effects, and anti-social effects. Although empirical research has failed to provide adequate support for the notion that guilty parties desire punishment, research has provided evidence that guilt can be associated with both pro- and anti-social outcomes (see Baumeister et al., 1994). The underlying mechanism is that individuals, when experiencing guilt, change their behavior in order to meet perceived expectations and norms. Pro-social effects of guilt include effort to make amends or apologize for the perceived transgression (Baumeister et al., 1994). Furthermore, guilt may make individuals want to do something for another person such as a favor. Tangney (1991) has argued that there are many positive outcomes of guilt, especially empathy, as it acts as our moral compass and tells us when we are behaving inappropriately. Thus, although the experience of guilt is unpleasant for the individual, it can motivate changes in behavior and ultimately result in positive outcomes.

In the context of the work–family interface, individuals who feel guilty that their family responsibilities have interfered with their performance at work may attempt to restore balance through acts of kindness, or pro-social behavior. In effect, the individual may "make amends" through acts that demonstrate their consideration of the situation and attempt to reconcile the perceived transgression. Research with children demonstrates that a way to alleviate experienced guilt is through pro-social behaviors (e.g., apology, kind acts) (Estrada-Hollenbeck & Heatherton, 1998). When family-to-work guilt arises from conflict-based experiences (e.g., late to work due to a sick child; late to work due to spouse being in emergency room) employees may feel that they have wronged, for example, their coworkers (e.g., not pulling their weight on interdependent tasks) and will try to make amends by performing pro-social behaviors. The individual may attempt to compensate for their perceived transgressions by performing such discretionary behaviors toward individuals (e.g., supervisors, subordinates, coworkers, clients).

We propose the source of guilt and the target of its consequences determine the direction of the individual's behavioral response. Specifically, we propose that when an emotion-generating event occurs (e.g., family-to-work conflict) and the individual has an emotional response (e.g., family-to-work guilt), the individual will be aware of the target of their perceived transgression. When the source of the guilt comes from individuals (e.g., the victims of the perceived transgression were coworkers), attempts to redress this experience might also be targeted toward individuals. Thus, we suggest an individual experiencing family-to-work guilt may look to make amends for the perceived transgression to other individuals within the organization (e.g., coworkers, subordinates). This behavioral response may be an effort to compensate or prove to other individuals in the work environment that they can manage both work and family. This rationale suggests that when an individual experiences family-to-work guilt they may be most likely to direct OCBs toward other individuals rather than the organization.

Hypothesis 1: Family-to-work guilt is positively associated with OCB directed toward individuals.

Anti-Social Work Behavior

Another class of behaviors, antisocial behaviors, has been classified as an alternative dimension of workplace performance, CWB. CWB includes a variety of domains (e.g., misuse of information, time or resources; poor attendance, poor quality work) (Gruys & Sackett, 2003; Sackett, DeVore, Anderson, Ones, Sinangil, & Viswesvaran, 2002). Like OCB, CWB can be directed both at the individual and organization (Robinson & Bennett, 1995). Although there has been growth in this line of research, there is an incomplete understanding as to why individuals may engage in CWBs. Similar to theorizing regarding determinants of OCB, disposition, job attitudes, and contextual/situational variables have been found to predict CWB (Marcus & Schuler, 2004). Exchange-based and equity perspectives can be applied to CWBs; individuals may enact CWB when they perceive inequity to restore balance (Weiss, Suckow, & Cropanzano, 1999). For example, experiencing a negative event at work can trigger feelings of inequity and ultimately lead to negative behaviors toward the organization (e.g., leaving work early). We focus here on emotion as a proximal predictor of CWB.

The Role of Work–Family Guilt in Anti-Social Work Behavior

Guilt gives rise to antisocial effects such as a desire to avoid the victims of one's transgression or to withdraw from the situation all together (Baumeister et al., 1994; Tangney, 1995). This behavior is believed to occur because the individual is either trying to avoid prolonging the guilt experience, or as an act of aggression toward the individual. Furthermore, it is believed that particularly high levels of guilt may be associated with antisocial behaviors given that such intense emotions can become overwhelming and produce worry, anxiety, or rumination (Siegle, Moore, & Thase, 2004). Thus, we argue that guilt experienced at work may motivate CWBs.

Guilt research suggests the most common antisocial response to the feeling of guilt is avoidance (Baumeister et al., 1994). In the workplace, we typically call this behavior withdrawal. This may be in the form lateness, working slowly, dragging out work, or putting forth little effort. When an individual experiences a conflict-based experience that produces work–family guilt, the individual may respond by trying to avoid work-related responsibilities either through mental or physical withdrawal. Following an equity or justice perspective, withdrawal may redress perceived inequity from the conflict experience (e.g., stayed late at work one night, arrive late to work the next day). In fact, Barclay, Skarlicki, and Pugh (2005) demonstrated that emotion mediated the relationship between fairness perceptions and retaliation (i.e., reaction to a lay-off).

Withdrawal behavior could be explained as a form of retaliation, however, Baumeister et al. (1994) suggest that avoidance is an effort to reduce the guilt because the individual is able to remove themselves from the situation that caused this unpleasant feeling. In the case of guilt related to work and family, antisocial behavior at work is expected to be affected by the perception that work has interfered with family (rather than the opposite); when individuals feel guilty that work has taken something away from their family, they may retaliate against the organization or engage in behaviors to redress the perceived inequity. In summary, when an individual experiences work–family guilt the individual will attempt to avoid or withdraw from the source of guilt.

Similar to the rationale for OCB, we propose that when an emotion-generating event occurs (e.g., work-to-family conflict) and the individual has an emotional response (e.g., work-to-family guilt), the individual will evaluate the source or make an effort to assign blame for the negative emotional responses. In the case of work-to-family guilt, the source of the negative emotion is most likely the organization as an entity. Therefore, the individual may respond by performing a negative behavior (i.e., CWB) directed toward the organization. This may be a strategic way to punish the organization for causing the conflict and negative emotion, or even retaliate against the organization, as it is to blame for the perceived transgression toward the family. This rationale suggests that guilt about work interfering with family may be more likely to give rise to CWBs directed toward the organization rather than individuals within the organization. Thus,

Hypothesis 2: Work-to-family guilt is positively associated with CWB directed toward the organization.

Method

We employed a triangulation of qualitative and quantitative methodologies to explore the construct of work–family guilt and test the current hypotheses. Triangulation of methodologies involves combining more than one method in order to achieve a comprehensive understanding of the research question(s) (Tucker, Powell, & Meyer, 1995). Although qualitative and quantitative research are often pitted against one another, when used in conjunction with one another these methodologies can be complementary (Locke, Golden-Biddle, & Rogelberg, 2002). Thus, by implementing a triangulation of methodologies we attempt to compensate for each method's shortcomings and strengthen the conclusions.

Participants and Procedure

Participants consisted of 245 working adults in the Washington D.C. Metropolitan Area. Of the 245 participants, 180 were women and 65 were men. Participants were Caucasian (53%), Hispanic (13%), African American (8%), Asian (6%), and Mixed (6%). Participants ranged in age from 18 to 66 years with a mean of 29 years. The majority, 52% of participants, were single, however, 23% were married and approximately 50% had children. Forty-eight (48%) percent of the participants had one or more children. And, 56% of the participants had a Bachelor's degree and 32% had been working in their current position between 1 and 2 years.

Participants were recruited through two methods. The first method was through three listservs for professional women's societies in the Washington D.C. Metropolitan Area ($N = 38$). The second method was through the undergraduate research pool at a large Mid-Atlantic University ($N = 207$). In order to complete the study, undergraduate participants had to be at least 18 years of age and work a minimum of 25 hours per week. If undergraduate participants who desired to complete the study did not meet the criteria for participation (i.e., work hours), they were asked to nominate a working adult to complete the online survey. Participants who agreed to participate in the study clicked on a link to an online survey.

Qualitative Measures

Participants responded to two sets of open-ended questions that targeted specific instances in which they experienced guilt that was related to their work and family life, one related to work and one related to family. Specifically, participants read and responded to the following: "Think of a time during the past month when you felt guilt related to your work (family). Try to recall as many details of the incident as you can." The participants typed their responses with regard to guilt about work as well as guilt about family. For the purpose of this study, we were interested in the behavioral responses described with regard to the guilt experience in the work domain; "How did you respond to the situation?"

The open-ended responses were coded according to predetermined categories: pro- and anti-social behaviors. In addition to the predetermined categories new themes were identified throughout the coding process in order to attain a complete understanding of the behavioral responses of the guilt experience. The responses were content coded by two graduate students who were trained in content analytic procedures. There was an inter-rater agreement of .77. Inter-rater agreement was calculated by dividing the number of identically coded items by the total number of coded items. Any discrepancies (23%) were settled by the first author.

Quantitative Measures

Work–family guilt. The experience of work–family guilt was assessed using an eight-item measure adapted from Netemeyer, Boles, and McMurrian (1996) and also used in research by Dorio, Bryant, and Allen (2008). The purpose of adapting a current measure of work–family conflict was to appropriately and reliably capture elements of work and family responsibilities. This was accomplished by adding in the stem "I feel guilty when" before each of the eight items in the work–family conflict measure (e.g., I feel guilty when the demands of my work interfere with my home and family life). This approach to measuring work–family guilt was intended to capture the extent to which an individual feels guilty when his or her behavior is inconsistent with the norms of how he or she should balance work and family responsibilities. In effect, we are capturing the extent to which one feels guilty when he or she does not balance work and family (Dorio et al., 2008). All items were assessed on a five-point Likert scale ranging from 1 (*strongly disagree*) to (*strongly agree*). The reliability for the family interfering with work scale was .93, and the work interfering with family scale was .93.

Organizational citizenship behaviors. Organizational citizenship behaviors were assessed with a 15-item measure from Podsakoff and MacKenzie (1994). There were eight items that assessed behaviors directed at the organization and seven items that assessed behaviors directed at the individual. All items were measured on a five-point Likert scale from 1 (*strongly disagree*) to (*strongly agree*). The reliability for these scales were .84 (OCB-Individual) and .68 (OCB-Organizational).

Counterproductive work behaviors. Workplace deviance was assessed using a 19-item measure from Bennett and Robinson (2000). There were 12 items that assessed behaviors directed at the organization and seven items that assessed behaviors directed at the individual. All items were measured on a five-point Likert scale ranging from 1 (*strongly disagree*) to (*strongly agree*). The reliability for these scales were .81 (CWB-Individual) and .80 (CWB-Organizational).

Counterproductive work behaviors—withdrawal subset. A subset of the 19-item measure from Bennett and Robinson (2000) was used to assess withdrawal or avoidance. There were three items that assessed withdrawal or avoidant behaviors including: "spent too much time fantasizing or daydreaming instead of working, and come in late to work without permission." All items were measured on a five-point Likert scale from 1 (*strongly disagree*) to (*strongly agree*). The reliability for this scale was .76.

Negative affect. The guilt subset (six items) from Waston and Clark's (1994) Positive and Negative Affect Schedule (PANAS-X) was used to capture and control for guilt related to general negative affectivity. Participants were asked to report the extent to which they felt (guilty, lively, ashamed, angry at self, blameworthy, dissatisfied with self) during the past few weeks while at work. The reliability for this scale was .75.

Demographics. Information on the participants' gender, age, race, education, marital status, and number of children, as well as work tenure was collected.

Results

Qualitative

Of the 245 participants, 131 completed the open-ended questions and of those responses 111 (42%) were considered codeable (i.e., related to work or family).

For the pro-social behaviors, two themes appeared to dominate responses. The first theme was *working harder* or *putting more effort toward work*. A total of 33 responses (30%) were representative of this theme. Sample responses include the following: "I worked harder the next few days to over compensate for the goals not met earlier in the week," "I tried to finish my work ASAP," and "I offered to work on a new plan to redefine the project plan." These quotes are examples of responses indicative of a desire to work harder in an effort to make amends or compensate for their guilt experience. The second theme was *helping a coworker* or *giving of physical time*. A total of 11 responses (10%) were representative of this theme. Sample responses include the following: "I volunteered to take [my coworker's] shift," "I offered to work on the weekend," "I offered to help my supervisor for free," and "I did some of her [coworker's] job so she could leave early." This theme tapped a notion of helping coworkers or supervisors, as well as the organization. Helping others is one of the key factors of OCBs and consistent with what was found in this thematic analysis.

Turning toward antisocial behaviors, there was only one dominant theme that appeared in the responses: *withdrawal*. A total of 18 responses (16%) were representative of this theme. Sample responses include the following: "I left work early," "I tried my best to ignore it by avoiding the situation," and "I waited until things blew over and then put effort back into my work." These responses represented other participants' responses and were suggestive of withdrawing from the actual situation or organization as well physically leaving the workplace all together presumably in an effort to avoid the guilt experience.

Quantitative

The overall scale means, standard deviations, and correlations are provided in Table 1. To control for systematic differences in the frequency of work–family conflict as a function of gender, as well as potential individual differences in tendencies to report negative moods, both gender and the guilt subscale of the PANAS-X (Watson & Clark, 1994) were entered as controls in regression analyses. In Step 1, the controls were entered. In Step 2, the respective work–family guilt measures were entered. Consistent with Hypothesis 1, there was a positive relationship between high levels of family-to-work guilt and OCBs directed toward the individual ($\beta = .14$, $p < .05$, $\Delta R^2 = .02$). Hypothesis 2 predicted a positive relationship between high levels of work-to-family guilt and CWBs directed toward the organization. Work-to-family guilt was not related to employees' reports of CWB directed toward the organization at the .05 level ($\beta = .13$, $p = .06$, $\Delta R^2 = .02$), but the trend in the data suggests support for Hypothesis 2. In an exploratory analysis, we identified a subset of CWB directed toward the organization items that represented withdrawal, a primary consequence of guilt, as outlined by Baumeister et al. (1994) and suggested by the current thematic coding

Table 1. Scale Means, Standard Deviations, and Intercorrelations

	M	SD	1	2	3	4	5	6	7	8	9
1. Gender	1.73	0.44									
2. PANAS-X (NA)	9.94	3.42	−.01								
3. FIW guilt	11.88	4.09	.03	.26**							
4. WIF guilt	16.61	4.49	−.08	.28**	.54**						
5. WF guilt (FIW/WIF)	25.35	7.58	.02	.31**	.36**	.40**					
6. OCB–I	30.85	4.19	.19**	−.05	.13*	.05	.04				
7. OCB–O	22.43	3.24	.07	−.23**	−.07	−.04	−.12	.55**			
8. CWB–I	10.47	4.88	−.26**	.03	−.15*	.02	.07	−.26**	−.25**		
9. CWB–O	19.87	8.87	−.16*	.15	.05	.15*	.22**	−.27**	−.34**	.64**	
10. CWB withdrawal	6.70	3.34	−.11	.21**	.14*	.20*	.18**	−.12	−.22**	.43**	.83**

Note. $N = 245$, $^*p < .05$, $^{**}p < .01$.

Table 2. Relationships between Predictors and Dependent Variables

	OCB-I		CWB-O		CWB-O-withdrawal	
	β	ΔR^2	β	ΔR^2	β	ΔR^2
FIW Guilt	.14*	.02*				
WIF Guilt			.13*	.02*		
WIF Guilt					.15*	.02*

$N = 245$, $^*p < .05$.

of open ended responses. Hypothesis 2 was tested using withdrawal behaviors as a dependent variable. This exploratory analysis was supported ($\beta = .15, p < .05$, $\Delta R^2 = .02$). See Table 2.

Discussion

Overall, the results of the current study suggest that work–family guilt is a motivational antecedent of both pro- and anti-social behaviors in workplaces in the United States. The qualitative data clarify the types of behaviors that reflect pro- and anti-social behaviors in the workplace that may be associated with guilt about work and family. Specifically, when individuals reflected on experiences of family-to-work guilt, they reported responding with helping behaviors directed toward individuals either in the form of exerting greater effort to support others or by giving their time to help others. When individuals experienced work-to-family guilt, they reported a general shirking of work responsibilities that included avoiding or ignoring the situation or in some cases a removing themselves from the work environment. The quantitative data echoed these findings by demonstrating that family-to-work guilt produced OCB directed toward individuals and work-to-family guilt produced CWB directed toward the organization, mostly in the form of withdrawal. This pattern of results suggests that individuals respond to emotion-generating events in effortful behavioral displays that seek to redress the perceived violation of work–family norms. This finding aligns with Kailasapathy and Metz's (2012) study that revealed women in an Eastern culture (Sri Lanka) sought to identify the source of stress (i.e., conflict arising from violation of societal norms) that was perceived as changeable and therefore attempted to change the source of stress by negotiating roles to resolve work–family conflict. Our study findings suggest that U.S. workers are responding to the common emotional experience of guilt in effortful ways that are both pro- and anti-social, and thus may ultimately strain their cognitive resources and ability to sustain work and family roles.

These findings can be understood through social exchange and equity (see Adams, 1965; Blau, 1964) frameworks that emphasize balance. Exchange-based equity perspectives suggest that individuals engage in behaviors (e.g., OCB; Konovsky, Organ, & Dennis, 1996; CWB; Weiss, Suckow, & Cropanzano, 1999) when they perceive inequity in an effort to restore balance. This suggests that when individuals feel guilty that their family has interfered with their work responsibilities, they are motivated to compensate for their perceived wrongdoing. These pro-social behaviors may be viewed as an adaptive strategy on behalf of the individual to demonstrate that they are committed and interested in the work environment. In effect, perceived transgressions (family-to-work guilt) motivate individuals to engage in pro-social, or compensatory, behaviors. This is particularly interesting as Baumeister et al. (1994) suggests that people can induce guilt on others. This can be used as a strategy to achieve what one wants, or knowingly make a person feel badly in order to garner an apology or some form of compensatory behavior. Due to continued normative expectations surrounding work and family, dual earners with children are likely be in positions of risk because others may attempt to capitalize on individuals' perceived transgressions in an effort to induce desired behavioral responses to emotion-generating events. Such a strategy may result in extrarole behaviors that may be perceived to facilitate (i.e., OCB) or hinder (i.e., CWB) an individual's success in their career. Moreover, extant empirical research shows that there are differential expectations held for women (i.e., women are expected to perform OCBs and when they do not they are denigrated) may result in negative work outcomes (Heilman & Chen, 2005) further complicating perceptions of women's success in the workplace (e.g., performance evaluation) and women's ability to advance in the workplace and more generally sustain career and care roles over the long term.

When individuals experience an event where work interferes with their family time, they may feel guilty because of perceived normative violations of being a "good" mother, father, spouse, parent, etc. The performance of CWB (in particular, withdrawal behaviors) may be viewed as a punitive act or a means to adapt or alleviate the negative emotion (work-to-family guilt). In other words, employees who experience guilt about work negatively affecting their family lives engage in CWB directed toward the organization. This finding is consistent with Baumeister et al.'s (1994) theoretical emphasis on withdrawal as a key antisocial behavior.

Consistent with hypotheses, the results of both the qualitative and quantitative analyses also suggest that, generally speaking, individuals' behavioral responses to work–family guilt varied with regard to their target; OCBs associated with guilt tended to be directed toward individuals, but CWBs were directed toward the organization as a whole. Consonant with our argument that the source of guilt and the target of its consequences determine the direction of the response, if the source of the guilt came from individuals (e.g., the victims of the perceived transgression were coworkers), attempts to redress this experience might also be targeted toward individuals. However, if the source of the guilt was more general (i.e., the organization as the cause of guilt-inducing event) we anticipated and found that the response would also be targeted toward the organization. Indeed, when work interfered with family, it was the organization as a whole that may be seen as the source of the guilt experience, whereas when family interfered with work, individuals may feel that they have let down specific individuals (e.g., coworkers, subordinates).

Limitations

These findings should be interpreted in light of several limitations. A first limitation of this study is the sample is primarily comprised of nontraditional undergraduate students. It could be argued that students do not fully experience or understand incompatibility between work and family roles. In other words, students may not have the conflict-based experiences that traditional working adults with children may experience. Alternatively, students may not be as sensitive to societal norms therefore reducing the likelihood of perceived violation, triggering work–family guilt. However, these concerns over the sample may make it more difficult to find significant effects and therefore this study may, in fact, be a conservative test of this finding. Also, it is important to note that although a primarily student-based sample, the students were nontraditional working more than 25 hours a week and approximately half had one or more children. Therefore, it can be argued that these individuals are ripe to experience conflict and therefore guilt as they are juggling multiple roles (e.g., paid work, school, family).

A second limitation of this research is that we do not include direct measures of the mechanism underlying the guilt–behavior relationship. Although we build a theoretical argument as to why work–family guilt may trigger citizenship or CWB, we are unable to assess the accuracy of this rationale. Specifically, this study lacks direct measures of perceptions of equity and compensatory or retaliatory thought processes to accurately capture the mechanism driving behavior. Third and finally, this study used cross-sectional data creating the possibility that the variables of interest may be connected along a different timeline. For example, inequity or imbalance between employee and organization could trigger negative or positive acts toward others, followed by guilt over this action. However, there is strong theoretical evidence drawing from affective events theory on emotions and scholars' research on guilt that suggests the ordering of variables proposed in this study is representative of how they are experienced.

Implications and future research

Recognition of the importance of emotion in organizational behavior has provided new perspectives on important topics including leadership (Lewis, 2000), group processes (George, 1990), employee violence and justice (Cropanzano, Weiss, Suckow, & Grandey, 2000), and emotional labor (Grandey, 2000). The current article responds to recent calls to better integrate linkages between work and family experiences and emotions (e.g., Judge et al., 2006; Williams & Alliger, 1994). Integrating previously disconnected streams of research on the work–family interface and the emotion of guilt, this article conceptualizes work–family guilt as an internal emotion-based response rooted in one's evaluation of perceived wrongdoing or violation of norms.

This emotion is particularly meaningful in the context of the work–family interface, as employees with care responsibilities often feel as though they may fall short at home, work, or both. Upon experiencing work–family conflict employees use normative expectations to judge their ability to manage work and family. When employees do fall short they are apt to experience negative emotions (i.e., guilt) triggering behavioral responses that are an attempt to sustain these, oftentimes, competing roles. We propose employees experiencing such emotional discomfort seek to restore balance in an effort to sustain multiple roles, however, these attempts to create balance may or may not facilitate a truly sustainable lifestyle. Therefore, it is critical to raise awareness of the connections between conflict and emotion as it may lead to unintended behavioral responses (i.e., CWB directed toward the organization) that do not foster sustainability in career and care.

Our findings have important implications for the work–family interface, as they exemplify the bidirectional nature of work and family research and underscore the behavioral consequences that may be associated with involvement in work and family. By definition, elements of the family domain can influence the work domain and elements of the work domain can influence the family domain (Gutek et al., 1991). We explore outcomes only within the work domain, but demonstrate that emotion related to both work-to-family and family-to-work guilt may result in behavioral outcomes in the work domain within the United States. By establishing that emotions generated from the work–family interface may result in critical workplace behaviors, this study highlights important future research directions in the area of work–family emotions and behavioral consequences that may facilitate a more complete understanding of how to achieve sustainability in careers and care.

Future research should continue to explore the linkages between work–family conflict-based experiences, emotions, and behavioral responses. One avenue for future research is to explore how time-, strain-, and behavior-based conflict influence emotional responses, specifically guilt. Perhaps one form of conflict (e.g., time-based) is a stronger predictor of emotional responses than other forms of conflict (e.g., strain-based). Identifying more specific predictors of guilt may be a first step at knowing when (or perhaps even reducing) peoples' emotional responses. Also, future research should explore behavioral responses to work–family guilt in the family domain to gain a better understanding of whether (and how) this emotion triggers behavioral responses among family members. Cross-over research would allow for a more complete understanding of how work–family guilt may reduce sustainability in the care role. Future research should also explore whether work–family guilt is a U.S.-based phenomenon or whether this emotional response extends to other cultures, as norms for familial roles and responsibilities may vary widely. Furthermore, emotional responses, in addition to guilt, should be explored. Perhaps other inward emotions such as shame or outward emotions such as anger should be included in this research to more fully capture the range of possible responses to work–family (time-, strain-, and behavior-based) conflict. Similarly, perhaps certain emotions predict different behaviors. This study demonstrates guilt has the potential to motivate pro- or anti-social behavior, but perhaps anger only motivates anti-social behavior whereas empathy only motivates pro-social behavior. Future research should also specifically consider the rise in "nontraditional" families, as there is reason to believe that both parents and nonparents may experience work–family guilt. Moreover, there should be consideration for the varied private life contexts—whether an individual has a (working) partner and/or children—of today's workers. Consideration for these varied private life contexts should be addressed in future research, as a preliminary study demonstrates differential effects of private life context on self-reported work–family conflict (Van Veldhoven & Beijer, 2012).

Future research should look to explicitly measure the underlying mechanisms or processes in this conflict–emotion–behavioral response model. Measures of social exchange, specifically targeting feelings of needing to "make up for" would be important to illustrate the proposed theory of perceived inequity and restoring balance. Additionally, future research may consider further developing the proposed model by including an attributions component to the model. Part of the evaluation process may be to assign blame as to why an individual is experiencing this negative emotion. A person's behavioral response may vary depending on whether an individual blames him/herself versus his/her supervisor. Therefore, this attribution may determine how an individual reacts to this perceived "failure" by compensating (i.e., restoring equity because it was his/her fault) versus withdrawing from the organization (i.e., restoring equity because it was the organization's fault). Thus, the inclusion of explicit measures testing these notions may add further insight into work–family emotions and behavioral responses that may provide clarity in how workers attempt to sustain both career and care roles.

References

Adams, J. S. (1965). Inequity in social exchange. *Advances in Experimental Social Psychology, 62*, 335–343.

Barclay, L. J., Skarlicki, D. P., & Pugh, S. D. (2005). Exploring the role of emotions in injustice perceptions and retaliation. *Journal of Applied Psychology, 90*, 629–643. doi: 10.1037/0021-9010.90.4.629

Barnett, R. C., & Hyde, J. S. (2001). Women, men, work, and family: An expansionist theory. *American Psychologist, 56*, 781–1796. doi: 10.1037/0003-066X.56.10.781

Baumeister, R. F., Stillwell, A. M., & Heatherton, T. F. (1994). Guilt: An interpersonal approach. *Psychological Bulletin, 115*, 243–267. doi: 10.1037/0033-2909.115.2.243

Bennett, R. J., & Robinson, S. L. (2000). Development of a measure of workplace deviance. *Journal of Applied Psychology, 85*, 349–360. doi: 10.1037/0021-9010.85.3.349

Blau, P. M. (1964). *Exchange and power in social life.* New York: Wiley.

Cropanzano, R., Weiss, H. M., Suckow, K. J., & Grandey, A. A. (2000). Doing justice to workplace emotion. In N. M. Ashkanasy, C. E. J. Hartel, & W. J. Zerbe (Eds.), *Emotions in the workplace: Research, theory, and practice.* Westport, CT: Quorum Books.

Dorio, J. M., Bryant, R., & Allen, T. D. 2008). *Guilt and self-regulatory skills: Moderators of the demands-WFC relationship.* Paper presented at the 23rd annual conference for the Society for Industrial Organizational Psychology, San Francisco, CA.

Eby, L. T., Casper, W. J., Lockwood, A., Bordreaux, C., & Brinley, A. (2005). Work and family research in IO/OB: Content analysis and review of the literature (1980–2002). *Journal of Vocational Behavior, 66*, 124–197. doi: 10.1080/13668800902779023

Estrada-Hollenbeck, M., & Heatherton, T. F. (1998). Avoiding and alleviating guilt through prosocial behavior. In J. Bybee, *Guilt and children* (pp. 215–231). San Diego, CA: Academic Press.

Friede, A., & Ryan, A. M. (2005). The importance of the individual: How self-evaluations influence the work-family interface. In E. E. Kossek & S. J. Lambert (Eds.), *Work and life integration: Organizational cultural, and individual perspectives* (pp. 193–209). Mahwah, NJ: Erlbaum.

Frone, M. R., Russell, M., & Cooper, M. L. (1992). Prevalence of work family conflict: Are work and family boundaries asymmetrically permeable? *Journal of Organizational Behavior, 13*, 723–729. doi:10.1002/job.4030130708

Fuegen, K., Biernat, M., Haines, E., & Deaux, K. (2004). Mothers and fathers in the workplace: How gender and parental status influence judgments of job-related competence. *Journal of Social Issues, 60*, 737–754. doi: 10.1111/j.0022-4537.2004.00383.x

George, J. M. (1990). Personality, affect, and behavior in groups. *Journal of Applied Psychology, 35*, 352–364. doi: 10.1037/0021-9010.78.5.798

Grandey, A. A. (2000). Emotion regulation in the workplace: A new way to conceptualize emotional labor. *Journal of Occupational Health Psychology, 5*, 95–110. doi. 10.1037/1076-8998.5.1.95

Greenhaus, J. H., & Beutell, N. J. (1985). Sources and conflict between work and family roles. *Academy of Management Review, 10*, 76–88. doi: 10.2307/258214

Gruys, M. L., & Sackett, P. R. (2003). Investigating the dimensionality of counterproductive work behavior. *International Journal of Selection and Assessment, 11*, 30–42. doi: 10.1111/1468-2389.00224

Guendouzi, J. A. (2004). "The Guilt Thing": Balancing individual needs and domestic social roles. Paper presented at the annual meeting of the International Communication Association, New Orleans Sheraton, New Orleans, LA.

Gutek, B. A., Searle, S., & Klepa, L. (1991). Rational versus gender role explanations for work-family conflict. *Journal of Applied Psychology, 76*, 560–568. doi: 10.1037/0021-9010.76.4.560

Heilman, M. E., & Chen, J. J. (2005). Same behavior, different consequences: Reactions to men's and women's altruistic citizenship behavior. *Journal of Applied Psychology, 90*, 431–441. doi 10.1037/0021-9010.90.3.431

Hochschild, A., & Machung, A. (2003). *The second shift: Working parents and the revolution at home.* New York: Viking-Penguin.

Judge, T. J., Ilies, R., & Scott, B. A. (2006). Work-family conflict and emotions: Effects at work and at home. *Personnel Psychology, 59*, 779–814. doi: 10.1111/j.1744-6570.2006.00054.x

Kahn, R. L., & Byosiere, P. (1992). Stress in Organizations. In M. D. Dunnette & L. M. Hough (Eds.), *Handbook of industrial and organizational psychology* (2nd ed., Vol. 3, pp. 572–650). Palo Alto, CA: Consulting Psychologists Press, Inc.

Kailasapathy, P., & Metz, I. (2012). Work-family conflict in Sri Lanka: Negotiations of exchange relationships in family and at work. *Journal of Social Issues, 68*(4), 790–813.

Konovsky, M. A., & Organ, D. W. (1996). Dispositional and contextual determinants of organizational citizenship behavior. *Journal of Organizational Behavior, 17*, 253–266. doi: 10.1002/(SICI)1099-1379(199605)17:3<253::AID-JOB747>3.0.CO;2-Q.

Lee, K., & Allen, N. J. (2002). Organizational citizenship behavior and workplace deviance: The role of affect and cognitions. *Journal of Applied Psychology, 87*, 131–142. doi: 10.1037/0021-9010.87.1.131

Lewis, K. M. (2000). When leaders display emotion: how followers respond to negative emotional expression of male and female leaders: *Journal of Organizational Behavior, 21*, 221–234. doi: 10.1002/(SICI)1099-1379(200003)21:2<221::AID-JOB36>3.0.CO;2-0.

Livingston, B. A., & Judge, T. A. (2008). Emotional responses to work-family conflict: An examination of gender role orientation among working men and women. *Journal of Applied Psychology, 93*, 207–216. doi: 10.1037/0021-9010.93.1.207

Locke, K., Golden-Biddle, K., & Rogelberg, S. G. (2002). An introduction to qualitative research: Its potential for industrial and organizational psychology. In *Handbook of research methods in industrial and organizational psychology* (pp. 99–118). Malden, MA: Blackwell Publishing.

MacDermind, S. M., Seery, B. L., & Weiss, H. M. (2002). An emotional examination of the work-family interface. In R. G. Lord, R. J. Klimoski, & R. Kanfer (Eds.), *Emotions in the workplace.* New York: Jossey-Bass.

Marcus, B., & Schuler, H. (2004). Antecedents of counterproductive behavior at work: A general perspective. *Journal of Applied Psychology, 89*, 647–660. doi: 10.1037/0021-9010.89.4.647

Miles, D. E., Borman, W. E., & Spector, P. E. (2002). Building an integrative model of extra role work behaviors: A comparison of counterproductive work behavior with organizational citizenship behavior. *International Journal of Selection and Assessment, 10*, 51–57. doi: 10.1111/1468-2389.00193

Netemeyer, R. G., Boles, J. S., & McMurrian, R. (1996). Development and validation of work-family conflict and work-family conflict scales. *Journal of Applied Psychology, 81*, 400–410. doi: 10.2307/1251791

Oatley, K., & Jenkins, J. M. (1992). Human emotions: Function and dysfunction. *Annual Review of Psychology, 43*, 55–85. doi: 10.1146/annurev.ps.43.020192.000415

Okimoto, T. G., & Heilman, M. E. (2012). The "bad parent" assumption: How gender stereotypes affect reactions to working mothers. *Journal of Social Issues, 68*(4), 704–724.

Organ, D. W. (1997). Organizational citizenship behavior: It's construct clean-up time. *Human Performance, 10*, 85–97. doi: 10.1207/s15327043hup1002_2

Podsakoff, P. M., & MacKenzie, S. B. (1994). Organizational citizenship behavior and sales unit effectiveness. *Journal of Marketing Research, 31*, 351–363.

Podsakoff, P. M., MacKenzie, S. B., Moorman, R. H., & Fetter, R. (1990). Transformational leader behaviors and their effects on followers' trust in leader, satisfaction, and organizational citizenship behaviors. *Leadership Quarterly, 1*, 107–142. doi: 10.1016/1048-9843(90)90009-7

Robinson, S. L., & Bennett, R. J. (1995). A typology of deviant workplace behaviors: A multidimensional scaling study. *Academy of Management Journal, 38*, 555–572. doi: 10.2307/256693

Rodell, J. B., & Judge, T. A. (2009). Can "good" stressors spark "bad" behaviors? The mediating role of emotions in links of challenge and hindrance stressors with citizenship and counterproductive behaviors. *Journal of Applied Psychology, 94*, 1438–1451. doi: 10.1037/a0016752

Rotundo, M., & Sackett, P. R. (2002). The relative importance of task, citizenship, and counterproductive performance to global ratings of job performance: A policy-capturing approach. *Journal of Applied Psychology, 87*, 66–80. doi: 10.1037/0021-9010.87.1.66

Sackett, P. R., DeVore, C. J., Anderson, N., Ones, D. S., Sinangil, H. K., & Viswesvaran, C. (2002). Counterproductive behaviors at work. In *Handbook of industrial, work and organizational psychology, Volume 1: Personnel psychology* (pp. 145–164). Hoboken, New Jersey: Sage Publications Ltd.

Siegle, G. J., Moore, P. M., & Thase, M. E. (2004). Rumination: One construct, many features in healthy individuals, depressed individuals, and individuals with lupus. *Cognitive Therapy and Research, 28*, 645–668. doi: 10.1023/B:COTR.0000045570.62733.9f

Sommer, K., & Baumeister, R. (1997). Making someone feel guilty: Causes, strategies, and consequences. In R. Kowalski (Ed.), *Aversive interpersonal behaviors* (pp. 31–54). New York: Plenum.

Tangney, J. P. (1991). Moral affect: The good, the bad, and the ugly. *Journal of Personality and Social Psychology, 61*, 598–607. doi: 10.1037/0022-3514.61.4.598

Tangney, J. P. (1995). Shame and guilt in interpersonal relationships. In J. P. Tangney & K. W. Fisher (Eds.), *Self-conscious emotions: Shame, guilt, embarrassment, and pride* (pp. 114–139). New York: Guilford.

Tiedje, L. B. (2004). Processes of change in work/home incompatibilities: Employed mothers 1986–1999. *Journal of Social Issues, 60*, 787–800. doi: 10.1111/j.0022-4537.2004.00386.x

Tucker, M. L., Powell, K. S., & Meyer, G. D. (1995). Qualitative research in business communication: A review and analysis. *Journal of Business Communication, 32*, 383–399.

U.S. Census Bureau (2008). *Statistical abstract of the United States: 2008* (127th ed.). Washington, DC: U.S. Census Bureau. Retrieved from http://www.census.gov/statab/www/

Van Veldhoven, M. J. P. M., & Beijer, S. E. (2012). Workload, work-to-family conflict, and health: Gender differences and the influence of private life context. *Journal of Social Issues, 68*(4), 665–683.

Watson, D., & Clark, L. A. (1994). Emotions, moods, traits, and temperaments: Conceptual distinctions and empirical findings. In P. Ekman & R. J. Davidson (Eds.), *The nature of emotion: Fundamental questions* (pp. 89–93). New York: Oxford University Press.

Weiss, H. M., & Cropanzano, R. (1996). Affective events theory: A theoretical discussion of the structure, causes, and consequences of affective experiences at work. In B. M. Staw & L. L. Cummings (Eds.), *Research in Organizational Behavior: An annual series of analytical essays and critical reviews* (Vol. 18, pp. 1–74). Greenwich, CT, US: Elsevier Science/JAI Press.

Weiss, H. M., Suckow, K., & Cropanzano, R. (1999). Effects of justice conditions on discrete emotions. *Journal of Applied Psychology, 84*, 786–794. doi: 10.1037/0021-9010.84.5.786

Williams, K. J., & Alliger, G. M. (1994). Role stressors, mood spillover, and perceptions of work-family conflict in employed parents. *Academy of Management Journal, 37*, 837–868. doi: 0.2307/256602

Williams, L., & Anderson, S. (1991). Job satisfaction and organizational commitment as predictors of organizational citizenship and in-role behaviors. *Journal of Management, 1*, 601–617. doi: 10.1177/014920639101700305

WHITNEY BOTSFORD MORGAN received her doctorate in Industrial and Organizational Psychology from George Mason University in 2009. She is an Assistant Professor at the University of Houston–Downtown in the Department of Management, Marketing, and Business Administration. The overarching goal of her program of research is to provide theoretical and empirical evidence guiding the advancement of women and mothers in the workplace. Her line of research touches a variety of content areas including performance appraisal, developmental opportunities, extra-role behavior, and retention. She has published in *Human Resource Management Review*, *Journal of Occupational Health Psychology*, *Equal Opportunities International*, *and Sex Roles*. In addition to her research, she consults for EASI·Consult® on applied projects including competency modeling, role clarification, workforce analysis, and entry-level selection systems.

EDEN B. KING joined the faculty of the Industrial-Organizational Psychology program at George Mason University after earning her PhD from Rice University in 2006. Dr. King is pursuing a program of research that seeks to guide the equitable and effective management of diverse organizations. Her research, which has appeared in outlets such as the *Journal of Applied Psychology*, *Human Resource Management*, *Perspectives of IO Psychology*, *and Group and Organization Management*, integrates organizational and social psychological theories in conceptualizing social stigma and the work–life interface. This research addresses three primary themes: (1) current manifestations of discrimination and barriers to work–life balance in organizations, (2) consequences of such challenges for its targets and their workplaces, and (3) individual and organizational strategies for reducing discrimination and increasing support for families. In addition to her academic positions, Dr. King has consulted on applied projects related to climate initiatives, selection systems, and diversity training programs, and has worked as a trial consultant. She is currently on the editorial board of the *Journal of Management* and the *Journal of Business and Psychology*.

The "Bad Parent" Assumption: How Gender Stereotypes Affect Reactions to Working Mothers

Tyler G. Okimoto[*]
The University of Queensland

Madeline E. Heilman
New York University

Although balancing work and family commitments is a significant source of strain for working parents, working mothers in traditionally male positions face additional anxiety due to unfounded assumptions about their competence as employees, assumptions rooted in gender stereotypes. However, stereotype-based assumptions can also bias competence impressions of these working mothers in family domains, depicting them as bad parents. In four experimental studies, we documented evidence that working mothers are seen as less effective parents than nonworking mothers. Consistent with the argument that gender stereotypes underlie these findings, the bad parent assumption was apparent only for mothers and not fathers (Study 1), only when working in a male sex-typed occupation (Study 2), more intensely when job success was clear (Study 3), and only when working out of personal choice (Study 4). Similar patterns were observed in ratings of interpersonal appeal (e.g., likability, friend desirability, coworker desirability), relational judgments suggesting that there are also negative social consequences for working mothers.

Commonly cited pressures facing working parents are often attributed to the time constraints imposed by both work and family obligations and the commitment trade-off they produce (e.g., Cooke & Rousseau, 1984; Gutek, Repetti, & Silver, 1988; Kandel, Davies, & Raveis, 1985). Consequently, many of the work/family policies instituted by organizations focus on alleviating (or being flexible with) the time demands of their employees who have children. But working parents face

---

[*]Correspondence concerning this article should be addressed to Tyler G. Okimoto, UQ Business School, The University of Queensland, Brisbane QLD 4072, Australia [e-mail: t.okimoto@business.uq.edu.au].

problems even when time management is not actually an issue—they are assumed to have commitment deficits. Family obligations are assumed to reduce working parents' commitment to the job (Fuegen, Biernat, Haines, & Deaux, 2004), and work obligations are assumed to reduce working parents' commitment to their families (Bridges & Etaugh, 1995; Etaugh & Nekolny, 1990).

These assumptions can be troubling for mothers and fathers alike. However, mothers have been shown to face an additional problem. On top of the assumption that they lack commitment, they are also assumed to be less capable as employees than nonworking mothers or working fathers, particularly in management and other male sex-typed occupations (Cuddy, Fiske, & Glick, 2004; Heilman & Okimoto, 2008). These beliefs about job ineffectiveness are a consequence of cultural stereotypes depicting women as relationship-oriented or, as termed in the literature, "communal" (i.e., warm, caring, sensitive, and emotional), characteristics that are thought to be inconsistent with the attributes necessary for job success (i.e., assertive, strong, dominant and task-focused), resulting in a perceived "lack of fit" (Heilman, 1983, 2001; see also Eagly & Karau, 2002). Research has indicated that this perceived lack of fit is particularly stark for working mothers, as motherhood epitomizes our cultural conception of being a woman and thus exaggerates perceptions of a mother's embodiment of stereotypically feminine characteristics (Cuddy et al., 2004; Heilman & Okimoto 2008). As a result, working mothers are seen as ill-equipped to handle male sex-typed organizational roles and less deserving of these positions than nonmothers.

Importantly, these findings suggest that gender stereotypes and the lack of fit perceptions they produce can give rise to yet another negative consequence for mothers working in male sex-typed occupations. If, despite incompetence assumptions, a working mother is successful at obtaining and holding a traditionally male job, this implies that she in fact has the attributes necessary for success in a male field. However, because there is a perceived inconsistency between the attributes believed critical for success in male sex-typed work and the communal characteristics associated with women, her success also implies a deficit in the attributes believed to be essential for being a good mother. This can produce a lose-lose dilemma for working mothers; motherhood prompts assumptions about their work ineffectiveness, but if those assumptions are proven wrong by evidence of job competence, they are assumed to be ineffective as parents.

Assumptions of working mothers' parental ineffectiveness (Bridges, 1987; Bridges & Orza, 1992; Etaugh & Study, 1989) can serve as an additional source of psychological stress. Concerns about maternal inadequacy can be disturbing and debilitating, distracting working mothers from being effective both at home and at work. The perception that work impinges on the family can also lead to feelings of guilt and counterproductive work behaviors (Morgan & King, 2012). Even more concerning is the research linking perceptions of parental self-efficacy to depression and mother–child attachment problems (see Teti & Gelfand, 1991).

In addition, assumptions about working mothers' lack of communality are likely to lead to dislike and the ascription of harsh and unflattering characterizations (Heilman & Okimoto, 2007; Heilman, Wallen, Fuchs, & Tamkins, 2004; Rudman, 1998). This negativity in interpersonal appeal can promote social isolation from both coworkers and parental peers, resulting in the absence of the social support that can be crucial to the mental health and well-being of new parents (LaRocco, House, & French, 1980).

The Bad Parent Assumption

In four experimental studies, we investigated the "bad parent" assumption, attempting to determine whether, why and under what conditions working women employed in traditionally male jobs are denigrated as mothers. We examined beliefs about the parental effectiveness of working and nonworking mothers, and also assessed their interpersonal appeal. We predicted:

Hypothesis 1 (The Bad Parent Assumption Hypothesis): Working mothers will be seen as less effective parents and as less interpersonally appealing than nonworking mothers.

Each of the four studies tested this primary hypothesis. In addition, we sought to demonstrate the importance of gender stereotypes and the lack of fit perceptions they produce in provoking the bad parent assumption. We have proposed that the diminished evaluations of working mothers' effectiveness are driven by a presumed deficit in communal traits that derives from the perceived lack of fit between the attributes believed necessary for career success in a male sex-typed job and the attributes believed necessary to be a good mother. Therefore, we also predicted that beliefs about a target's lack of communal traits would mediate evaluations of parental effectiveness, accounting for the bad parent assumption over and above perceptions of insufficient family commitment:

Hypothesis 2 (Mediation Hypothesis): The effect of mothers' employment status on parental evaluations and interpersonal appeal ratings will be mediated by perceived lack of communality, even when controlling for the variance explained by diminished perceptions of family commitment.

Taken together, the four studies were designed to provide converging evidence for the role of gender stereotypes in evaluations of and reactions to working mothers, impressions that serve as an understudied barrier for working mothers' effectiveness in both work and family domains.

Table 1. Studies 1–4: Descriptive Statistics and Intercorrelations between Dependent Measure Scales

Study 1 (N = 105)		Scale reliability	1	2	3
Study 1 (N = 105)					
Mean age = 36.8 (13.2)	1. Family commitment	r = .87	–		
% female = 70%	2. Communality	α = .82	.65*	–	
% with children = 51%	3. Parental evaluations	r = .88	.83*	.70*	–
	4. Interpersonal appeal	α = .89	.69*	.71*	.78*
Study 2 (N = 188)					
Mean age = 35.9 (13.3)	1. Family commitment	r = .82	–		
% female = 69%	2. Communality	α = .87	.64*	–	
% with children = 45%	3. Parental evaluations	r = .82	.86*	.69*	–
	4. Interpersonal appeal	α = .90	.63*	.66*	.70*
Study 3 (N = 256)					
Mean age = 35.4 (13.2)	1. Family commitment	r = .83	–		
% female = 64%	2. Communality	α = .90	.65*	–	
% with children = 50%	3. Parental evaluations	r = .89	.88*	.71*	–
	4. Interpersonal appeal	α = .94	.74*	.71*	.81*
Study 4 (N = 196)					
Mean age = 35.0 (12.8)	1. Family commitment	r = .83	–		
% female = 71%	2. Communality	α = .89	.63*	–	
% with children = 50%	3. Parental evaluations	r = .76	.81*	.68*	–
	4. Interpersonal appeal	α = .94	.70*	.74*	.79*

*$p < .05$. Standard deviations appear in parentheses.

General Methodology

Participants for the studies were U.S. volunteers who were recruited for online research participation in exchange for a 1/40 chance of winning a $10 lottery reward. Although susceptible to many of the limitations of online research (Skitka & Sargis, 2006), the participant pool from which these participants were drawn was more representative than most online or student samples: only 13% students, 50% without a college degree, median household income $50K–$75K, 75% Caucasian, 14% Asian, 4% Hispanic, 4% Black, and normally distributed in political orientation. Descriptive statistics for each individual study are presented in Table 1.

In all four studies, participants were told the study investigated first impressions, and were asked to read one short description of a target:

> "Jennifer is 38 years-old. She is married and the mother of two children ages 4 and 8. She is originally from the San Francisco Bay area, and first moved to Illinois when she attended

the University of Illinois at Chicago. She currently lives in the suburbs of Chicago. In her free time, Jennifer enjoys reading and is an avid tennis player."

The target description varied depending on experimental condition, but all other details were held constant and all targets were described as being parents.

After reading about the target, participants were asked to report their impressions. *Family commitment* was evaluated on two 7-point scale items (1 = not at all, 7 = very much): "How committed do you think this person is to his/her family?" and "How family oriented do you think this person is?" *Communality* was evaluated using four 7-point bi-polar adjective ratings: "not supportive-supportive," "insensitive-sensitive," "not understanding-understanding," and "cold-warm." *Parental evaluations* were assessed by two 7-point scale items: "How good of a parent do you think this person is? (1 = very bad, 7 = very good)," and "Do you feel like this person is a good parent? (1 = not at all, 7 = very much)." *Interpersonal appeal* was assessed by four 7-point scale items (1 = not at all, 7 = very much): "Would you want this person to be your neighbor?", "Would you want to be friends with this person?", "Would you want your children to be friends with this person's children?", and "Would you want to work with this person?" Ratings within each multi-item scale were averaged to form a composite measure. See Table 1 for reliability statistics and inter-scale correlations.

Study 1

In the first study we sought to demonstrate the existence of the "bad parent assumption" for working mothers (Hypothesis 1) and show that it is mediated by a perceived lack of communality (Hypothesis 2), implicating the underlying "lack of fit" process. To this end, we compared evaluations of working mothers to nonworking mothers, as well as to mothers with no employment information provided (reflecting baseline beliefs about mothers in general). We also examined reactions to working mothers as compared to working fathers. Because there is a lack of fit between the attributes thought necessary for employment success and the attributes thought necessary to be a good mother, but *not* the attributes thought necessary to be a good father, information about employment status should only diminish evaluations of mothers.

Hypothesis 3: Information about employment status will negatively affect the parental evaluations and interpersonal appeal ratings of mothers but not fathers.

Since working fathers were included solely to provide another comparison group for working mothers, we did not fully cross the study design to include a condition of nonworking (full-time parent) fathers. Reactions to this relatively

Table 2. Study 1: Means and Standard Deviations by Condition for Each Dependent Measure Scale

		No info	Working	Nonworking
Family commitment	Mother	5.81 (0.91)$_a$	4.69 (1.15)$_b$	6.48 (0.66)$_c$
	Father	5.31 (0.75)$_a$	5.29 (1.09)$_a$	–
Communality	Mother	5.60 (0.84)$_a$	4.69 (0.68)$_b$	5.56 (1.05)$_a$
	Father	4.94 (0.73)$_b$	4.85 (0.82)$_b$	–
Parental evaluations	Mother	5.79 (1.01)$_a$	4.62 (1.25)$_b$	6.07 (1.04)$_a$
	Father	5.07 (0.68)$_b$	5.12 (0.88)$_b$	–
Interpersonal appeal	Mother	5.62 (1.02)$_a$	4.64 (0.86)$_b$	5.54 (0.91)$_a$
	Father	5.15 (0.68)$_{ab}$	5.21 (0.95)$_a$	–

Note. Standard deviations appear in parentheses. Cell means that do not share subscripts differ at $p < .05$.

scarce group, while no doubt interesting, are immaterial to our purpose and beyond the scope of this investigation.

We experimentally varied the target description to create the five conditions in our between-subjects design: nonworking mother (i.e., full-time parent), working mother, mother with no job information, working father, and father with no job information. *Target gender* was manipulated by altering the names and pronouns to reflect "Jennifer" or "Jason." In the *no job information* conditions, only the filler information was provided (as above). In the *working* conditions, the target was described as working full-time as a Financial Advisor (a male sex-typed occupation). Finally, in the *nonworking* condition (mothers only) the target was described as having decided to put her career on hold to stay home and raise her children.

Results and Discussion

Preliminary analysis indicated no participant gender differences on any of the rating scales. There was, however, a significant interaction between the manipulations and participant parental status (i.e., whether or not they have children) on parental evaluations, $F(4,93) = 2.76, p < .05$ ($\eta^2 = .107$). The effects of the manipulations appeared to be stronger when participants were parents themselves. Nonetheless, the overall pattern was similar, and including participant parental status as a covariate did not change the results of the analysis; thus, participant responses were combined for all subsequent analyses. Table 2 presents all cell means, standard deviations, and intercell comparisons as indicated by planned Fisher's LSD tests.

Comparisons between mothers. For each dependent measure, we conducted a one-way ANOVA to test for differences between the three motherhood conditions. Analyses of variance for each dependent variable consistently indicated a significant effect of condition on parental evaluations, $F(4,100) = 7.36$, $p < .001$ ($\eta^2 = .23$), interpersonal appeal, $F(4,100) = 3.94$, $p = .005$ ($\eta^2 = .14$), communality, $F(4,100) = 5.37$, $p = .001$ ($\eta^2 = .18$), and family commitment, $F(4,100) = 10.81$, $p < .001$ ($\eta^2 = .30$). Consistent with our predictions, when the target mother was presented as being employed, she was seen as a worse parent than when no employment information was mentioned or when it was made clear that she was a nonworking mother. This pattern of data was the same for ratings of commitment and communality. Employed mothers were also rated as having less interpersonal appeal than other mothers, suggesting that the negative consequences for working mothers may go beyond parental disapproval, having potential implications for social ostracism.

Mediation analyses. We then conducted mediation analysis to test for the predicted mediation effects. We dummy-coded the three mother conditions (with no information mothers reflected in the constant) and examined the indirect effect of working motherhood, simultaneously considering both family commitment and communality as competing mediators in a multiple mediator model using bootstrapping techniques that facilitate the examination of indirect effects with small samples (see Preacher & Hayes, 2008).

Analysis indicated a significant negative indirect effect of working motherhood on parental evaluations, through family commitment ratings, $B = -.74$, $SE = .23$ (95%CI $= -.326$ to -1.303), and also through communality ratings, $B = -.29$, $SE = .10$ (95%CI $= -.129$ to $-.552$). Similarly, there was a negative indirect effect of working motherhood on interpersonal appeal, through family commitment, $B = -.44$, $SE = .15$ (95%CI $= -.191$ to $-.794$), and communality, $B = -.42$, $SE = .14$ (95%CI $= -.182$ to $-.715$). These results showed that, consistent with our mediation prediction (Hypothesis 2), perceived communality was partially responsible for working mothers' lower parental evaluations and ratings of interpersonal appeal, even when controlling for family commitment; each explained independent variance when considered together in a multiple mediator model. This finding supported our assertion that the bad parent assumption is a consequence of a perceived lack of fit between the requisite attributes for an employee in a male sex-typed position and for a good mother.

Comparisons of mothers to fathers. In a separate analysis excluding the nonworking mother condition, we conducted a 2×2 ANOVA to test for the interaction between work information and target gender (Hypothesis 3). The analyses for each dependent variable consistently indicated no main effect of target gender on parental evaluations, $F(1,80) = 0.25$, $p = .62$, interpersonal appeal, $F(1,80) = 0.08$, $p = .78$, communality, $F(1,80) = 2.22$, $p = .14$, or family commitment, $F(1,80) = 0.05$, $p = .83$. In contrast, there was a consistent main effect of work information on parental evaluations, $F(1,80) = 6.89$, $p = .01$ ($\eta^2 = .08$), interpersonal appeal, $F(1,80) = 5.61$, $p < .05$ ($\eta^2 = .07$), communality, $F(1,80) = 8.87$, $p < .005$ ($\eta^2 = .10$), and family commitment, $F(1,80) = 7.03$, $p = .01$ ($\eta^2 = .08$). However, these main effects were qualified by significant interactions on each measure: parental evaluations, $F(1,80) = 8.11$, $p < .01$ ($\eta^2 = .09$), interpersonal appeal, $F(1,80) = 7.17$, $p < .01$ ($\eta^2 = .08$), communality, $F(1,80) = 5.81$, $p < .05$ ($\eta^2 = .07$), and family commitment, $F(1,80) = 6.46$, $p = .01$ ($\eta^2 = .08$). For mothers, the provision of employment information significantly lowered her parental evaluations, as well as ratings of her interpersonal appeal, communality, and family commitment. However, this same information had no effect on any of the ratings of fathers. Further scrutiny of these data indicated that the parental evaluations and perceived communality of mothers was *higher* than that of fathers when no information about work was provided; however, this advantage disappeared when they were explicitly depicted as employees. This pattern was slightly different for ratings of interpersonal appeal and family commitment; working mothers were rated as the lowest of all the parents in interpersonal appeal and family commitment.

These results provided support for Hypothesis 3; only mothers faced the bad parent assumption implied by employment in male sex-typed work. While the provision of work information diminished the parental evaluations and interpersonal appeal of mothers, this same information had no effect on equivalently described fathers. The specific pattern of these results was also notable. Consistent with past research (Kobrynowicz & Biernat, 1997), mothers were actually seen as better parents than fathers when no information about employment was available; however, this perceived superiority was eliminated by information about employment. By contrast, employment information appeared to create a difference between mothers' and fathers' interpersonal appeal where none existed in absence of employment information. In other words, when said to be employed, mothers lost their traditional edge and were viewed to be no better than fathers in parental skills, but they slipped from equivalence in their ratings of interpersonal appeal, coming to be seen as the least appealing of all the experimental targets. Despite different starting points for these comparisons, both patterns demonstrated that employment information can degrade evaluations of mothers.

Scope of the Bad Parent Assumption

As argued earlier, we believe that the diminished evaluations of working mothers' effectiveness as parents are driven by the perceived lack of fit (Heilman, 1983) between the attributes required for career success and the communal attributes required to be a good mother. If our reasoning is correct, the bad parent assumption should be moderated by variables that affect this lack of fit perception.

Hypothesis 4: Working mothers will be seen as less effective parents and less interpersonally appealing than nonworking mothers when there is a greater lack of fit between the attributes believed to be necessary for the job and the attributes believed to be necessary for parental success.

In other words, the bad parent assumption should only occur in conditions where the stereotype of a good mother is inconsistent with necessary job attributes. Thus, we should be able to *diminish* the bad parent assumption by manipulating situational characteristics that increase perceived fit. Likewise, we should also be able to *exacerbate* the bad parent assumption by manipulating situational characteristics that decrease perceived fit.

To test this hypothesis in the remaining studies, in addition to replicating the "bad parent assumption" (Hypothesis 1) and documenting the underlying mediating processes (Hypothesis 2), we examined different moderating variables that influence the degree of perceived fit. In Study 2, we examined the effects of job sex-type. We expected mothers employed in male sex-typed jobs to face stronger bad parent assumptions because the attributes of a good mother are a greater mismatch with the attributes deemed necessary for success in male sex-typed roles than in female sex-typed roles. In Study 3, we examined the effects of evidence attesting to work success in a male sex-typed job. We expected the bad parent assumption to be exacerbated with indisputable evidence of a working mother's career success because that success increases the perceived lack of fit by further substantiating her embodiment of the job-relevant attributes believed to be incongruent with those attributes believed necessary to be a good mother. Lastly, in Study 4, we examined reactions to mothers in male sex-typed jobs working out of necessity versus choice. We expected that mothers working out of choice would face stronger bad parent assumptions than those working out of necessity because information suggesting external constraints on a mother's employment decreases the perceived lack of fit by providing an excuse for behaviors that are thought to be incongruent with the attributes of a good mother (i.e., this is not what she really is like). Taken together, these follow-up studies were designed to provide convergent evidence that lack of fit perceptions underlie the bad parent assumption.

Study 2

In Study 2, we again tested for the "bad parent assumption" while also determining whether this assumption was elicited more when working mothers were employed in male sex-typed occupations. The "bad parent assumption" should be more apparent in male sex-typed occupations because the attributes assumed to be necessary to be a successful mother (e.g., warmth, sensitivity) are mismatched with the attributes deemed necessary for success in male sex-typed roles (e.g., toughness, dominance), but are congruent with the attributes deemed necessary for success in female sex-typed roles (e.g., relational aptitude, compassion). Likewise, perceptions of communality should follow this same pattern and mediate the effect of the manipulations on parental evaluations and interpersonal appeal. However, regardless of the sex-type of the job, working mothers should be seen as less committed to their families than nonworking mothers, as commitment impressions are likely to vary as a function of the time constraints associated with employment rather than role congruity.

In Study 2, all targets were described as mothers (Jennifer), but we experimentally varied the target mother's employment status in a 3-cell between-subjects design: nonworking, working in a female sex-typed job, or working in a male sex-typed job. Manipulations were identical to those used in Study 1, although we included a female sex-typed condition that varied the target's job title. Following from past research examining job sex-type (Heilman & Wallen, 2009; Heilman et al., 2004), targets in the *female sex-typed job* were described as an "Employee Assistance Counselor," while targets in the *male sex-typed job* were, as in Study 1, described as a "Financial Advisor." A manipulation check asking participants to rate the job (1 = masculine, 7 = feminine) indicated that the "Financial Advisor" job ($M = 3.78$, $SD = 0.96$) was significantly more masculine than the "Employee Assistance Counselor" job ($M = 4.46$, $SD = 0.89$), $t(119) = 4.03$, $p < .001$. It is worth noting that additional checks indicated the "Financial Advisor" job was also seen as higher in prestige ($t = 4.38$, $p < .001$) and salary ($t = 5.03$, $p < .001$), but the two jobs did not differ in perceived difficulty or time investment ($ts < 1.4$).

Results and Discussion

Preliminary analysis indicated a main effect of participant gender on evaluations of family commitment, $F(2,182) = 5.55$, $p < .05$ ($\eta^2 = .03$), and communality, $F(2,182) = 4.19$, $p < .05$ ($\eta^2 = .02$). Regardless of condition, female participants rated targets more favorably. There was also a main effect of participant parental status on parental evaluations, $F(2,182) = 4.69$, $p < .05$ ($\eta^2 = .03$), and interpersonal appeal, $F(2,182) = 5.77$, $p < .05$ ($\eta^2 = .03$). Again regardless of condition, participants with children rated targets more favorably. Notably, these demographic variables did not interact with the manipulations, and including them as covariates did not change the results; thus, participant responses were combined for all subsequent analyses.

The data analysis scheme was the same as that used to compare ratings between mothers in Study 1. Cell means, standard deviations, and inter-cell comparisons are presented in Table 3. Analyses of variance indicated a significant effect of condition for each dependent variable: parental evaluations, $F(2,185) = 20.82$, $p < .001$ ($\eta^2 = .18$), interpersonal appeal, $F(2,185) = 5.29$, $p < .01$ ($\eta^2 = .05$), communality, $F(2,185) = 7.41$, $p = .001$ ($\eta^2 = .07$), and family commitment, $F(2,185) = 24.25$, $p < .001$ ($\eta^2 = .21$). Mothers working in a male sex-typed job

Table 3. Study 2: Means and Standard Deviations by Condition for Each Dependent Measure Scale

	Nonworking mother	Mother working in a female sex-typed job	Mother working in a male sex-typed job
Family commitment	6.30 (0.85)$_a$	5.43 (1.14)$_b$	5.14 (0.94)$_b$
Communality	5.59 (0.92)$_a$	5.34 (0.95)$_a$	4.97 (0.84)$_b$
Parental evaluations	5.93 (0.92)$_a$	5.22 (1.03)$_b$	4.86 (0.93)$_c$
Interpersonal appeal	5.46 (1.00)$_a$	5.24 (0.97)$_a$	4.88 (1.06)$_b$

Note. Standard deviations appear in parentheses. Cell means that do not share subscripts differ at $p < .05$.

were rated as worse parents than mothers working in a female sex-typed job, and both were rated as worse parents than nonworking mothers. Mothers working in a male sex-typed job were also evaluated as less interpersonally appealing and less communal than both nonworking mothers and mothers working in a female sex-typed job. In contrast, working mothers were seen as less committed to their family compared to nonworking mothers, regardless of their job sex-type.

Mediation analyses. For the bootstrapping analysis, we dummy-coded conditions to examine the indirect effect of male and female sex-typed employment (with nonworking mothers reflected in the constant). Analysis indicated that perceived communality was partially responsible for the lower parental evaluations and interpersonal appeal of working mothers, even when controlling for family commitment. There was a significant negative indirect effect of *male* sex-typed employment on interpersonal appeal, through family commitment, $B = -.44$, $SE = .12$ (95%CI $= -.223$ to $-.698$), and through communality, $B = -.28$, $SE = .09$ (95%CI $= -.141$ to $-.535$). Similarly, there was a negative indirect effect of male sex-typed employment on parental evaluations, through family commitment, $B = -.76$, $SE = .12$ (95%CI $= -.530$ to -1.034), and communality, $B = -.17$, $SE = .06$ (95%CI $= -.073$ to $-.293$). In contrast, the parental evaluations of mothers working in the *female* sex-typed job were only mediated by family commitment; there was a negative indirect effect through commitment, $B = -.57$, $SE = .12$ (95%CI $= -.348$ to $-.853$), but not communality, $B = -.07$, $SE = .05$ (95%CI $= +.020$ to $-.176$).

These results replicated Study 1, again showing that mothers' employment in a male sex-typed job resulted in lower parental evaluations. Moreover, the results demonstrated that these effects were stronger when the mother was employed in a male sex-typed rather than a female sex-typed job. This finding provided critical information about the processes underlying the bad parent assumption ascribed to working women. If our assertions are correct, negativity toward working mothers should be strongest when there is lack of fit between the attributes thought necessary for motherhood and attributes thought necessary to do the job. Our data supported this idea, as did the meditational analyses. The parental evaluations and interpersonal appeal of mothers employed in male sex-typed work, which is inconsistent with maternal attributes, reflected judgments of communality. In contrast, the evaluations of mothers employed in female sex-typed work, which is more consistent with maternal attributes, only reflected concerns about job commitment, not about communality. Moreover, only mothers in male sex-typed jobs suffered from diminished interpersonal appeal. Evidently, it was not working per se that decreased working mothers' social acceptance, but working in a gender-inconsistent job.

Study 3

In Study 3, we examined another variable implicating perceived lack of fit as underlying the "bad parent" assumption faced by working mothers. When there is clear information that a working mother is successful in male sex-typed employment, the lack of fit between motherhood and employment is particularly stark. Clear work success implies greater congruence with the masculine attributes required for male sex-typed jobs, exacerbating the perception of lack of fit between the characteristics implied by employment and the feminine characteristics assumed necessary to be a good mother. As a result, the negative parental evaluations of working mothers should be amplified when there is clear information that a working mother is successful.

Holding male sex-type job constant, we experimentally varied the target mother's employment success in a 3-cell between-subjects design: nonworking, working with no job success information, or working with clear job success information. The first two conditions were identical to those used in Studies 1 and 2. However, in the third *job success* condition, the sentence describing the target's job included additional information stating that she recently received an award from the company CEO for her excellent track record. A single item manipulation check asked participants, "How successful do you think this person has been in his/her career? ($1 =$ not at all successful, $7 =$ very successful). Participants in the success condition ($M = 6.32$, $SD = 0.78$) indicated that the target was significantly more successful than participants in the no success information condition ($M = 5.71$, $SD = 1.12$), $t(166) = 4.09$, $p < .001$, although all targets were rated as fairly successful. Note that in Studies 3 and 4, the measure of *interpersonal appeal* was expanded to eight items, including: "How much do you think you would like this person?" ($1 =$ not at all, $7 =$ very much), "Would you want to get to know this person better?" ($1 =$ not at all, $7 =$ very much), "How good of a friend do you think this person is?" ($1 =$ very bad, $7 =$ very good), and a 7-point bipolar adjective "not likeable-likeable." See Table 1 for reliability statistics and inter-scale correlations.

Table 4. Study 3: Means and Standard Deviations by Condition for Each Dependent Measure Scale

	Nonworking mother	Working mother without success info	Working mother with success info
Family commitment	6.26 (0.80)$_a$	5.17 (1.38)$_b$	4.65 (1.41)$_c$
Communality	5.63 (0.89)$_a$	5.08 (1.16)$_b$	4.66 (1.12)$_c$
Parental evaluations	5.82 (0.99)$_a$	5.19 (1.39)$_b$	4.61 (1.40)$_c$
Interpersonal appeal	5.45 (0.98)$_a$	5.09 (1.08)$_b$	4.59 (1.17)$_c$

Note. Standard deviations appear in parentheses. Cell means that do not share subscripts differ at $p < .05$.

Results and Discussion

Preliminary analysis indicated no effects of participant gender on any of the ratings. There was, however, a significant main effect of participant parental status on interpersonal appeal, $F(1,246) = 4.83, p < .05$ ($\eta^2 = .019$). Regardless of condition, participants with children rated targets more favorably than participants without children. There was also a significant interaction between participant parental status and the manipulations on parental evaluations, $F(2,246) = 3.11$, $p < .05$ ($\eta^2 = .025$). Similar to Study 1, the effects of the manipulations appeared to be stronger when participants were parents themselves. Nonetheless, the overall pattern was similar, and including participant parental status as a covariate did not change the results of the analysis; thus, participant responses were combined for all subsequent analyses.

The data analysis scheme comparing mothers was the same as in the previous two studies. Cell means, standard deviations, and inter-cell comparisons are presented in Table 4. Analyses of variance indicated a significant effect of condition for each dependent variable: parental evaluations, $F(2,253) = 20.82, p < .001$ ($\eta^2 = .14$), interpersonal appeal, $F(2,253) = 5.29, p < .001$ ($\eta^2 = .10$), perceived communality, $F(2,253) = 7.41, p < .001$ ($\eta^2 = .13$), and family commitment, $F(2,253) = 39.21, p < .001$ ($\eta^2 = .24$). For all measures, all three conditions were significantly different from one another. Successful working mothers were evaluated less favorably than working mothers for whom no additional success information was provided, and both working mothers were evaluated less favorably than nonworking mothers.

Mediation analyses. For the bootstrapping analysis, we used a stepwise coding scheme examining the effect of employment and, separately, the effect of job success information. Analysis indicated that perceived communality was partially responsible for the lower parental evaluations and interpersonal appeal of working mothers, even when controlling for family commitment. There was a significant negative indirect effect of employment on parental evaluations, through family commitment, $B = -1.00$, $SE = .12$ (95%CI $= -.793$ to -1.285), and through communality, $B = -.22$, $SE = .06$ (95%CI $= -.117$ to $-.338$). Similarly, there was a significant negative indirect effect of employment on interpersonal appeal, through family commitment, $B = -.58$, $SE = .08$ (95%CI $= -.433$ to $-.772$), and communality, $B = -.30$, $SE = .07$ (95%CI $= -.169$ to $-.436$). Communality was also partially responsible for the negative effects of job success information, even when controlling for family commitment. There was a significant negative indirect effect of success information on parental evaluations, through family commitment, $B = -.20$, $SE = .08$ (95%CI $= -.036$ to $-.367$), and through communality, $B = -.06$, $SE = .06$ (95%CI $= -.012$ to $-.123$). Similarly, there was a significant negative indirect effect of success information on interpersonal appeal, through family commitment, $B = -.12$, $SE = .05$ (95%CI $= -.012$ to $-.224$), and communality, $B = -.08$, $SE = .04$ (95%CI $= -.007$ to $-.158$).

These results again replicated the basic findings of the earlier studies, while also demonstrating that providing information of clear job success amplified the effects. A mother's employment in a male sex-typed occupation again led to the bad parent assumption and lower interpersonal appeal, and this effect was exacerbated by additional information underscoring employment success. These findings were partly due to the greater time and attention needed to achieve work success. However, even when controlling for these commitment ratings, the additional decrements instigated by employment success could be accounted for by further decreases in perceptions of communality. Thus, these findings provided further support for our theoretical arguments, illustrating how variations in perceived lack of fit, in this case sparked by clarity of success in a male sex-typed role, can influence reactions to working mothers. At the same time, these results highlighted the more general trade-off between perceptions of likeability and perceptions of competence often faced by working women (see Rudman & Glick, 2008).

Study 4

Study 4 expanded on the previous studies by examining whether or not the "bad parent" assumption is reduced when a working mother is believed to be working out of necessity rather than choice. The belief that a mother's employment is indicative of a stereotype-inconsistent disposition that implies parental ineffectiveness is likely to be contingent on observers making an internal attribution (Weiner, 1995), crediting her employment in male sex-typed work to her true character. Ambiguity about the cause of a mother's employment provides her with an excuse, facilitating a process of "attributional rationalization" that allows observers to ignore evidence that is incongruent with gender stereotypes (Heilman & Haynes, 2005). Indeed, research has shown that information suggesting external causes of stereotype-incongruent behavior can elicit perceptions that a target is more stereotype-congruent (e.g., Deaux & Emswiller, 1974; Heilman & Haynes, 2005; Swim & Sanna, 1996). In other words, information suggesting external constraints on employment should help to mitigate the poor parental evaluations of working mothers because it reduces the perceived lack of fit between the traits implied by employment and those required to be a good mother. This prediction is consistent with past research showing that mothers described as working out of choice are less liked than mothers working out of financial necessity (Brescoll & Uhlmann, 2005; Bridges & Etaugh, 1995); however, it remains unclear whether or not this negativity was due, as we propose, to assumptions about a working mother's lack of communal characteristics believed so critical to being a good mother.

We experimentally varied women's employment preferences in a 3-cell between-subjects design: nonworking, working full-time because of financial need, or working full-time by choice. The nonworking condition was similar to the previous studies, indicating that, "when she became pregnant she decided to put her career on hold to stay home and raise her children." The employment information provided in both working conditions was identical to the previous studies (no success info, male sex-typed job held constant). However, in the *choice* condition, this information was accompanied by the additional statement: "when she became pregnant she decided that she wanted to continue working full-time." In contrast, in the *need* condition, it was accompanied by the additional statement: "she had planned to put her career on hold to stay home and raise her children, but when she became pregnant her family's financial situation required that she continue to work full-time."

In the subsequent questionnaire, when asked, "Was this person in this occupation by choice?" (1 = not at all, 4 = completely), participants in the choice condition ($M = 3.33$, $SD = 0.80$) provided significantly higher ratings than participants in the need condition ($M = 2.17$, $SD = 0.78$), $t(127) = 8.33$, $p < .001$. Similarly, when asked, "How career oriented do you think this person is?" (1 = not at all, 7 = very much), participants in the choice condition ($M = 5.72$, $SD = 0.94$) viewed the target as significantly more career oriented than participants in the need condition ($M = 5.02$, $SD = 1.25$), $t(129) = 3.66$, $p < .001$.

Results and Discussion

Preliminary analysis indicated no participant gender differences on any of the rating scales. There were also no effects of participant parental status, although a nonsignificant trend suggested that the observed effects were stronger for participants with children. Thus, as with the previous studies, participant responses were combined for all subsequent analyses.

The analytic approach was the same as in the previous studies. Cell means, standard deviations, and inter-cell comparisons are presented in Table 5. Analyses

Table 5. Study 4: Means and Standard Deviations by Condition for Each Dependent Measure Scale

	Nonworking mother	Mother working because of necessity	Mother working because of choice
Family commitment	6.22 (0.85)$_a$	5.62 (1.15)$_b$	5.01 (1.12)$_c$
Communality	5.68 (0.95)$_a$	5.41 (0.99)$_a$	4.90 (1.10)$_b$
Parental evaluations	5.81 (1.09)$_a$	5.58 (1.09)$_a$	4.92 (1.02)$_b$
Interpersonal appeal	5.48 (0.95)$_a$	5.41 (0.96)$_a$	4.84 (0.99)$_b$

Note. Standard deviations appear in parentheses. Cell means that do not share subscripts differ at $p < .05$.

of variance indicated a significant effect of condition for each dependent variable: parental evaluations, $F(2,193) = 12.03, p < .001$ ($\eta^2 = .11$), interpersonal appeal, $F(2,193) = 8.43, p < .001$ ($\eta^2 = .08$), perceived communality, $F(2,193) = 9.82, p < .001$ ($\eta^2 = .09$), and family commitment, $F(2,193) = 21.88, p < .001$ ($\eta^2 = .19$). Working mothers were rated as worse parents, having less interpersonal appeal, and being less communal than nonworking mothers, but only when their employment was described as a personal choice; mothers working because of need were rated similarly to nonworking mothers and more favorably than mothers working by choice. In contrast, both types of working mothers were rated as less committed than nonworking mothers, and the commitment ratings of all three mothers were significantly different from one another.

Mediation analyses. For the bootstrapping analysis, conditions were dummy-coded to reflect nonworking mothers in the constant. Consistent with the earlier ANOVAs, the parental evaluations and interpersonal appeal of mothers working out of necessity were not different than nonworking mothers. However, analysis indicated that communality was partially responsible for the lower parental evaluations and interpersonal appeal of mothers working because of personal choice, even when controlling for family commitment. There was a significant negative indirect effect of choice on parental evaluations, through family commitment, $B = -.78, SE = .13$ (95%CI $= -.544$ to -1.067), and through communality, $B = -.23, SE = .07$ (95%CI $= -.123$ to $-.399$). Similarly, there was a significant negative indirect effect of work choice, through family commitment, $B = -.45, SE = .10$ (95%CI $= -.285$ to $-.671$), and communality, $B = -.36, SE = .09$ (95%CI $= -.181$ to $-.544$).

These results showed that when a working mother's career, and the assumed lack of communality suggested by its pursuit, could be attributed to an external cause (in this case financial need) they did not suffer the negative parental and interpersonal evaluations typically ascribed to mothers who elect to work. This pattern of findings supported the view that intent ambiguity leads to the attributional rationalization of stereotype-inconsistent information (Heilman & Haynes, 2005), while also illustrating that such rationalization can reduce the perceived lack of fit between the characteristics implied by employment in male sex-typed work and the communality that is believed to be necessary for success as a mother.

General Discussion

Taken together, this series of studies indicated that people assume that mothers working in male sex-typed occupations are worse parents than nonworking mothers. This basic finding is not surprising, and past research has already documented the existence of this "bad parent" assumption. However, in contrast to past research suggesting that perceptions of reduced family commitment underlies the harsher parental evaluations of working mothers (Etaugh & Nekolny, 1990), the current research provided consistent and converging evidence that these evaluations are *also* driven by a perceived deficiency in communality that is implied by success in male sex-typed jobs, communality that cultural beliefs dictate to be essential for success as a mother.

In addition to consistent evidence of mediation, the results of all four studies helped to elucidate the process underlying the bad parent assumption. Supporting the notion that this effect is particularly relevant for mothers because it is grounded in female gender stereotypes, Study 1 showed that employment information had a negative effect for mothers but not fathers. We then demonstrated three different corroborating patterns of moderation aimed at increasing or decreasing the perceived lack of fit between the attributes associated with employment and the attributes associated with mothers, conditions that reduced or exacerbated assumptions about working mothers' lack of communality and their ineffectiveness as parents. In Study 2, the bad parent assumption was particularly apparent for mothers working in male sex-typed occupations. In Study 3, the unequivocal achievement of success in a male sex-typed job exacerbated the bad parent assumption. Finally, in Study 4, when provided with evidence suggesting an external determinant of their decision to work full-time, working mothers were "excused for their careers" and were seen as no less effective as parents than nonworking mothers.

Although the primary intent of the current research was to provide evidence of the processes underlying the "bad parent" assumption faced by working mothers, we also documented similar patterns of results for ratings of interpersonal appeal, indices meant to capture participants' willingness or desire to interact with the targets. Although these additional ratings should be cautiously interpreted because of their reliance on self-reported behavioral intentions, they offer preliminary evidence that employment in male sex-typed occupations may have social costs for working mothers. Further research is still needed to determine whether the attitudes reported here translate into behavior, and whether these interactional biases are yet an additional source of stress on the emotional well-being of working mothers.

Despite the clarity of our results, caution should be exercised in their interpretation. Our methods of investigation were designed to allow for controlled and systematic experimentation, but like any method of investigation, they also put limits on the implications that we can draw from the data. Participants were provided with very little information about the targets, and their reactions might have been very different had they known more about them. Therefore, it is important to test the current ideas in more natural settings with actual parents as targets. Although such research would not allow for the control offered by this set of studies, it would test the validity of our findings and may also suggest other critical moderators of our effects.

It is also important to note some possible limitations in the generalizability of the current research. Although perceptions of communality may underlie standards of motherhood regardless of culture (Cuddy et al., 2008), it is possible that findings derived from our U.S. sample may differ from countries in which governments provide more ample support for working parents or in which working mothers have served as head of state. Widespread legitimization of working mothers may weaken their perceived communal deficit, affecting the degree to which their role at work is seen as inconsistent with their role as a mother. Also, the current research examines only nonworking and full-time working parents. People may respond to mothers with alternative work arrangements (e.g., flextime, part-time) differently than to full-time working mothers (see Hall, Lee, Kossek, & Las Heras, 2012; Vinkenburg, Van Engen, Coffeng, & Dikkers, 2012). To the extent their employment goals are seen differently than women who work full-time, mothers with alternative work arrangements may be less vulnerable to the bad parent assumption. Additional research is necessary to address these questions and to obtain more information about the full scope of the bad parent assumption and its consequences.

These issues aside, the potential implications of this research are disheartening for working women in traditionally male fields. Our findings indicate yet another problem for women who strive for career success, contributing to their well-documented angst concerning the balance between work and family. Even if they feel that they can successfully manage both sets of obligations, our results suggest that third parties may assume otherwise and further disparage mothers for fully engaging in male sex-typed career pursuits. This assumed ineffectiveness as parents puts working mothers in a very difficult position, particularly in light of parallel assumptions about their incompetence at work (Heilman & Okimoto, 2008).

In conclusion, this research highlights the need to recognize that the distress experienced by working parents stems from issues other than just time constraints and commitment trade-offs. Gender stereotypes and reactions to stereotype-inconsistent behavior can impact not only how working mothers are viewed as workers but also how they are viewed as parents, adding the burden of having to combat assumptions about their personal life as well as their work life. Failing to attend to this added stressor may hinder the success of work/family programs, particularly for working mothers, and may partly underlie the mixed findings about the effectiveness of these programs to significantly impact women's career advancement or alleviate the family–life demands that drive mothers from the workplace. Our findings suggest the need for work/family programs that acknowledge these problems and provide ways for working mothers to validate their effectiveness in both career and family domains, possibly by building a sense of community or work/family culture that recognizes and provides support in the face of assumptions about work or parental ineptitude. Only by helping working mothers understand and cope with these negative impressions can such programs have a significant and positive impact. The data reported here leave little doubt that, to achieve maximum sustainability, work/family programs must aid working mothers in impression management as well as time management, while focusing on stressors arising from family as well as work domains.

References

Brescoll, V. L., & Uhlmann, E. L. (2005). Attitudes toward traditional and nontraditional parents. *Psychology of Women Quarterly, 29*, 436–445. doi: 10.1111/j.1471-6402.2005.00244.x

Bridges, J. S. (1987). College females' perceptions, of adult roles and occupational fields for women. *Sex Roles, 16*, 591–604. doi: 10.1007/BF00300375

Bridges, J. S., & Etaugh, C. (1995). College students' perceptions of mothers: Effects of maternal employment–child rearing pattern and motive for employment. *Sex Roles, 32*, 735–751. doi: 10.1007/BF01560187

Bridges, J. S., & Orza, A. M. (1992). The effects of employment role and motive for employment on the perceptions of mothers. *Sex Roles, 27*, 331–343. doi: 10.1007/BF00289943

Cooke, R. A., & Rousseau, D. M. (1984). Stress and strain from family roles and work role expectations. *Journal of Applied Psychology, 69*, 252–260. doi: 10.1037/0021-9010.69.2.252

Cuddy, A. J. C., Fiske, S. T., & Glick, P. (2004). When professionals become mothers, warmth doesn't cut the ice. *Journal of Social Issues, 60*, 701–718. doi: 10.1111/j.0022-4537.2004.00381.x

Cuddy, A. J. C., Fiske, S. T., & Glick, P. (2008). Warmth and competence as universal dimensions of social perception: The stereotype content model and the BIAS map. In M. P. Zanna (Ed.), *Advances in experimental social psychology* (Vol. 40, pp. 61–149). New York, NY: Academic Press.

Deaux, K., & Emswiller, T. (1974). Explanations of successful performance on sex-linked tasks: What is skill for the male is luck for the female. *Journal of Personality and Social Psychology, 29*, 80–85. doi: 10.1037/h0035733

Eagly, A. H., & Karau, S. J. (2002). Role congruity theory of prejudice toward female leaders. *Psychological Review, 109*, 573–598. doi: 10.1037//0033-295X.109.3.573

Etaugh, C., & Nekolny, K. (1990). Effects of employment status and marital status on perceptions of mothers. *Sex Roles, 23*, 273–280. doi: 10.1007/BF00290048

Etaugh, C., & Study, G. G. (1989). Perceptions of mothers: Effects of employment status, marital status, and age of child. *Sex Roles, 20*, 59–70. doi: 10.1007/BF00288027

Fuegen, K., Biernat, M., Haines, E., & Deaux, K. (2004). Mothers and fathers in the workplace: How gender and parental status influence judgments of job-related competence. *Journal of Social Issues, 60*, 737–754. doi: 10.1111/j.0022-4537.2004.00383.x

Gutek, B. A., Repetti, R., & Silver, D. (1988). Nonwork roles and stress at work. In C. Cooper & R. Payne (Eds.), *Causes, coping and consequences of stress at work* (2nd ed., pp. 141–174). New York: Wiley.

Hall, D. T., Lee, M. D., Kossek, E. E., & Las Heras, M. (2012). Pursuing career success while sustaining personal and family well being: A study of reduced-load professionals over time. *Journal of Social Issues, 68*(4), 742–766.

Heilman, M. E. (1983). Sex bias in work settings: The lack of fit model. In B. Staw & L. Cummings (Eds.), *Research in organizational behavior* (Vol. 5, pp. 269–298). Greenwich, CT: JAI Press.

Heilman, M. E. (2001). Description and prescription: How gender stereotypes prevent women's ascent up the organizational ladder. *Journal of Social Issues, 57*, 657–674. doi: 10.1111/0022-4537.00234

Heilman, M. E., & Haynes, M. C. (2005). No credit where credit is due: Attributional rationalization of women's success in male-female teams. *Journal of Applied Psychology, 90*, 905–916. doi: 10.1037/0021-9010.90.5.90

Heilman, M. E. & Okimoto, T. G. (2007). Why are women penalized for success at male tasks? The implied communality deficit. *Journal of Applied Psychology, 92*, 81–92. doi: 10.1037/0021-9010.92.1.81

Heilman, M. E. & Okimoto, T. G. (2008). Motherhood: A potential source of bias in employment decisions. *Journal of Applied Psychology, 93*, 189–198. doi: 10.1037/0021-9010.93.1.189

Heilman, M. E. & Wallen, A. S. (2009). Wimpy and undeserving of respect: Penalties for men's gender-inconsistent success. *Journal of Experimental Social Psychology, 46*, 664–667. doi: 10.1016/j.jesp.2010.01.008

Heilman, M. E., Wallen, A. S., Fuchs, D., & Tamkins, M. M. (2004). Penalties for success: Reactions to women who succeed at male tasks. *Journal of Applied Psychology, 89*, 416–427. doi: 10.1037/0021-9010.89.3.41

Kandel, D. B., Davies, M., & Raveis, V. H. (1985). The stressfulness of daily social roles for women: Marital, occupational and household roles. *Journal of Health and Social Behavior, 26*, 64–78. Retrieved from http://www.jstor.org/stable/2136727

Kobrynowicz, D., & Biernat, M. (1997). Decoding subjective evaluations: How stereotypes provide shifting standards. *Journal of Experimental Social Psychology, 33*, 579–601. doi: 10.1006/jesp.1997.1338

LaRocco, J. M., House, J. S., & French, J. R. P., Jr. (1980). Social support, occupational stress, and health. *Journal of Health and Social Behavior, 21*, 202–218. Retrieved from http://www.jstor.org/stable/2136616

Morgan, W. B., & King, E. B. (2012). The association between work-family guilt and pro-and antisocial work behavior. *Journal of Social Issues, 68*(4), 684–703.

Preacher, K. J., & Hayes, A. F. (2008). Asympotic and resampling procedures for assessing and comparing indirect effects in multiple mediator models. *Behavior Research Methods, 40*, 879–891. doi: 10.3758/BRM.40.3.87

Rudman, L. A. (1998). Self-promotion as a risk factor for women: The costs and benefits of counterstereotypical impression management. *Journal of Personality and Social Psychology, 74*, 629–645. doi: 10.1037/0022-3514.74.3.629

Rudman, L. A., & Glick, P. (2008). *The social psychology of gender: How power and intimacy shape gender relations*. New York, NY: Guilford.

Skitka, L. J., & Sargis, E. G. (2006). The Internet as psychological laboratory. *Annual Review of Psychology, 57*, 529–555. doi: 10.1146/annurev.psych.57.102904.19004

Swim, J. K., & Sanna, L. J. (1996). He's skilled, she's lucky: A metaanalysis of observers' attributions for women's and men's successes and failures. *Personality and Social Psychology Bulletin, 22*, 507–519. doi: 10.1177/0146167296225008

Teti, D. M., & Gelfand, D. M. (1991). Behavioral competence among mothers of infants in the first year: The mediational role of maternal self-efficacy. *Child Development, 62*, 918–929. doi: 10.1111/j.1467-8624.1991.tb01580.x

Vinkenburg, C. J., Van Engen, M. L., Coffeng, J., & Dikkers, J. S. E. (2012). Bias in employment decisions about mothers and fathers: The (dis)advantages of sharing care responsibilities. *Journal of Social Issues*, 68(4), 725–741.

Weiner, B. (1995). *Judgments of responsibility: A foundation for a theory of social conduct.* New York, NY: Guilford.

TYLER G. OKIMOTO is a Lecturer in Management in the business school at the University of Queensland, Australia. He received his PhD in social and organizational psychology from New York University in 2005, and has worked as a postdoctoral researcher in the School of Management at Yale University, and in the School of Psychology at Flinders University in Australia. Dr. Okimoto's research investigates the conditions under which the deviant attitudes and behaviors of others are threatening to an individual's sense of self and identity, eliciting feelings of outrage, injustice, indignation, and/or a desire for some sanctioning response. His research uses experimental social-psychological approaches to explore interdisciplinary questions fundamental to criminology, management, and public policy. Dr. Okimoto's work in the area of stereotyping and bias has been published in *Personality and Social Psychology Bulletin* and the *Journal of Applied Psychology*.

MADELINE E. HEILMAN is Professor of Psychology at New York University. For over 20 years she was Coordinator of the Industrial/Organizational Psychology program which is now part of the University's Social Psychology program. She is currently serving as the Director of Graduate Studies of the Psychology Department. After receiving her PhD from Columbia University in 1972, she spent eight years as a member of the faculty at Yale's School of Organization and Management. She also spent the 1998–99 academic year as a Visiting Professor at Columbia University's Graduate School of Business. She has been on the editorial boards of the *Journal of Conflict Resolution, Organization Dynamics, Journal of Applied Behavioral Science, Academy of Management Review*, and *Organizational Behavior and Human Decision Processes,* and currently serves on the editorial board of the *Journal of Applied Psychology.* Her research has focused on sex bias in work settings, the dynamics of stereotyping, and the unintended consequences of preferential selection processes.

Bias in Employment Decisions about Mothers and Fathers: The (Dis)Advantages of Sharing Care Responsibilities

Claartje J. Vinkenburg[*]
VU Amsterdam

Marloes L. van Engen
Tilburg University

Jennifer Coffeng
VU Amsterdam

Josje S. E. Dikkers
University of Applied Sciences Utrecht

Bias against mothers in employment decisions has often been explained by the assumption that mothers are less committed and competent than fathers and nonparents. In a simulated employment context, we studied whether this "motherhood bias" can be attenuated by different ways of dividing care responsibilities between partners. We contrasted a main provider model to a shared model in which both partners equally share work and care responsibilities. In the Netherlands, where part-time work is encouraged and available, sharing work and care is increasingly considered "normal." As predicted, we found less favorable perceptions of full-time working mothers who are main providers than of mothers who share responsibilities with their partner. In contrast, we found least favorable perceptions of fathers who share responsibilities. Our findings show how normative beliefs about parenting dictate that we applaud mothers—and punish fathers—who combine career and care by working reduced hours.

Working mothers are disadvantaged compared to working fathers or employees without children because decision makers, i.e., those who make hiring and

---

[*]Correspondence concerning this article should be addressed to Faculty of Economics & Business Administration, VU University Amsterdam, De Boelelaan 1105, 1081 HV Amsterdam, The Netherlands [e-mail: c.j.vinkenburg@vu.nl].

promotion decisions in organizational settings, have reduced expectations about mothers' professional commitment and competence. This phenomenon has been labeled "motherhood bias" (Cuddy, Fiske, & Glick, 2004; Heilman & Okimoto, 2008). Earlier research in simulated employment contexts has shown evidence of this motherhood bias in employment decisions (Benard & Correll, 2010; Heilman & Okimoto, 2008; Okimoto & Heilman, 2012), and motherhood bias is found in studies of "real" selection and promotion decisions as well (King, 2008; Williams & Segal, 2003). As this special issue is about sustainability in combining career and care, we set out to study if motherhood bias is attenuated by different ways of dividing care responsibilities between partners. We contrast a main provider model in which one partner is the primary earner to a shared model in which both partners equally share work and care responsibilities. Under which conditions do decision makers consider mothers (and fathers) most committed and competent, and thus most likely to be hired for a managerial position? We designed an experiment concerning employment decisions which closely follows the design of the simulated employment context described by Heilman and Okimoto (2008), and which incorporates different ways of dividing work and care between partners typical to the Netherlands, the country in which this study was carried out.

Part-Time Work in the Netherlands

The Netherlands is, according to Mainiero and Sullivan (2005, p. 120), a prime example of those few countries that "have initiated policies that provide considerable support for working parents" by providing employees with the legal right to reduce the length of their workweek and by offering quality part-time jobs with pro-rated pensions and benefits. The Netherlands has the highest rate of part-time work throughout the OECD (Organisation for Economic Co-operation and Development) countries for both women and men (OECD, 2009), with more than 60% of Dutch women and 15% of Dutch men working part time. In the Netherlands, 56% of couples with children fit the "one-and-a-half-income" model, in which one partner (typically the mother) works "half time," and one partner (typically the father) works full time (Janssen & Portegijs, 2011). Twenty-four percent of Dutch couples with children fit the "breadwinner-homemaker" model with one income. Families with children in which both partners work full time, both work part time, or both are unemployed are rare (8%, 7%, and 2%, respectively). The standard one-and-a-half-income (or main provider) model is quite normative, in that women with pre-school aged children are not expected to work more than 3 days per week (Cloïn & Souren, 2011). The shared model, in which both partners work 4 days per week, while not yet common, is rapidly becoming more popular, with 49% of Dutch men saying they prefer sharing responsibilities while both mothers and fathers work reduced hours (Cloïn & Souren, 2011).

Bias in Employment Decisions: Sharing Care

In this study, we focus on the effect of the shared versus the main provider model of distributing work and care responsibilities between partners on commitment and competence evaluations and screening recommendations by decision makers in a simulated employment context, i.e., when considering a potential candidate for a managerial position. Heilman and Okimoto (2008) showed that motherhood bias can be triggered by merely providing decision makers with information about parental status of job candidates. If a mother is the main provider, and her partner works half time (i.e., a reversed version of the standard one-and-a-half income model), will she be considered more committed and competent, and thus more hireable for a managerial position, than a mother who shares care responsibilities equally with her partner by both working 4 days per week? Or, will mothers who work full time be treated more harshly for not adhering to prescriptive norms of being a good mother? And how does sharing care responsibilities by working part time versus being the main provider (i.e., the standard one-and-a-half-income model) affects the anticipated commitment and competence of fathers?

Stereotype maintenance theory (Rudman & Fairchild, 2004) suggests that perceivers protect their stereotypes by condemning mothers who work full time, as well as fathers who work part time and are not the main provider. Below, we discuss how normative beliefs about parenting that stem from gender stereotypes affect employment decisions about mothers and fathers who have different ways of dividing care responsibilities, by contrasting main providers, i.e., those who work full time with a partner who works half time, with those that equally share care responsibilities with their partner by both working reduced hours.

Normative Beliefs about Parenting

Gender stereotypes are consensually held beliefs about the typical traits, characteristics, and behaviors of women and men (Eagly & Karau, 2002). These stereotypes hold that women in general are attributed communal characteristics, e.g., being warm and nurturing, and men are attributed agentic characteristics, e.g., being assertive and competitive. Gender stereotypes are not only descriptive (in that they describe how women and men, mothers and father typically behave), but also prescriptive, in that they provide information on how people are supposed to behave (Heilman, 2001). As has been substantially demonstrated, the female gender stereotype is often at odds with stereotypical images we have of the "typical," and particularly the "ideal" worker (Acker, 1990; Burgess & Borgida, 1999; Eagly & Karau, 2002; Heilman, 2001). As a consequence, gender stereotypes have been shown to introduce bias into hiring and promotion decisions (Heilman, Wallen, Fuchs, & Tamkins, 2004; Rudman, 1998; Rudman & Glick, 2001; Vinkenburg, Van Engen, Eagly, & Johannesen-Schmidt, 2011).

The degree to which inferences made about women are based on gender stereotypes varies with the extent to which a woman is believed to be a typical representative of her sex (Fiske & Taylor, 1991). As being a mother "virtually embodies our cultural conception of being a woman" (Heilman & Okimoto, 2008, p. 189), gender stereotypes particularly influence inferences made about mothers. More specifically, gender stereotypes reflect the image of fathers as breadwinners and providers, and of mothers as caregivers and homemakers. Therefore, career making does not match with the stereotypical nurturing role of mothers. Working mothers tend to be viewed negatively in their role as parents (Bridges & Etaugh, 1995; Etaugh & Nekolny, 1990), particularly when they are successful in their working role (Benard & Correll, 2010), and when they are believed to work out of personal choice or career aspirations instead of out of economic necessity (Okimoto & Heilman, 2012). Brescoll and Uhlmann (2005) show that prescriptive gender role stereotypes result in negative evaluations of nontraditional parents (i.e., full-time employed mothers and stay-at-home fathers).

According to stereotype maintenance theory social perceivers tend to reinforce stereotypes by sanctioning or sabotaging people that violate role prescriptions (Rudman & Fairchild, 2004). When women become mothers they are generally expected to prioritize their family above their work. Many employers want to be supportive by offering mothers more time-off and reduced work hours, assuming that is what they wish for (Porter, 2006). By doing so, organizations, perhaps unintentionally, reinforce social pressures on women to reduce their working hours. In the Dutch context of the normative "one-and-a-half-income" model, the legal right to work part time implicitly reproduces maternalism (Orloff, 2006). Research by Rudman and Fairchild (2004) has shown that perceivers (un)consciously sabotage people violating stereotypes, causing them to be unsuccessful. In the context of normative beliefs about parenting this would suggest that decision makers, when making employment decisions about a candidate for a managerial position, would prefer mothers who share care responsibilities and fathers who are main providers. Indeed, Padgett, Harland, and Moser (2009) found that women who did not reduce their work hours when their children were young, received lower ratings of advancement motivation and capability compared to women who did reduce their hours temporarily. Padgett et al. (2009) argued that women who return to a regular schedule after a temporary reduction are perceived to be more committed to their career than women who continued working full time. By behaving in conformity with their prescribed gender role the women who worked reduced hours "made the right choice" and as a consequence suffered fewer negative career consequences than women who did not reduce their hours when they became mothers.

As the one-and-a-half income model is the norm in the Netherlands, both for fathers (working full time) and for mothers (working part time), we argue that mothers who share care responsibilities with their partner by both working reduced hours will be penalized less by decision makers who consider them for a managerial position than mothers who are main providers while their partner works half time. Thus we hypothesize that:

Hypothesis 1: Mothers who are main providers and work full time will be rated less favorable (less committed, less competent, and less hirable) when applying for a managerial position than mothers who share care responsibilities equally with their partner by both working reduced hours.

In contrast, men who become fathers are generally expected to work even harder than before in order to provide for their fledgling family, and they often do (Burnett, Gatrell, Cooper, & Sparrow, 2011; Gatrell & Cooper, 2008). A longitudinal study of Dutch couples' work–home task division in the transition to parenthood revealed that women indeed reduced work hours whereas men worked more hours when they became parents, despite expectations and negotiations before the child was born that both would reduce their work hours (Kluwer, 1998). Dutch census data show that indeed fathers of young children work more hours than men without children. Despite the fact that 49% of Dutch men in a recent census panel data study indicate they prefer shared responsibilities (Cloïn & Souren, 2011), fathers who would like to work fewer hours however may still "face resistance from colleagues and employers who can neither understand nor accept the paternal desire to reduce working hours so as to improve work–life balance" (Gatrell & Cooper, 2008, p. 77). Fathers mention fear of this resistance and negative career consequences as the main reason for not wanting to (or deciding not to vocalize their desire to) work fewer hours (Burnett et al., 2011; Sheridan, 2004; Van der Horst & De Jongh, 2008). In sum, for fathers, the gender role prescriptions are that they should take up the role of main provider. Therefore, we expect negative career consequences of fathers sharing care responsibilities with their partner by reducing their work hours. Thus we hypothesize that:

Hypothesis 2: Fathers who are main providers and work full time will be rated more favorable (more committed, more competent, and more hirable) when applying for a managerial position than fathers who share care responsibilities equally with their partner by both working reduced hours.

Method

Overview

Following the research tradition of the simulated employment context (Davison & Burke, 2000; Olian, Schwab, & Haberfeld, 1988), participants in this experimental study were asked to make employment decisions based on a resume of a candidate for a managerial position. Male and female participants were presented with a written vignette which included a job description of a senior marketing manager and a resume of a male or a female target job candidate interested in this position. The target candidate's work–home task division in the vignette was described as either a main provider (i.e., one-and-a-half-income) situation or a shared (i.e., both working 4 days) work–home situation. Participants were asked to rate the anticipated commitment and competence as well as provide a screening recommendation for the target candidate.

Design and Participants

The design was a 2 (target sex) × 2 (target work–home task division) × 2 (participant sex) between-subjects factorial design, in which male and female participants were randomly assigned to one of four experimental conditions. A total of 81 participants (41 women and 40 men), varying in age from 21 to 60 years ($M = 40–45$, $SD = 1.76$), were recruited through professional contacts of the third author from five different Dutch companies. Of these 81 participants, 22.9% occupied a top management position, 34.6% a middle management position, 7.4% lower management positions, and 25.9% nonmanagerial positions. Of these participants, 21% worked 16–32 hours, and 77.8% of the participants worked 33–40 hours. More female than male participants worked part time (36% and 5%, respectively). We do not have information about the respondent race or ethnicity. In the Netherlands, asking someone's ethnic background is considered unethical and may lead to reduced response rates.

Procedure

Participants were sent an e-mail with a link to an online survey. In the online survey it was explained the study was about recruitment and employment decisions based on limited information of target candidates. Participants were asked to review the information of one candidate. In the instruction it was mentioned that the target candidate had applied for a senior marketing manager position at a commercial organization which offered several growth opportunities. Participants first read a short description of the target candidate. The candidate was described as holding a degree in Economics from Utrecht University, having 13 years of work experience, and working 2.5 years in their current position. The description furthermore included the candidate's current supervisor's reference, which indicated excellent performance. Next, personal background information about the target candidate was provided. The sex of the target was indicated by the first name, either Jan (male), or Marieke (female). As the average age difference between male and female partners in the Netherlands is two years (men being older) and women on average have their first child at age 30, Jan was always depicted as 38 and Marieke as 36 years old. Respondents received either a description of a main provider (working full time with a partner who works 2.5 days), or of someone who is sharing care responsibilities (both partners working 4 days per week). The vignette read: "[Jan/Marieke (target candidate)] and [Marieke/Jan (partner)] have been together for 12 years and have been married since 2005. They have two children of 4 and 6 years old and they live in Amsterdam. At the moment, [Jan/Marieke (target)] works [full time/4 days per week] and [Marieke/Jan (partner)] works [2.5 days/4 days per week]. [Jan/Marieke] is the candidate for the position."

Employment Decisions

After reading the vignette, the participants rated the target candidate on different scales measuring anticipated commitment and anticipated competence. Next, the participants indicated their screening recommendation of the candidate. All items had a Likert scale answering format ranging from 1 = do not agree at all, 5 = very much agree (unless otherwise mentioned).

Anticipated commitment. The participants' rating of the target's anticipated commitment consisted of three indicators: ambition, commitment, and availability. Ambition was measured with a nine-item scale developed by Dikkers, Van Engen, and Vinkenburg (2010), including items such as "The candidate has the ambition to grow to a higher position," "The candidate would like to fulfill a top position," "The candidate sets high goals for his/her career." Factor analyses revealed one underlying factor explaining 56% of the variance. Based on reliability analyses we removed one (reversed) item. The remaining eight items form a reliable scale of anticipated ambition ($\alpha = .88$). Commitment of the candidate if selected was measured using three items (Heilman & Okimoto, 2008): "The candidate will be loyal to the company," "The candidate is willing to make sacrifices for the job," and "The candidate will give the job top priority." These three items were averaged into a reliable commitment scale ($\alpha = .79$). Availability of the target candidate if selected (Fuegen, Biernat, Haines, & Deaux, 2004; Heilman & Okimoto, 2008) was measured using three items: "The candidate will be able to work a lot," "The candidate will have a low number of sick days," and "The candidate will not be late for work or leave early." These three items were averaged into a reliable anticipated availability scale ($\alpha = .80$).

Anticipated competence. The participants' rating of the target's anticipated competence consisted of two indicators, namely competence and career success. Competence of the candidate if selected was measured using six items, including "The candidate will be competent," "... effective," "... productive," etc. (adapted from Heilman & Okimoto, 2008). These items were averaged into a reliable anticipated competence scale ($\alpha = .83$). Furthermore, the participants rated target's future career success of the candidate using two items: "The candidate's salary will raise quickly," and "The candidate will be promoted quickly." These two items together form a scale of career success ($r = .65$).

Screening recommendation. Finally, participants gave a screening recommendation by answering the following three questions about the target: "How strongly would you recommend that this candidate goes to the next stage of the selection process?" (answers ranging from 1 = not at all to 5 = very strongly), "I think that this candidate is suitable for the job," and "The candidate should be eliminated from the selection process" (reversed item) (Heilman & Okimoto, 2008). These items were averaged into a reliable screening recommendation scale ($\alpha = .86$).

Results

Hypotheses were tested by means of a full factorial MANOVA with anticipated commitment (i.e., ambition, commitment, and availability), anticipated competence (i.e., competence and career success), and screening recommendation as dependent variables, and target sex, work–home task division, and participant sex as independent variables. The multivariate analyses indicated a significant effect for target sex ($F(6, 68) = 2.83, p = .016, \eta^2 = .20$), which was qualified by a significant target sex by task division interaction ($F(6, 68) = 4.51, p < .001, \eta^2 = .29$). No significant main effect was found for participant sex ($F(6, 68) = .86, p = .53, \eta^2 = .07$) or for task division ($F(6, 68) = 1.66, p = .145, \eta^2 = .13$). Furthermore, no significant interaction effect was found for target sex and participant sex ($F(6, 68) = 2.31, p = .36, \eta^2 = .09$), or for the three-way interaction of participant sex, target sex, and work–home task division ($F(6, 68) = .86, p = .53, \eta^2 = .07$). The multivariate analyses revealed a significant effect for participant sex by task division ($F(6, 68) = 2.31, p < .044, \eta^2 = .17$). Univariate analyses showed that female respondents rated main provider targets as somewhat less committed ($M = 3.10$) than targets who shared responsibilities ($M = 3.48, F(1, 37) = 4.73, p < .04$). No other significant effects for participant sex were found. Consequently, for further analyses we collapsed data across participant sex.

The upper part of Table 1 presents the means and standard deviations of the three anticipated commitment ratings (ambition, commitment, and availability) by target sex and task division. The lower part of Table 1 presents the anticipated competence ratings (competence, and career success) and the screening recommendation by target sex and task division. The main target sex effects for ambition ($F(1, 80) = 12.07, p < .001, \eta^2 = .14$), availability ($F(1, 80) = 4.16, p < .045, \eta^2 = .05$), competence ($F(1, 80) = 7.45, p < .008, \eta^2 = .09$), and career success ($F(1, 80) = 15.37, p < .001, \eta^2 = .17$) were qualified by significant target sex by target work–home division interaction effects (ambition $F(1, 80) = 10.94, p < .001, \eta^2 = .12$; availability $F(1, 80) = 8.73, p < .002, \eta^2 = .10$; competence $F(1, 80) = 15.60, p < .001, \eta^2 = .17$; career success $F(1, 80) = 16.33, p < .001, \eta^2 = .18$). The interaction effects are displayed in Figure 1. As was hypothesized, mothers are rated as more ambitious, available, competent, and more successful in their

Table 1. Anticipated Ambition, Commitment, Availability, Competence, Career Success, and Screening Recommendations as a Function of Target Sex and Work–Home Task Division [Means (std. dev.)]

	Ambition			Commitment			Availability		
	Main provider	Shared responsible	Total	Main provider	Shared responsible	Total	Main provider	Shared responsible	Total
Father	3.52 (.71)	3.09 (.49)	3.32 (.65)	3.05$_a$ (.79)	2.95$_a$ (.52)	3.00 (.67)	3.30 (.67)	3.19$_a$ (.56)	3.27 (.61)
Mother	3.54 (.39)	3.89 (.46)	3.72 (.46)	3.05 (.83)	3.48 (.72)	3.27 (.79)	3.20 (.86)	3.92 (.48)	3.57 (.77)
Total	3.53 (.57)	3.51 (.62)	3.52 (.59)	3.05 (.80)	3.23 (.68)	3.14 (.74)	3.27 (.76)	3.58 (.63)	3.42 (.71)

	Competence			Career success			Screening Recommendation		
	Main provider	Shared responsible	Total	Main provider	Shared responsible	Total	Main provider	Shared responsible	Total
Father	3.85 (.51)	3.53 (.55)	3.70 (.55)	3.46 (.67)	3.00 (.53)	3.24 (.64)	3.94$_a$ (.76)	3.67$_a$ (.79)	3.81 (.77)
Mother	3.73 (.44)	4.21 (.31)	3.97 (.45)	3.45 (.39)	3.94 (.49)	3.70 (.50)	3.98$_b$ (.60)	4.16$_b$ (.68)	4.07 (.64)
Total	3.79 (.48)	3.88 (.55)	3.84 (.51)	3.46 (.54)	3.49 (.69)	3.48 (.62)	3.96 (.68)	3.93 (.76)	3.94 (.72)

Subscripts $_a$ (fathers) and $_b$ (mothers) indicate within target sex post hoc comparison of the effect of task division. Means that share a subscript do not differ, $p > .05$. #$_a$ The difference is marginally significant, $p < .09$. #$_b$ The difference is marginally significant, $p < .06$.

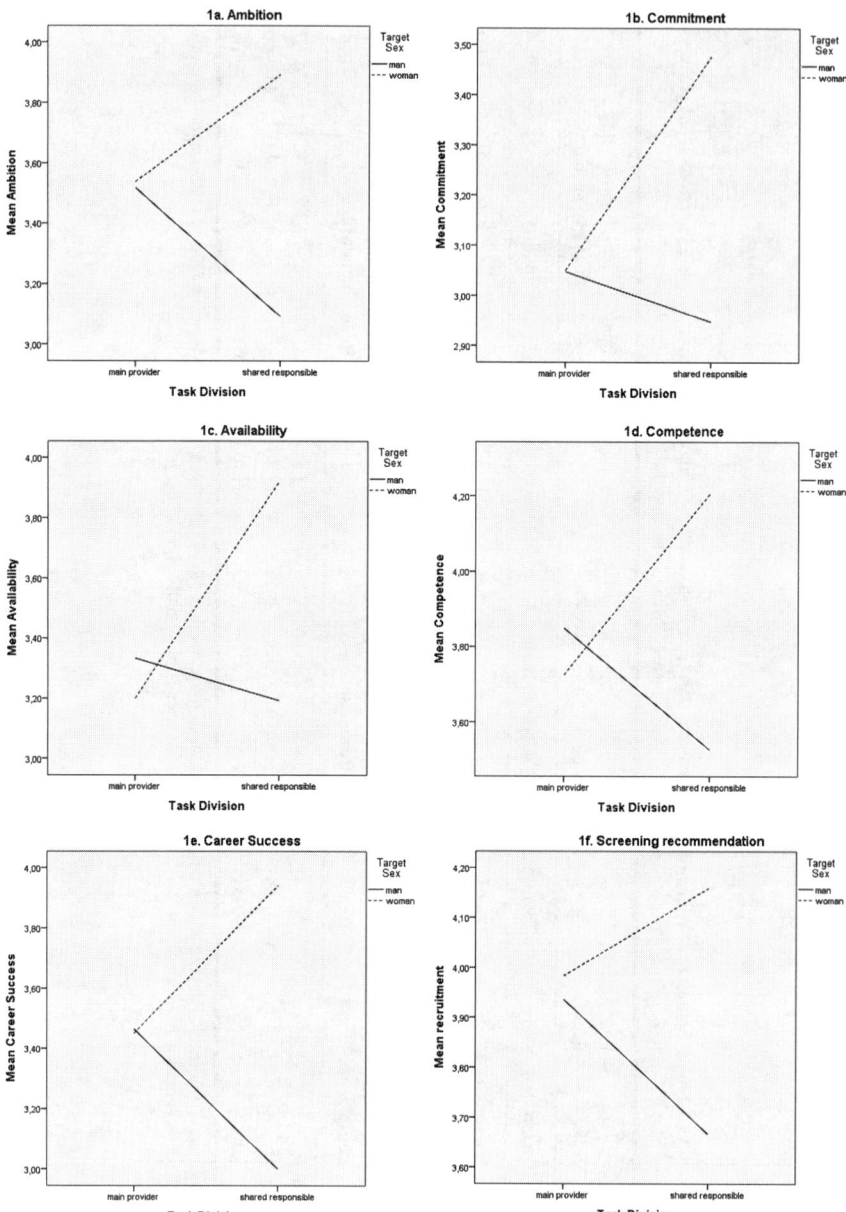

Fig. 1. Interaction effects of target sex and task division for anticipated ambition, commitment, availability, competence, career success, and screening recommendation.

career when they share care responsibilities with their partner and work reduced hours (shared work–home task division) than when they are main providers and work full time (Figure 1a, 1c, 1d, and 1e). Although the trends for commitment and screening recommendations are in the same direction (Figure 1b and 1f), the interaction effects were marginally significant ($F(1, 80) = 2.66$, $p = .06$, $\eta^2 = .03$; $F(1, 80) = 2.00$, $p = .08$, $\eta^2 = .03$, respectively). Post hoc contrasts for task division for mothers did show that mothers who shared responsibilities were rated as more committed than mothers who are portrayed as main providers. Thus (partial) support was found for Hypothesis 1.

Consistent with Hypothesis 2, fathers who share care responsibilities with their partner and work reduced hours (shared work–home division) were rated as less ambitious and less successful in their career compared to fathers that are main providers with a partner who works half time (see Figure 1). Again, while the trends for availability, commitment, competence, and screening recommendations were in the same direction, the task division effects for fathers did not reach significance. Post hoc analyses showed that out of all four target candidates, the mother who shares care responsibilities was rated most, and the father who shares care responsibilities was rated least ambitious, available, competent, and successful.

Discussion

Our results show that prescriptive norms for mothers in the Netherlands to work reduced hours spill over to the workplace, even for managerial positions that generally have a strong full-time prescriptive norm in and of themselves. Mothers who share work and care responsibilities equally with their partner are considered more ambitious and competent than mothers who work full time, supposedly because mothers who share work and care meet the requirements of the "good" mother. Similarly, our results also show the reinforcement of the main provider or breadwinner norm for fathers. Fathers who share care responsibilities and work reduced hours suffer a penalty in the sense that they are evaluated less positively when applying for a managerial position than full-time working fathers. Our study therefore shows that gender stereotypes and normative beliefs about parenting are reinforced by those making employment recommendations, with potentially large consequences for careers of mothers and fathers. The motherhood bias as evidenced in earlier studies resulting in lower commitment and competence ratings of mothers is attenuated by the degree to which partners share care responsibilities. The mother who takes on care responsibilities but works 4 days per week and has a partner who does the same is seen as more competent and successful than a mother who is the main provider and works full time. Furthermore, this mother is clearly perceived as the most likely to succeed in a senior management position.

However, there is a clear penalty for the "daddy track"—a father who shares care responsibilities and works 4 days per week is considered less competent and successful than a father who is the main provider and works full time. Apparently, in the Dutch context of the normative one-and-a-half income model, this type of father is still considered a failure when it comes to career consequences. As expected, stereotype maintenance theory states that we condemn actors who show behavior that is not in conformity with traditional gender roles.

While policymakers in the Netherlands view the "both parents work four days" model as a sustainable solution for combining career and care and as a viable alternative for the current norm of working 24 hours for women, gender roles and normative beliefs about parenting may prove to be a considerable source of resistance. While there is growing evidence of changes in gender roles and normative beliefs about parenting in the Netherlands (Cloïn & Souren, 2011) as well as elsewhere (Barnett, 2004), an increase in labor force participation of women and, consequently, an increase in sharing of care responsibilities by parents may not automatically lead to a normalization of the notion that mothers (also) work and fathers (also) care. As Goldberg, Kelly, Matthews, Kang, Li, & Sumaroka (2012) show, "the more things change, the more they stay the same." It will take a considerable shift (both in people's minds as well as in the common models of work–home task division) before beliefs start following policy and practice.

We expected that mothers as main providers would be penalized in comparison to fathers as main providers, but this was not the case. This finding might suggest that, in contrast to earlier research, we did *not* find evidence for motherhood bias. While our research design was too limited to give definite explanations for this unexpected outcome, it could point to subtle changes in normative beliefs about working mothers (i.e., working 4 days is becoming more accepted), in contrast to fathers who are still held to the main provider norm and who may thus suffer especially from "flexibility stigma" (Williams, 2000).

Future Research Agenda

Further research should help to investigate the conditions under which decision makers in organizations as well as the general public are more likely to see the long term advantages of sharing care responsibilities and work hours equally between mothers and fathers. This study was a first attempt at investigating the consequences of different ways of dividing work and care responsibilities between partners in the Dutch context. Future studies into this topic could build upon these findings by using a more elaborate experimental design which includes gradual differences in work–home task division beyond the (reversed) provider and shared conditions. Studies of the long term career effects of different ways of sharing care responsibilities of "real" dual earner couples may also shed light on the question which combination is most advantageous in terms of both joined and individual income (e.g., Budig & Hodges, 2010). Moreover, it would be interesting to study the effects of changes in legislation and availability of family-friendly policies on the uptake of part-time work by Dutch parents over time. For example, the Dutch government is currently considering reducing the subsidy for childcare to parents. In case this plan is followed through, would this lead to more Dutch mothers opting out of the labor force (i.e., returning full time to their caregiving role) or—in contrast—increasing numbers of fathers taking on caregiving responsibilities? The (long-term) effects of these behavioral patterns on gender roles and normative parenting beliefs can also be examined in large-sample, longitudinal studies.

A final route for further research would be to study country specific normative beliefs about the division of work and care and the career consequences of prevalent and changing models of sharing care responsibilities between parents. While part-time work is "normal" in the Netherlands (Portegijs & Keuzekamp, 2008), parents trying to sustainably combine career and care may have different options to challenge norms in different countries (Poelmans, 2012).

Practical Implications

Based upon this study's findings, we would advise managers and employers to look into their own attitude and behavioral responses toward their employees with children. Do they make distinctions in their reactions to a call for part-time work put forward by fathers versus mothers, and—if so—would this be a profitable, sustainable approach in the long run for attracting and retaining talented staff? In addition, another recent Dutch study indicated that the uptake of flexible family-friendly arrangements (e.g., working from home) is positively related to employees' career success (Dikkers et al., 2010). Using these policies does not necessarily imply pushing on the brakes of one's career, although the exact type of arrangement used does affect this relationship.

To conclude, this Dutch vignette study showed that employees rated mothers sharing work and care responsibilities with their partners as most ambitious, available, competent, and likely to succeed. In contrast, fathers who shared responsibilities with their partners were considered failures. Our findings show how current gender roles and normative beliefs about parenting in the Netherlands have shifted somewhat in the sense that we now *applaud* mothers who try to combine career and care by working reduced hours instead of stigmatizing them as "bad" mothers (Okimoto & Heilman, 2012). However, our frame-of-reference has shifted disproportionately as this study also showed that Dutch fathers who attempt to break through the ruling gender stereotypes and normative parenting beliefs in opposite direction, by working part time in order to share caregiving responsibilities with their partners, are *punished* with respect to their career prospective.

References

Acker, J. (1990). Hierarchies, jobs, bodies: A theory of gendered organizations. *Gender and Society*, *4*(2), 139–158. doi: 10.1177/089124390004002002

Barnett, R. C. (2004). Preface: Women and work: Where are we, where did we come from, and where are we going? *Journal of Social Issues*, *60*(4), 667–674. doi: 10.1111/j.0022-4537.2004.00378.x

Benard, S., & Correll, S. J. (2010). Normative discrimination and the motherhood penalty. *Gender & Society*, *24*(5), 616–646. doi: 10.1177/0891243210383142

Brescoll, V. L., & Uhlmann, E. L. (2005). Attitudes toward traditional and non-traditional parents. *Psychology of Women Quarterly*, *29*(4), 436–445. doi: 10.1111/j.1471-6402.2005.00244.x

Bridges, J. S., & Etaugh, C. (1995). College students' perceptions of mothers: Effects of maternal employment–child rearing pattern and motive for employment. *Sex Roles*, *32*, 735–751. doi: 10.1007/BF01560187

Budig, M. J., & Hodges, M. J. (2010). Differences in disadvantage. *American Sociological Review*, *75*(5), 705–728. doi: 10.1177/0003122410381593

Burgess, D., & Borgida, E. (1999). Who women are, who women should be: Descriptive and prescriptive gender stereotyping in sex discrimination. *Psychology, Public Policy, and Law*, *5*(3), 665–692. doi: 10.1037/1076-8971.5.3.665

Burnett, S., Gatrell, C., Cooper, C., & Sparrow, P. (2011). Fatherhood and flexible working: A contradiction in terms? In S. Kaiser, M. J. Ringlstetter, D. R. Eikhof, & M. Pina e Cunha (Eds.), *Creating balance?* (pp. 157–171). Berlin: Springer.

Cloïn, M., & Souren, M. (2011). Onbetaalde arbeid en de combinatie van arbeid en zorg. In A. Merens, M. van den Brakel, M. Hartgers, & B. Hermans (Eds.), *Emancipatiemonitor 2010* (pp. 108–147). SCP-publicatie 2011–4. Den Haag: SCP/CBS.

Cuddy, A. J. C., Fiske, S. T., & Glick, P. (2004). When professionals become mothers, warmth doesn't cut the ice. *Journal of Social Issues*, *60*, 701–718. doi: 10.1111/j.0022-4537.2004.00381.x

Davison, H. K., & Burke, M. J. (2000). Sex discrimination in simulated employment contexts: A meta-analytic investigation. *Journal of Vocational Behavior*, *56*, 225–248. doi: 10.1006/jvbe.1999.1711

Dikkers, J. S. E., Van Engen, M. L., & Vinkenburg, C. J. (2010). Flexible work: Ambitious parents' recipe for career success in the Netherlands. *Career Development International*, *15*(6), 562–582. doi: 10.1108/13620431011084411

Eagly, A. H., & Karau, S. J. (2002). Role congruity theory of prejudice toward female leaders. *Psychological Review*, *109*, 573–598. doi: 10.1037//0033-295X.109.3.573

Etaugh, C., & Nekolny, K. (1990). Effects of employment status and marital status on perceptions of mothers. *Sex Roles*, *23*, 273–280. doi: 10.1007/BF00290048

Fiske, S. T., & Taylor, S. E. (1991). *Social cognition* (2nd ed.). New York: McGraw-Hill.

Fuegen, K., Biernat, M., Haines, E., & Deaux, K. (2004). Mothers and fathers in the workplace: How gender and parental status influence judgements of job-related competence. *Journal of Social Issues*, *60*(4), 737–754. doi: 10.1111/j.0022-4537.2004.00383.x

Gatrell, C. J., & Cooper, C. L. (2008). Work-life balance: Working for whom? *European Journal for International Management*, *2*(1), 71–86. doi: 10.1504/08.16929

Goldberg, W. A., Kelly, E., Matthews, N. B., Kang, H., Li, W., & Sumaroka, M. (2012). The more things change, the more they stay the same: Gender, culture, and college students' views about work and family. *Journal of Social Issues* [Special Issue], *68*(4), 814–837.

Heilman, M. E. (2001). Description and prescription: How gender stereotypes prevent women's ascent up the organizational ladder. *Journal of Social Issues*, *57*, 657–674. doi: 10.1111/0022-4537.00234

Heilman, M. E., & Okimoto, T. G. (2008). Motherhood: A potential source of bias in employment decisions. *Journal of Applied Psychology*, *93*(1), 189–198. doi:10.1037/0021-9010.93.1.189

Heilman, M. E., Wallen, A. S., Fuchs, D., & Tamkins, M. M. (2004). Penalties for success: Reactions to women who succeed at male tasks. *Journal of Applied Psychology*, *89*, 416–427. doi: 10.1037/0021-9010.89.3.416

Janssen, B., & Portegijs, W. (2011). Betaalde arbeid. In A. Merens, M. van den Brakel, M. Hartgers, & B. Hermans (Eds.). *Emancipatiemonitor 2010*. (pp. 72–107). SCP-publicatie 2011–4. Den Haag: SCP/CBS.

King, E. B. (2008). The effect of bias on the advancement of working mothers: Disentangling legitimate concerns from inaccurate stereotypes as predictors of advancement in academe. *Human Relations*, *61*(12), 1677–1711. doi: 10.1177/0018726708098082

Kluwer, E. S. (1998). *Marital conflict over the division of labor: When partners become parents.* Dissertation, University of Groningen, Groningen, the Netherlands.

Mainiero, L. A., & Sullivan, S. E. (2005). Kaleidoscope careers: An alternative explanation for the "opt-out" revolution. *Academy of Management Executive*, *19*(1), 106–123. doi: 10.5465/AME.2005.15841962

OECD (2009). Incidence of part-time employment, from Organisation for Economic Co-operation and Development (OECD) family database indicators, LMF1.6 Gender differences in employment outcomes. Downloaded on May 14, 2012, from http://www.oecd.org/social/family/database.

Okimoto, T. G., & Heilman, M.E. (2012). The "bad parent" assumption: How gender stereotypes affect reactions to working mothers. *Journal of Social Issues* [Special Issue], *68*(4), 704–724.

Olian, J. D., Schwab, D. P., & Haberfeld, Y. (1988). The impact of applicant gender compared to qualifications on hiring recommendations: A meta-analysis of experimental studies. *Organizational Behavior and Human Decision Processes*, *41*(2), 180–195. doi: 10.1016/0749-5978(88)90025-8

Orloff, A. S. (2006). From maternalism to "employment for all": State policies to promote women's employment across the affluent democracies. In J. D. Levy (Ed.), *The state after statism: New state activities in the age of liberalization* (pp. 230–268). Cambridge, MA: Harvard University Press.

Padgett, M., Harland, L., & Moser, S. B. (2009). The bad news and the good news: The long-term consequences of having used an alternative work schedule. *Journal of Leadership & Organizational Studies*, *16*(1), 73–84. doi: 10.1177/1548051809333241

Poelmans, S. (2012). The "Triple-N" model: Changing normative beliefs about parenting and career success. *Journal of Social Issues* [Special Issue], *68*(4), 838–847.

Portegijs, W., & Keuzekamp, S. (2008). *Nederland Deeltijdland: vrouwen en deeltijdwerk*. Sociaal en Cultureel Planbureau and Centraal Bureau voor de Statistiek, Den Haag.

Porter, N. B. (2006). Re-defining superwoman: An essay on overcoming the "maternal wall" in the legal workplace. *Duke Journal of Gender Law & Policy*, *13*, 55–84. Available at SSRN: http://ssrn.com/abstract = 959691

Rudman, L. A. (1998). Self-promotion as a risk factor for women: The costs and benefits counterstereotypical impression management. *Journal of Personality and Social Psychology*, *74*, 629–645. doi: 10.1037//0022-3514.74.3.629

Rudman, L. A., & Fairchild K. (2004). Reactions to counterstereotypic behavior: The role of backlash in cultural stereotype maintenance. *Journal of Personality and Social Psychology*, *87*(2), 157–176. doi: 10.1037/0022-514.87.2.157

Rudman, L. A., & Glick, P. (2001). Prescriptive gender stereotypes and backlash toward agentic women. *Journal of Social Issues*, *57*, 743–762. doi: 10.1111/0022-4537.00239

Sheridan, A. (2004). Chronic presenteeism: The multiple dimensions to men's absence from part-time work. *Gender, Work and Organization*, *11*(2), 207–225. doi: 10.1111/j.1468-0432.2004.00229.x

Van der Horst, T., & De Jongh, M. (2008). *(Voor)oordelen over parttimers–Echte mannen werken fulltime*. Report: TNS NIPO.

Vinkenburg, C. J., Van Engen, M. L., Eagly, A. H., & Johannesen-Schmidt, M. C. (2011). An exploration of stereotypical beliefs about leadership styles: Is transformational leadership a route to women's promotion? *The Leadership Quarterly*, *22*, 10–21. doi: 10.1016/j.leaqua.2010.12.003

Williams, J. C. (2000). *Unbending gender: Why family and work conflict and what to do about it*. New York: Oxford University Press.

Williams, J. C., & Segal, N. (2003). Beyond the maternal wall: Relief for family caregivers who are discriminated against on the job. *Harvard Journal of Law and Gender*, *26*, 77–162.

CLAARTJE J. VINKENBURG is Associate Professor of organizational behavior and development at the VU University Amsterdam. She studied social psychology at the University of Groningen, and earned her PhD in Business Administration in 1997 at the VU University Amsterdam on gender differences in managerial behavior and effectiveness. From 1997 to 2001 she worked as a management consultant (at Berenschot and independently) and a visiting scholar and adjunct lecturer at Northwestern University (USA). As managing director of the Amsterdam Center for Career Research (www.accr.nl), Claartje's research focuses on gender, leadership, and career advancement, including the effects of normative beliefs about parenting on women's career patterns and outcomes, with Josje Dikkers (VU) and Marloes van Engen (UvT). She has published several book chapters and articles (e.g., *Journal of Vocational Behavior*, *Journal of Occupational and Organizational Psychology*, *Leadership Quarterly*) on her research, as well as edited a book on "Top potentials" for the Dutch Foundation of Management Development.

MARLOES L. VAN ENGEN is Assistant Professor at the Department of Human Resource Studies, Tilburg School of Social and Behavioral Sciences at Tilburg University where she lectures in Diversity in Organizations and Human Resource Studies. She studied social psychology with a minor in the psychology of culture and religion at the Radboud University in Nijmegen. She lectured at Communication Sciences before she moved to Tilburg University. Her research interests are in the area of gender in organizations, gender and careers, work–family issues in organizations, diversity in teams and organizations, effectiveness of diversity practices and policies and methodology such as meta-analysis, multilevel analysis, qualitative research, and intervention studies. She earned her PhD in 2001 on gender and leadership. She was a visiting academic at Northwestern University (USA), the University of Queensland (Australia), and Monash University (Australia). She has published in *Psychological Bulletin*, the *Journal of Organizational and Occupational Psychology*, *Organizational Behavior and Human Decision Processes*, and *Leadership Quarterly*.

JENNIFER COFFENG studied Business Administration and Social Psychology at the VU University. Shortly after graduating from the master of Business Administration (December 2008), she started with working by EMGO+ as a research assistant for the project Balance@Work. In October 2009, she started her PhD project at the EMGO Institute within the department of Public and Occupational Health, on the development and evaluation of an RCT to improve physical activity and to reduce stress among office workers. The project is part of VIP (vitality in practice).

JOSJE S. E. DIKKERS works at the Department of Human Resource Management, University of Applied Sciences Utrecht. She studied Work & Organizational

Psychology at Tilburg University and completed this study with honors (Cum Laude). In 2008, she earned her PhD on "Work–home interference in relation to work, organizational, and home characteristics" at the Department of Work & Organizational Psychology of the Radboud University Nijmegen. From 2006 to 2012, she worked at VU University Amsterdam within the Department of Management & Organization Studies. Josje Dikkers has published several (inter)national articles and book chapters based on her research. Since 2004 she has also worked part time at Qidos as a research consultant. Her research interests primarily focus on the interaction between people's work and private lives and work–home culture.

Pursuing Career Success while Sustaining Personal and Family Well-Being: A Study of Reduced-Load Professionals over Time

Douglas T. Hall[*]
Boston University

Mary Dean Lee
McGill University

Ellen Ernst Kossek
Michigan State University

Mireia Las Heras
IESE Business School

This study examines the experiences, over 6 years, of 73 managers and high level professionals who reduced their workloads to achieve more sustainable career and family outcomes. We compared personal, family, and career success outcomes for people who maintained reduced loads over time with those who went back to full time work, and we found few differences, except for more promotions for the full-timers. To further understand our results, we identified four groups with all four possible combinations of extreme success (either very high or very

---

[*]Correspondence concerning this article should be addressed to Douglas T. Hall, Department of Organizational Behavior, School of Management, Boston University, 595 Commonwealth Avenue, Boston, MA 02215 [e-mail: dthall@bu.edu].

We thank the Alfred P. Sloan Foundation (1996–98 and 2002–04) and the Social Sciences and Humanities Council of Canada (1996–99) for financial support making this research possible. We are also grateful to other members of two research teams for their contributions to data collection and analysis, as well as ideas generated in periodic research team retreats: Shelley MacDermid Wadsworth, Carol Schreiber, Margaret Williams, Michelle Buck, Leslie Haugen, Sharon Leiba O'Sullivan, and Connie J. G. Gersick. We are also very appreciative for the technical assistance of Sung Soo Kim and Christine Bataille of McGill University for their help with statistical analyses. McGill University, Michigan State University, and Boston University are thanked for their institutional support of this research.

low) on our two measures of success, objective and subjective. *The groups were labeled Aligned Achievers, Alienated Achievers, Happy Part Timers, and Hard Luck Strivers. Subsequent qualitative analysis of group members' reflections on the meaning of career success as well as the occurrence of significant life events helped explain the variation in their success in sustaining desired career and life arrangements over time.*

Not enough is known about how individuals adapt to changing demands in their careers and personal lives in order to create sustainable and psychologically successful lives over time. Careers are increasingly nonlinear and more customized (Benko & Weisberg, 2007; Cascio, 2007; Valcour, Bailyn, & Quijada, 2007), as individuals around the world, particularly professionals, seek to better balance rising workloads and career advancement with care-giving demands and other personal life interests (Briscoe, Hall, & Mayrhofer, 2012; Herman & Lewis, 2012; Kailasaphy & Metz, 2012; Tiedje, 2004). This growing variation in how individuals synthesize career and personal life priorities has occurred in part because the demography of professionals, particularly in major corporations, has shifted to include more women and employees in dual earner or single parent households (Blair-Loy & Wharton, 2002). Many of these individuals are not only juggling care-giving for children with demanding careers but also elder care, comprising sandwiched generation households (Neal & Hammer, 2007).

Despite this shift in the demographic composition of the professional workforce, professionals are still typically expected to work long hours, sometimes as much as 60–70 hours a week, as a means to demonstrate their devotion to their jobs despite the fact that they have families competing for time and energy (Blair-Loy, 2003). Customizing jobs to reduce workloads and deviate from traditional norms about professional working time and workload is a growing trend in many industrialized nations (Briscoe et al., 2012; Valcour et al., 2007). This way of working is also often referred to as part-time work but is distinct from part-time in that it is not paid on an hourly basis, and it is pursued on a voluntary basis. However, it is worth noting that one-fifth of the U.S. workforce and 39% in the Netherlands work part-time (see Kossek & Michel, 2010, for a review of flexible schedules).

Specifically, then, in this article we will be addressing three key questions, which we will discuss later in more detail:

(1) To what extent were individuals' career and life outcomes over 6 years related to their sustained pursuit of reduced-load work arrangements?
(2) What is the relationship between levels of objective and subjective career success for these individuals?
(3) How do different meanings of career success, along with work-related phenomena, personal and family events, relate to different patterns of high versus low objective and subjective career success?

Interactions among Work, Personal, and Family Life

Researchers have tried a number of different approaches to understanding how individuals are combining career with personal life. These include: work and family conflict as well as work/family enrichment (Greenhaus & Powell, 2006; Tiedje, 2004); boundary tactics and transition management (Ashforth, Kreiner & Fugate, 2000; Hall & Richter, 1989); kaleidoscope careers (Mainiero & Sullivan, 2006); and customized careers (Benko & Weisberg, 2007; Valcour et al., 2007). However, few of these have focused on examining both career and family outcomes simultaneously, and few have empirically examined the reconciliation of career and family commitments over time. In addition, none of these studies has studied these outcomes longitudinally. The study reported here attempts to fill these gaps and shed light on the inter-relationships between personal, family, and career well-being as well as career success.

We define "career" using Arthur, Hall, and Lawrence's (1989) definition, "the evolving sequence of a person's work experiences over time" (p. 8). This definition has two major elements: work and time. The term "career success" refers to an evaluation or assessment of accumulated work experiences in the context of time (Seibert & Kraimer, 2001). There are two sides to success (Hughes, 1958). One is objective success, which is made up of the objective indicators of attainment that other people can observe, such as income and position. The other is subjective success, which is the individual's own perception of the quality of his or her attainments. One need in the literature is to include both subjective and objective measures of career success in our research designs (Arthur, Khapova, & Wilderom, 2005). As Arthur et al. (2005) point out after reviewing 10 years of empirical research on career success and 68 studies, the preponderance of careers research has studied the objective career; but little research provides insight into both sides of the career or of how the individual defines career success. As the authors point out:

> ".... not one of the articles sampled involved listening directly to the research subjects, or even allowing them to nominate their own criteria for career success. While the purpose and design of any one paper may be worthy, the overall body of empirical work on career success seems to be sorely lacking in such qualitative input" (Arthur et al., 2005, p. 196).

Arthur et al. concluded with a call, to which we try to respond here, for more research on "how career success unfolds in a dynamic and uncertain world" (2005, p. 197). To promote this goal, they call for research designs that contain adequate measures of both objective and subjective success, as well as designs that can reveal "the two-way, time-dependent interaction between the two sides of career success" (2005, p. 194). They also call for a more holistic approach, involving a study of the developing person and different spheres of life.

The Current Study

In terms of this special issue, this article is crafted to contribute to the section labeled, "Work–home arrangements and individual career outcomes." Based on the changes of the landscape in which careers develop, and the growing tension that builds as people experiment with balancing work and family, we want to explore how different kinds of arrangements for managing the work—home relationship are related to well-being and different facets of career success as a particularly important type of career outcome.

In Phase 1 of our longitudinal study, we looked at people who had negotiated a reduced-load work arrangement in order to pursue personal and family priorities while continuing a demanding professional career. Reduced-load work is defined as working less than full-time (e.g., 3 days or 4 days a week), with a commensurate reduction in pay. Some people did this through job sharing, and others did it by cutting back the number of days they worked each week. It is an example of a career strategy that can be used to help individuals reconcile work and family demands by reducing hours or workload, while sustaining commitment to their careers (Lee, MacDermid, Williams, Buck, & Leiba-O'Sullivan, 2002; Russell, O'Connell, & McGinnity, 2009; Valcour et al., 2007). Russell et al. (2009) compared the effects of different kinds of flexibility on work pressure and work–life conflict, and they found that only reduced-load or part-time arrangements (compared to telework, job share, and flex-time) had a positive effect on the dependent measures.

In Phase 2 of our study, we went back 6 years later to see to what extent these reduced-load work arrangements had been sustained and to determine how our participants viewed their career and overall life outcomes with the passage of time. Because of the longitudinal nature of this unique sample, we also examined the relationships between objective career success (e.g., promotions, pay, and status) and subjective career success (psychological well-being) as a way to look in depth at sustainability of well-being in personal, family, and professional life.

Another paper from the current project (Lee, Kossek, Hall, & Litrico, 2011) identified five distinct career narratives and presented a model of the evolution of careers. The model suggested that individuals construct careers over time through their own sensemaking of constantly shifting entangled strands of their personal, family, work, and community lives and three key dynamics that are ongoing: external events, gradual developments, and individual actions.

In the current article, we analyze whether objective and subjective career success are correlated. If we find no correlation between subjective and objective success measures, this would support the idea that there may be quite different determining factors for each. Even if there is a positive relationship, the fact is that subjective and objective success are separate and distinct variables and experiences. Following the recommendation of Arthur et al. (2005), we wanted to examine objective and subjective success separately and in detail to explore which factors and events (organizational, personal, and familial) operating in a person's life relate differentially to objective and subjective career success. Specifically, we looked at different meanings of career success among case groups of individuals who reported different combinations of high versus low objective and subjective career success.

Method

The two phases of this research consisted of two periods of data collection with 73 managers and professionals who were initially interviewed in the late 1990s and then again approximately 6 years later. We refer to these two interview points as Phase 1 and Phase 2. The purpose of the first set of interviews was to learn about the negotiation and implementation of reduced-load work, how it had affected individuals' careers and lives, and what factors facilitated or hindered the success of these arrangements. The purpose of the second set of interviews was to determine how these individuals had fared over time and to see how they had continued to make choices to achieve their personal, career and family priorities.

Sample

Professionals working voluntarily on a reduced-load basis were initially recruited using personal and professional contacts with individuals as well as human resource managers and work–life administrators in organizations. About half of the firms approached agreed to participate; those that declined stated that either they had no employees who fit the criteria, or they were not able to do the research necessary to determine if they had potential participants. Of the professionals approached, 85% agreed to participate.

The study was designed in order to maximize variation along several variables, including industry at the organizational level; and at the individual level, age, gender, type and level of position, and success of the arrangement. Maximizing variation along multiple dimensions increases the likelihood of capturing rich contrasts in qualitative observation to support theory building (Patton, 2002). Because the research team sought a heterogeneous sample, the representation of industries and jobs was monitored throughout the recruitment process. Recruitment of participants also targeted achieving a minimum of 10% men as this was their estimated representation at the time in the population of reduced-load professionals, according to informed observers in the work–life field. No more than four cases were included from any one firm in order to increase the range of organizations in the sample.

During Phase 2, we made extensive efforts to locate the participants who had been interviewed in Phase 1. The response participation rate in Phase 2 was 93%, 81 of 87 original interviewees. We report data here on 73 of the 81, who also completed a timeline exercise that will be explained below. We compared the Phase 1 and Phase 2 samples and found no systematic differences on key variables such as gender, mean age, salary, industry distribution, etc. The average age of the participants at Phase 2 was 45. Eighty-nine percent were women, and 11% were men, which represented approximately the gender composition of professionals working part-time in the United States at that time. One participant was an Asian male, and all other participants were Caucasian. Ninety-three percent were married, and 47% were still working in a reduced load arrangement in Phase 2, averaging 29.9 hours per week. Thirty-eight percent were working full-time in Phase 2, averaging 47.4 hours per week, and 14% were not employed (of which about half were temporarily unemployed or retired and the other half taking a career break for family reasons). For the people on reduced load, the average load was 66% of full-time. The average full time equivalent salary for the sample was $109,057 (U.S. dollars).

Data Collection

Data were gathered in one-on-one confidential interviews in both Phases 1 and 2, mostly face-to-face during Phase 1, but more often by phone in the second interview. All interviews were audio-recorded and transcribed verbatim for analysis. The interviews lasted from 45 minutes to an hour and a half and were semi-structured in format.

In Phase 2 we asked participants to complete a timeline exercise to help us understand what had been happening in their careers and personal and family lives since the first interview. The timeline exercise involved a blank chart in which the vertical axis had a scale of 1 to 7, with 7 indicating "things working well," and 1 "things NOT working well;" the horizontal axis represented approximately 6 years in between the first and second interviews 1997–2003. Participants were asked to draw three lines to represent how well things had been working in their career, family, and personal lives since the first interview. The instructions for filling in the timelines were as follows:

> Draw a line from the time of your last interview with us to the present, indicating how well things have been working in (a) your career, (b) your family, and (c) your personal life. Mark each line with a "C," an "F," and a "P." Then think about any critical incidents, milestones, or turning points that have occurred and indicate the timing (approximately) with an X. Please also initial next to each X to remind you when we talk about this in the interview.

The interviewers then used the timelines in the interview process to probe for details about the person's experiences over time.

Measures

Personal and family well-being. The timelines were used to estimate participants' self-assessments of how things were working in their family and personal lives at the time of Phase 1 (which we call T1) and Phase 2 (which we call T3) and the mid-point in between (T2). These timeline coordinates served as measures of family and personal well-being at three different points in time, on a scale of 1 to 7.

Subjective career success. The timelines were also used to estimate participants' subjective career success. We created a summative measure based on the individual's perceived evaluation of "how well things were working" in their careers, as recorded at T1, T2, and T3 on the timeline. Thus, we defined subjective career success as the person's self-perceived assessment of how the career was going, averaged over the time span of the study [(T1 +T2 +T3)/3].

Objective career success. We used two measures of objective career success. First, we computed the percentage increase in the person's full time equivalent salary (i.e., if a person were working 80% of full-time and earning $80,000, the full-time equivalent salary would be equal to $100,000) based on self-reported salary in Phase 1 and Phase 2, in U.S. dollars. As a second measure of objective career attainment, we used the numbers of promotions that the person reported receiving in between the two interviews (i.e., for those who changed employers or careers during the 6 years, we assessed whether these moves should be counted as promotions based on whether there was an increase in responsibility and/or status of the new position). This promotions measure, while positively related to salary attained ($r = .38$, $p < .01$), gets at a different facet of success, which is the progress or change in position level and responsibility over the last 6 years.

It is important to note that the timeline exercise used to construct a measure of subjective career success was separate from the interview itself. Individuals were asked to complete the timeline in advance of the interview; then in the interview proper we collected salary and promotion self-report data. This separation in time and method decreases the likelihood that the collection of data for one measure of success would bias the data obtained for the other.

Data Analysis

To address the first research question, we used one-way ANOVAs to compare the experiences of people who sustained a reduced load arrangement and those who switched to full time, looking at the following outcomes: objective and subjective career success, family well-being at Phase 2, and personal well-being at Phase 2. For the testing of our second research question, about the relationship between objective and subjective career success, we computed the correlations among the measure of subjective career success and the two measures of objective career success (salary and number of promotions).

For the investigation of our third research question, an exploration of different individual conceptions of career success and other work-related phenomena and life events, we used both quantitative and qualitative methods. First, we created four groups of extreme cases, to maximize the differences among the groups. The four groups were: (1) those high on both objective success and subjective success; (2) those high on objective and low on subjective success; (3) those low on objective career success and high on subjective career success; and (4) those low on both objective and subjective success. The criteria for high objective success for the extreme case analysis were (a) being promoted once over the 6 years *and* (b) having a salary increase above the 60th percentile of the sample (31.85%) or being promoted two or more times over the 6 years. The criteria for low objective success were (a) experiencing no promotions *and* (b) a salary increase that fell below the median (26.04%) for the sample. For our criterion of subjective career success we took an average of each person's three ratings of how their career was going at T1, T2, and T3. Those with a mean greater than or equal to the sample mean of 4.67 were considered high on subjective career success; those with a mean below were considered low.

The numbers of cases in each quadrant of high and low objective and subjective success are shown, followed by the means and standard deviations in objective and subjective success measures used to create the groups (see Table 1). Second, a comparison of groups is provided using exploratory ANOVAs to examine differences on salient aspects of their experiences that had been recorded from the interviews: (a) demographic characteristics (e.g., age, age of youngest child, and spouse salary at Phase 2); (b) work characteristics (e.g., type of job (managerial vs. individual contributor), hours working per week at Phase 2, and employment status (full-time or reduced-load); (c) number of significant job-related events occurring between Phases 1 and 2 (e.g., periods of self-employment, leaves of absence, changes from reduced load to full time, organizational exit); (d) number of cases with instances of personal or close family member serious health problems between Phases 1 and 2 (Health was included because the interviews revealed that this had has important impact on people's experiences and choices in the years between Phase 1 and Phase 1). ANOVAs were used instead of MANOVA, because the dependent variables were not independent of one another, which is a required assumption that must be met with MANOVA. Some of the profile variables that we explored involved counts, or frequencies (e.g., type of job, employment status,

Table 1. Comparison of Extreme Case Success Groups

	Objective/subjective career success group				Statistics				
	High/High	High/Low	Low/High	Low/Low	F	χ^2	p	η^2	phi
Success group characteristics									
No. of cases	13	9	7	6			N/A	N/A	
Avg. FTE salary in USD (T2)	$149,41	$117,34	$75,80	$59,11	5.35		.004	.34	
Avg. % increase in FTE salary T1-T2	65	52	−11	−13	10.82		.000	.51	
Avg. no. of promotion since T1	1.6	1.7	0	0	31.97		.000	.76	
Subjective career success ratings (T1∼T2)	16	11	15	8	16.29		.000	.62	
Demographic characteristics									
Avg. age (T1)	38.8	41.1	41.1	38	.82		.494	.07	
Avg. age of youngest child (T1)	5.4	5.4	5.1	4.1	.11		.953	.01	
Avg. age (T2)	44.5	46.7	47.1	44	.74		.537	.07	
Avg. age of youngest child (T2)	9.1	9.5	7.4	8	.40		.757	.05	
Avg. spouse salary (T2)	$81,11	$180,66	$89,47	$152.38	2.19		.122	.26	
Work characteristics									
Avg. work hours/week (T2)	47	45	26	27	7.64		.001	.44	
Type of job (T2)						14.42	.002		.64
No. of professionals	3	3	7	5					
No. of managers	10	6	0	1					
Employment status (T2)						7.73	.052		.47
No. of employed FT	8	6	1	1					
No. of employed RL	5	3	6	5					

Continued.

Table 1. Continued

	Objective/subjective career success group				Statistics				
	High/High	High/Low	Low/High	Low/Low	F	χ^2	p	η^2	phi
Avg. no. of significant job-related events									
Self-employment	0.08	0.22	0.57	0.67	3.77		.02	.26	
Leave of absence	0.23	0	0.71	0.67	4.12		.014	.28	
Shift from RL to FT	0.69	0.67	0.14	0.17	2.79		.057	.21	
Organizational exit	0.31	0.33	1.14	1.17	4.08		.015	.28	
Significant health-related events									
Major health problem for self						3.46	.326		.32
No. of cases experienced	2	1	3	2					
No. of cases not experienced	11	8	4	3					
Major health problem for family						6.11	.106		.44
No. of cases experienced	7	1	2	4					
No. of cases not experienced	4	6	5	2					

major health problems for self and for family), and for these counts, we employed a Chi-square analysis to test for the significance of success group differences. Eta-squared values were used to measure effect size for the ANOVA results, and phi values were used for chi-square tests, instead of eta-squared, to report their effect sizes.

Once the groups were created, we conducted a qualitative analysis of the transcribed interview material to compare different conceptions of career success across the four extreme cases groups at Phase 1 and Phase 2. After the first set of interviews in Phase 1, the second author examined participants' responses to specific questions about what "career success" meant to them and what they wanted to accomplish in their careers.

Using a form of "axial coding" (Miles & Huberman, 1994) and through an iterative process of categorizing, collapsing, and re-categorizing predominant themes, eight distinct conceptions of career success were ultimately identified. They fell into three categories: (a) those related to organizational perceptions, judgments and actions ("organization-based"); (b) those involving individual respondents' perceptions and personal experiences, more or less independent of the objective work context (personal-based); and (c) those involving a mix of individual and organization-based perspectives on their personal outcomes rooted in objective organizational reality (organization and personal based). The organization-based themes included *upward mobility, peer respect,* and *organizational or supervisory recognition or appreciation.* The personal-based themes included *being able to have a life outside of work, being challenged or continuing to learn and grow professionally,* and *enjoying work*. The final category of themes was labeled organization and personal based, as these conceptions involved the individual's perceptions of personal outcomes but on organizational terms—specifically, *performing well* and *having an impact.*

These same themes were coded again at Phase 2, based on material from the second interviews. Two researchers read through each transcript using the eight different conceptions of success identified earlier and independently coded whether the individual referred to or used any of these meanings in descriptions of career outcomes and goals. There was no limit to the number of different conceptions that could be coded per respondent. After some initial training for consistency of coding, the two sets of coders reached 75% reliability in applying the criteria. Differences were discussed and resolved. See Table 2, which shows the profiles of career success meanings found among the extreme case groups at Phase 1 and Phase 2. In this analysis, which was exploratory, we were looking for distinct *patterns* in the meanings of career success over time for the different groups. As this was a qualitative analysis and exploratory in nature, we did not have specific hypotheses and did not do statistical tests comparing these groups on specific measures.

Table 2. Meaning of Career Success at Phase 1 and Phase 2 for Extreme Case Groups on Objective and Subjective Success

	Objective/subjective career success group							
	High/High		High/Low		Low/High		Low/Low	
	Phase 1	Phase 2	Phase 1	Phase 2	Phase 1	Phase 2	Phase 1	Phase 2
Organization-based themes								
Peer respect	31%	38%	44%	11%	57%	57%	67%	17%
Upward mobility	31%	31%	33%	11%	29%	14%	50%	33%
Appreciation/recognition	8%	58%	22%	22%	29%	14%	0%	17%
Personal themes								
Having a life outside work	77%	100%	100%	89%	57%	43%	67%	83%
Learning, growing, and being challenged	69%	46%	56%	67%	57%	71%	50%	67%
Fun and enjoyment/doing interesting work	0%	46%	44%	22%	0%	29%	0%	0%
Personal and organizational inter-linked								
Performing well	77%	31%	56%	11%	57%	29%	67%	17%
Having an impact/making a contribution	31%	58%	56%	56%	57%	86%	50%	50%

Results

Effects of Sustained Reduced-Load Work versus Return to Full-Time

To address our first research question, we used one-way ANOVAs to compare the experiences of the people who sustained their reduced load schedules with those who returned to full time work. Surprisingly, we found very few differences. There were no significant differences on subjective success, family well-being at Phase 2, and personal well-being at Phase 2. The only significant difference was that the group that had returned to full time work had received more promotions (1.27 for full time vs. 0.59 for part time, $p = .002$).

Relationship between Subjective and Objective Career Success

Addressing the second research question, we found that subjective career success and the two measures of objective career success were not correlated with one another. The correlation between subjective career success and the percentage salary increase between T1 and T3 was .09 (*n.s.*). The correlation between subjective career success and the number of promotions in this same time period was .007 (*n.s.*).

Findings from Analysis of Extreme Case Success Groups

Given this lack of relationship between subjective and objective career success, we proceeded to examine four extreme case groups of *High Objective and High Subjective*, *High Objective and Low Subjective*, *Low Objective and High Subjective*, and *Low Objective and Low Subjective*, in order to gain insight into the apparent independence of these constructs, at least in this sample. We compared their accounts of what career success meant to them at both Phases 1 and 2. Before describing these findings, we report on the results of our quantitative analysis of systematic differences across the extreme case success groups on demographic and work characteristics, as well as job and health-related events over time.

Table 1 shows that examination of differences in demographic and work characteristics of the four groups indicated either no significant effect across groups (e.g., on age, age of youngest child) or predictable effects based on how the extreme groups were constituted (e.g., groups with higher objective success worked longer hours and were more likely to be working full-time vs. reduced-load). However, there were significant differences across groups on frequency of several job-related events (e.g., period of self-employment, leave of absence). Furthermore, differences in spouse salary and frequency of serious family health problems across groups approached significance. These findings are addressed in relation to qualitative analysis of career success meanings across groups, which follows.

High objective and high subjective career success. This group included 13 women who were mostly managers with responsibility for a group of direct reports (10 of 13). Most were also working full-time (eight of 13), and the five working less were working between 80 and 90% of full-time. Five of the 13 were the sole or primary breadwinners in the family at the time of the second interview, and three had spouses who had spent a significant period of time, or were currently working on a reduced load basis, in order to help meet family commitments. Not surprisingly, the members of this group, on average, worked the most hours per week compared to the other groups (47).

The most frequently mentioned meaning of success theme in this group, at both Phases 1 and 2 was *having a life outside of work.* These participants' comments conveyed that they wanted to achieve, but within certain limits that allowed them to have a satisfying family life or personal life:

> "It has meant getting to this level...while also being able to have a big family... which I have in my life now. And I don't want to be a member of the senior management team. If they offered it to me, would I do it? It would depend on the circumstances. If I had to travel all the time at this stage in my life, no." *(Vice-President, Strategic Initiatives)*

The other two predominant themes at Phase 1 were *learning and growing* and *performing well.* An example of the theme of learning and growth was:

> "What means the most to me is having new challenges and growing professionally, not necessarily arriving at a particular position that I've been aiming for since college... No, it's more about what the job is than the title or level." (Asst. Comptroller and Vice President)

An example of the theme of performing well was,

> "I think it is doing the technical work and meeting the challenges." (Accountant)

At Phase 2, aside from the most frequently mentioned theme of *having a life outside work,* two different themes had replaced those dominant in Phase 1, *recognition* and *having an impact. Recognition and appreciation* was considered an organizational-based career success theme, as it was dependent on behavior of superiors in the workplace. For example,

> "I have to say that my ego has gotten stroked quite a bit at work from some of the things that I've been involved in, the successes I've gotten recognized for in the last two years." (Director of Clinical Trials Materials)

Having an impact was a meaning of career success that went beyond recognition and appreciation expressed by actions or words coming from a senior manager or leader. It meant being able to see for themselves the results or the effects of their initiatives or achievements.

"Success is feeling that I've made a difference, that I've done something really good, feeling that I'm giving something back" (Vice-President of Finance) and,

"Being able to be a mover and a shaker, to make things happen" (Asst. Comptroller and Vice President)

In addition, this group was the only one where a majority of the members (9 of 13) mentioned that career success has to do with upward mobility either at Phase 1, Phase 2 or both (i.e., the nine out of 13 represents nine different people over the two phases mentioning upward mobility. It is not a total of 9 mentions at a given point in time, so it does not show up in Table 2). However, at Phase 2 only four of the nine mentioned career advancement as critical to their definition of career success. These four clearly had specific goals about moving up in their organizations. Most of the rest in the group however explicitly said they did *not* want to go any higher than they already were, not wanting to make sacrifices in their family lives to succeed at a higher level.

> "I don't want to strive to be in a higher position in our organization. I have no desire to do that... I am content with what I do, and I think that goes into those three circles that I think I have... the kids and my husband and my work. And I think the danger is the work [at higher levels] becomes the bigger and bigger circle in your life." (Accounting Partner)

This group knew what it wanted and was working hard to succeed, while being aware of and accepting the trade-offs. We called them the *Aligned Achievers*.

High objective and low subjective career success. This group of nine cases included individuals who at Phase 1 were all managers with a group of subordinates. At Phase 2 seven of the nine were working for the same organization as 6 years earlier, but on a full-time rather than reduced load basis, except for one who was officially 75% but having great difficulty maintaining the appropriate hours. The other two had left their previous employers and were self-employed by choice and were working approximately 80% of a full-time equivalent position.

The striking feature of this group was that most had a preference for working part time; yet only two of the nine (those who were self-employed) were able to sustain a satisfactory reduced-load arrangement in the face of their personal and family life situations and career advancement opportunities. Four felt pressed by their employers to switch to full-time work, due to the nature of the work load and/or the career opportunities available contingent on full-time status. All four expressed regret or concern about the effects of this change on family life and their relationships with their children. Two others were partially motivated to return to full-time by their spouse's being laid off and the family needing the additional earning power. So the objective success of members of this group had been achieved at a cost, and they were clear about their preferences to be working less intensively. We labeled this group *Alienated Achievers*.

At Phase 1 there were four themes mentioned by more than half of this group's members: *having a life outside of work*; *learning and growing*; *performing well*; and *having an impact*. All nine mentioned the importance of *having a life outside of work*, and eight out of nine mentioned this theme at Phase 2. They wanted to be able to control the extent to which their work life infringed on family or personal time. *Learning and growing* was also a predominant theme at both points in time. *Performing well* and *having an impact* were both mentioned by more than half the group at Phase 1, but only *having an impact* was still predominant at Phase 2.

What distinguished this group was that they were the only group where more than half of all themes mentioned at both Phases 1 and 2 were in the personal-based category. It is ironic that these conceptions of success were very important to this group and are generally associated with subjective career success. Yet this group was low on subjective success. The very thing they cared most about—a part time schedule to give them more time for nonwork activities—most of them (7 of 9) did not have. Perhaps their objective success made it difficult for them to achieve what they really wanted, which could partially explain the lack of correlation between objective and subjective success. Alternatively, perhaps an acute health problem of a child at home could lead to more driven career behavior as an outlet removed from the difficulties at home. One such individual described her situation like this:

> "... my career has continued to move forward and upward even though my family life, you know, at times it felt like it was in a total shambles. And I can't explain that at all, except that work is a place where I don't have to deal with that ... " (Vice President Organization Development)

Low objective and high subjective success. This group of five women and two men were all professionals with specific expertise (e.g., engineer, research scientist), not managers. All members except one had continued to work on a reduced-load basis at the time of the second interview, by choice, and three of the seven were with the same employer; the one member of the group working full-time by choice had changed occupations and employer. The remaining three were self-employed, but only two of the three had chosen to leave their employers; the other one was laid off. Those who had chosen self-employment left their previous reduced-load positions because they had found it difficult and frustrating to try to perform their jobs to their satisfaction and maintain appropriate work hours.

This group also experienced important changes in their personal and family lives over the 6 years. Four of the seven experienced new family members (three births and one elderly parent moving in), and one experienced the sudden and unexpected death of her spouse. The other two described at least one serious personal illness they had to deal with. All seven talked about having made a choice about putting family or personal life first, above their careers, and being fairly comfortable with that tradeoff. However, it was clear that it had taken some time and struggle to get to that point. They were self-directed in their career and life choices, and they had been proactive when they had to be (e.g., making voluntary exits when necessary, choosing self-employment, etc.).

The three main meanings of success for this group help to explain why they rated their subjective career success high, even though they had not experienced notable career advancement or "objective" career success: *peer respect, learning and growing*, and *having an impact*. We called this group the *Happy Part Timers*. Their positive attitude can be heard in some of their comments:

> "What makes me feel most successful is that whenever I get put onto an assignment, all the other people around want to move onto it, because they want to work with me, because I try to coach and mentor and train as I go." (IT Consultant)

> "Doing things that make a difference and continuing to learn and grow while also working flexibly and according to my own rhythms." (Former executive, now a Principal in a consulting firm)

Low objective and low subjective success. This group consisted of six individuals, half of whom were managers and half independent contributors at Phase 1 of the study. They were all performing well then, and half of them wanted to advance. However, this group was dealt some difficult blows by life. Over the 6 years, two lost their jobs after mergers, and two had their jobs eliminated due to organizational financial downturn and reorganization. Of the other two, one lost her job in a reorganization and elimination of her department. The other did not lose her job, but a reorganization had a strong negative impact on the work climate. At the time of the second interview, four of the six in this category were self-employed and working part time and were feeling insecure.

This group also experienced significant challenges from personal and family life events that were difficult and disruptive. Three of the six experienced a child with serious health or behavioral problems, which in two cases were life-threatening. And two of the six changed employers three times over the 6 years as they struggled to recover from being laid off and find other suitable employment. We called this group the *Hard Luck Strivers*.

The most frequently mentioned success themes for this group include one organization-based theme (*peer respect*), one personal-based theme (*having a life outside of work*), and one organization and personal based theme (*performing well*). At Phase 2 *performing well* was no longer important, perhaps because it had not really helped their careers. Two themes that became more dominant at Phase 2 were *having a life outside of work* and *learning and growing*. We can imagine that these changes had to do with trying to come to terms with their situation and their identity in the context of what had happened over the 6 years. Two of the six talked about specific sacrifices they had made in their careers in order to be able to deal with family responsibilities and illnesses or special needs. A third talked about the difficult transition to being laid-off and her feeling of loss of identity.

"Everyone once in a while I get a twinge about, 'Well, when I'm 50 and my boys are maybe home in the summer, you know, or they're already off doing their own thing, 'am I still going to be content with that?' sort of thing. Or am I going to kind of regret that, by that point, you know, I don't know if you can ramp it back up, kind of thing?" (Accountant)

"I felt like when I walked out [of the firm], to some extent, that I left a piece behind. Because that is part of who I was, really. My first aspiration was my career... and I kind of gave that up... so I think I would be lying if I said my desire wouldn't be to get that person back." (Actuary)

Another distinguishing characteristic of this group was that at Phase 1 organization-based themes were mentioned by half or more of the members, more specifically *upward mobility* and *peer respect*. But at Phase 2 organization-based themes were mentioned by a third or less of the members, and the only themes mentioned by more than half were in the personal-based category: *having a life outside of work* and *learning and growing*. These individuals wanted the trappings of success in an organizational context; but for reasons beyond their control, due to organizational turmoil or family illnesses, they were facing difficult circumstances and feeling little sense of career success at the same time that their objective situation in their career was not very desirable.

Discussion

Relationship between Objective and Subjective Career Success

It was interesting what we did *not* find in our data on success. We did not find any relationship between subjective career success and either dimension of objective career success. Thus, even though Nicholson and de Waal-Andrews (2005) argue that it takes a high level of objective success to provide the basis for a high level of subjective success, we did not find that to be the case here. Perhaps one might make the argument that money may be necessary to provide for health and basic security and safety, a la Maslow (1954), but it may not be sufficient to produce high levels of subjective success. Also, the participants in this study had all given serious thought to what they were looking for in their lives and careers, and they may have had more clarity than most people about the distinction between their personal or subjective definitions of success and the external trappings of career achievement (i.e., objective career success).

Observations on the Extreme Case Success Groups

We did not find any direct relationship between the measures of well-being and either type of success, objective or subjective, nor, as we said before, did we find many links between these outcomes and work load arrangements. It appears that the links among well-being and success are more complex.

What did we learn about career success and well-being in the family and personal spheres through our examination of the extreme case success groups? One interesting group was those people who had done very well by objective indicators, such as pay and promotion, but who felt less successful subjectively. The people in this group were consistent in saying that having a life outside of work was very important to their sense of career success, with all members mentioning this at Phase 1. But they felt that they were involuntarily being pulled in the direction of pursuit of objective success.

Examination of the interviews of people in the Low Subjective/High Objective success group revealed some evidence for this phenomenon:

> "Well, I bought into the [game]: if you want this great responsibility, if you want the title of general manager, then you have got to play the game. And I gave up my four day work week to say, 'OK, I'm in.' And I took my Think Pad to the cottage on the weekend because I wanted to play. And I got really into the rewards of what that means. I mean, I get invited to, you know, women's leadership forums and all this stuff that I didn't have access to before... But, so where am I now?... I sold my soul to the devil is what I did. I really like being in the game but I just don't want to kill myself over it. And I'm feeling a lot of pressure to the point that most of my life is cracking into little bits and pieces, and I'm not sure I want that job." (General Manager, Learning Services)

One overall theme that emerges from all four of the extreme success groups is that many people manage to find their own ways, over time, to craft careers that work and that fit with what they value most in their family lives. That is certainly true of the two groups that are high on subjective career success. It may be that for those low on subjective career success, organizations could have been more supportive to employees trying to keep things going well on both fronts. Such an idea is consistent with Herman and Lewis's (2012) findings on the importance of managerial support in enabling scientists and engineers working reduced-load to achieve success without career penalties. More generally, as Tiedje (2004) found in a longitudinal study, this personal life-crafting process is also facilitated by factors such as personal coping, learning from experience, and social support.

In some ways, our results provide a more nuanced view of the "career mystique" (Moen & Roehling, 2005), which argues that when people get caught up in their career involvements, putting in long hours, etc., they make family and personal sacrifices that lead to negative outcomes. Our findings suggest that some career-oriented individuals (e.g., High Objective and Subjective Career Success) are able to navigate high commitment to careers at the same time as high commitment to family and still achieve objective and subjective career success. However, these individuals were the primary breadwinners in their families; they had spouses highly involved in family work. Thus, our findings reinforce van Veldhoven and Beijer's (2012) work that demonstrates the importance of understanding individuals' private life context, and in particular the spouse's employment situation.

We also saw that some career-oriented individuals are challenging the career mystique through sustained pursuit of reduced-load work, whether with an employer or through self-employment, and that they can achieve high subjective career success even if their objective success lags behind. The people in our Happy Part Timer group show that it is possible to step back from the career "rat race" and still to experience a pattern of sustained career success over time. But the people in this group had defined success on their own terms and were often achieving it outside the boundaries of the organization. This entails challenging negative societal stereotypes about gender, parental status, and job-related competence (Fuegen, Biernat, Haines, & Deaux, 2004). These individuals transcended the temptations of the career mystique and feel successful in their careers. An important question is, what enables some people to follow their own personal path, with a sense of personal agency, and what leads others to submit to the career mystique?

In general, the quantitative measures that distinguished the success groups included mostly work-related phenomena, with the exception of frequency of illness of family members. That is, those who were more successful objectively speaking tended to work longer hours, were in managerial jobs, experienced moving from a lower to higher work load at least once, and were less likely to have taken a leave of absence or exited an organization between Phase 1 and Phase 2. Those experiencing low objective success tended to have experienced more turbulence in their jobs—including a layoff and perhaps a period of self-employment. The low objective and low subjective group had significantly more family health crises over the 6 years. For the groups that were high on subjective success, their spouses (or partners) earned less than the spouses of the groups that felt less subjective success. And in fact, in the low subjective success groups, the partners' salaries were quite high ($180,658 and $152,375), suggesting that these participants had partners in highly demanding jobs, which meant that their partners might be less involved in the family "work," or that participants might have felt greater dissatisfaction with their own careers if they compared themselves with their partners.

In the many examples of people who bounced back from various kinds of setbacks (in the job, in the family, in personal life), there seems to be a general overall theme of resilience and thriving here. Most of the participants in Phase 1, including those in the low subjective/low objective success group, were able to come back from adversity and construct lives that provided a level of purpose and fulfillment. This is consistent with work by Voydanoff (2002), who finds the concept of adaptability and family resilience to be a strong factor related to positive personal and family outcomes. Family resilience is, "the successful coping of family members under adversity that enables them to flourish with warmth, support, and cohesion" (Black & Lobo, 2008). Black and Lobo (2008) conclude that prominent characteristics of resilient families include factors such as positive outlook, family member accord, flexibility, family communication, financial management, and support networks, among others.

Conclusions and Future Research

As the experiences of the participants in our study have shown, reduced load work arrangements can facilitate the process of crafting lives and careers that work. Tiedje (2004) came to a similar conclusion in her longitudinal study:

> "Alternative work arrangements (telecommuting, job sharing, flexible work hours) were very much in evidence in our sample, mirroring societal changes in the structure of work over the 13 years of data collection. Small, determined groups of women, men, and families who redefine work and family templates have changed things. Our study further revealed that, (a) there is no standard job template for women and new career/family templates are being slowly and incrementally created... and (b) more modest, incremental gains made by individuals can combat systemic forms of gender inequity in the workplace, for example, the example of leaving meetings early... Small, individual acts have the potential to inspire others who witness the possibilities and trigger large public consequences (see Myerson & Fletcher, 2000 for a discussion of this workplace phenomenon). How parents view parenting responsibilities is not only a result of company policies, but also the result of the workplace culture and practices (Lewis & Lewis, 1996)." (Tiedje, 2004, p. 798.)

Overall our study found that, while objective and subjective career success were not directly correlated with each other, they do relate to each other in more complex ways. We found major differences between the lives of individuals who have achieved high subjective success and those who experienced high objective success. People high on subjective success tend to be more self-directed and proactive in their choices. For example, people in the low objective and high subjective career success group made their own choices about remaining on reduced-load or about when and whether to leave their organizations, and many people in the high objective and high subjective career success group made their own decisions to limit their further upward mobility, for family reasons. These themes were similar to those found by Sturges (1999) in her study of the meanings of success in a group of UK managers, particularly among women (who represented 89% of our sample). People in our high subjective success group seem to have more of a boundaryless or protean career orientation, in that they are more self-directed and are driven more by their personal values. On the other hand, people who seem more motivated to strive for objective career success, whether by personal motivation or economic necessity, have careers that are more driven by their employing organizations. Since research has shown that the functioning of the traditional organization-based career contract seems stronger in some countries than others (Briscoe et al., 2012), comparative research in a variety of countries and cultures would provide more variance in organizational context and its influence on the nature of these career motivations.

Future research could build on the extreme case analysis method used here, with holistic longitudinal data on both objective and subjective success indicators. The fact that these were all people who had originally taken proactive measures to restructure their work arrangements, and had found ways to craft their lives in ways that worked for them (even members of low success groups), would make this type of research ideal ground for a Positive Organizational Scholarship (POS) approach (Cameron & Caza, 2004). A POS approach would lead us to examine the positive steps individuals and organizations can take to improve the sustainability of careers and families over time.

Research might also incorporate new measures of positive (and reduced negative) emotions linked to perceptions of work–family success. For example, Botsford and King's (2012) measure of work–family guilt may be useful to capture emotions as mediators of success perceptions as individuals attempt new career strategies, such as requesting a reduced-load work arrangement.

More research is also needed to examine how perceptions of objective and subjective success are embedded in institutional contexts. As several papers in this special issue suggest, future research should investigate the extent to which perceptions of success are linked to societal and policy contexts of what successful integration of parenting with sustainable careers looks like (Herman & Lewis, 2012). For example, multilevel research might investigate how prevailing societal norms regarding sanctioned strategies for combining parenting with career shape the perceived viability of reduced-load work arrangements as an adaptive strategy for achieving career success. Most of our sample was U.S. based, and working part-time was viewed as deviating from the norm. In contrast, Vinkenburg, van Engen, Coffeng, and Dikkers (2012) found that in the Netherlands part-time work allowing for greater "shared care" while maintaining career *was the preferred societal norm*. In fact, Dutch mothers (but not men) employed full-time were viewed less positively than part-time mothers. Research should investigate how societal norms and policy supports regarding successful career and parenting models, relate to individuals' success perceptions and personal strategies for achieving sustainable careers.

This multilevel approach may be particularly important when societies have individuals enacting new strategies that might violate prevailing gender and career norms. Research might study the extent to which mothers in the countries with social policies supportive of "shared care" (e.g., the Netherlands, Sweden, etc.) who work reduced load may have higher congruence between objective and subjective success than reduced-load mothers in contrasting policy contexts such as North America. To what extent does a supportive institutional and societal context for reduced-load career strategies make them a robust and vibrant vehicle for social change? [And even more fundamentally, how does a particular society value parental roles, especially motherhood, and to what extent are parents judged as equally agentic and career-committed compared to non-parents (Fuegen et al., 2004; Ridgeway & Correll, 2004).]

In summary, this study shows that while using work–home arrangements in and of themselves did not necessarily predict subjective career success or personal and family well-being, such arrangements were a valued support. Reduced-load work arrangements enabled talented professionals to remain in the labor force and sustain career involvement while maintaining the kind of engagement with family life they needed and/or desired. Our study results suggest that organizations and individuals should not look at these flexible work arrangements as a panacea in and of themselves or as necessarily ensuring psychological success. Rather the use of these arrangements should be studied in terms of their psychological meaning to individuals seeking cross-domain success across work, family and personal life, as they craft lives that work for them.

References

Arthur, M. B., Hall, D. T., & Lawrence, B. S. (1989). *Handbook of career theory*. New York: Cambridge University Press.

Arthur, M. B., Khapova, S. N., & Wilderom, C. P. M. (2005). Career success in a boundaryless career world. *Journal of Organizational Behavior, 26*(2), 177–202. doi:10.1002/job.290

Ashforth, B. E., Kreiner, G. E., & Fugate, M. (2000). All in a day's work: Boundaries and micro role transitions at work. *Academy of Management Review, 23*, 472–491. Retrieved from http://www.jstor.org/stable/259305

Benko, C., & Weisberg, A. (2007). *Mass career customization: Aligning the workplace with today's nontraditional workforce*. Boston, MA: Harvard Business School Press.

Black, K., & Lobo, M. (2008). A conceptual review of family resilience factors. *Journal of Family Nursing, 14*(1), 33–55. doi:10.1177/1074840707312237

Blair-Loy, M., & Wharton, A. (2002). The "overtime culture" in a global corporation: A cross-national study of finance professionals' interest in working part-time. *Work and Occupations, 29*(1), 32–63. doi:10.1177/0730888402029001003

Blair-Loy, M. (2003). *Competing devotions: Career and family and women executives*. Cambridge, MA: Harvard University Press.

Botsford, W., & King, E. (2012). The influence of work-family guilt on pro- and anti-social work behavior. *Journal of Social Issues, 68*, xx–xx.

Briscoe, J. P., Hall, D. T., & Mayrhofer, W. (2012). *Careers around the world: Individual and contextual perspectives*. New York and London: Routledge.

Cameron, K. S., & Caza, A. (2004). Introduction: Contributions to the discipline of positive organizational scholarship. *American Behavioral Scientist, 47*(6), 731–739. doi:10.1177/0002764203260207

Cascio, W. (2007). Trends, paradoxes, and some directions for research in career studies. In H. Gunz & M. Peiperl (Eds.), *Handbook of career studies* (pp. 549–557). Thousand Oaks, CA: Sage.

Fuegen, K., Biernat, M., Haines, I., & Deaux, K. (2004). Mothers and fathers in the workplace: How gender and parental status influence judgments of job-related competence. *Journal of Social Issues, 60*(4), 737–754. doi:10.1111/j.0022-4537.2004.00383.x

Greenhaus, J. H., & Powell, G. N. (2006). When work and family are allies: A theory of work-family enrichment. *Academy of Management Review, 31*(1), 72–92. Retrieved from http://search.proquest.com/docview/210951769?accountid = 12339

Hall, D. T., & Richter, J. (1989). Balancing work life and home life: What can organizations do to help? *Academy of Management Executive, 2*(3), 213–233. Retrieved from http://www.jstor.org/stable/4164832

Herman, C., & Lewis, S. (2012). Entitled to a sustainable career? Motherhood in science, engineering and technology. *Journal of Social Issues, 68*(4), 767–789.

Hughes, E. C. (1958). *Men and their work*. London: Free Press, Collier-Macmillan.

Kailasaphy, P., & Metz, I. (2012). Work-family conflict in Sri Lanka: Negotiations of exchange relationships in family and at work. *Journal of Social Issues, 68*(4), 790–813.

Kossek, E., & Michel, J. (2010). Flexible work scheduling. In S. Zedeck (Ed.), *Handbook of industrial and organizational psychology* (pp. 535–572). Washington, DC: American Psychological Association.

Lee, M. D., MacDermid, S. M., Williams, M. L., Buck, M. L., & Leiba-O'Sullivan, S. (2002). Contextual factors in the success of reduced-load work arrangements among managers and professionals. *Human Resource Management*, *41*(2), 209–223. doi:10.1002/hrm.10032

Lee, M, Kossek, E., Hall, D., & Litrico, J. (2011). Entangled strands: A process perspective on the evolution of careers in the context of personal, family, work, and community life. *Human Relations*, *64*(12), 1531–1553.

Lewis, S., & Lewis, J. (1996). *The work-family challenge: Rethinking employment*. Thousand Oaks, CA: Sage.

Mainiero, L. A., & Sullivan, S. E. (2006). *The opt-out revolt*. Mountain View, CA: Davis-Black Publishing.

Maslow, A. H. (1954). *Motivation and personality*. New York: Harper.

Miles, M. B. & Huberman, A. M. (1994). *Qualitative data analysis* (2nd ed.). Thousand Oaks, CA: Sage.

Moen, P., & Roehling, P. (2005). *The career mystique: Cracks in the American dream*. Oxford, UK: Rowman & Littlefield Publishers, Inc.

Myerson, D. E., & Fletcher, J. K. (2000). A modest manifesto for shattering the glass ceiling. *Harvard Business Review*, *78*, 127–236.

Neal, M. B., & Hammer, L. B. (2007). *Working couples caring for children and aging parents: Effects on work and well-being*. Mahwah, NJ: Lawrence Erlbaum Associates, Inc.

Nicholson, N., & de Waal-Andrews, W. (2005). Playing to win: Biological imperatives, self-regulation, and trade-offs in the game of career success. *Journal of Organizational Behavior*, *26*, 37–154. doi:10.1002/job.295

Patton, M. Q. (2002). *Qualitative research and evaluation methods*. Thousand Oaks, CA: Sage Publications, Inc.

Ridgeway, C. L., & Correll, S. J. (2004). Motherhood as a status characteristic. *Journal of Social Issues*, *60*(4), 683–700. doi:10.1111/j.0022-4537.2004.00380.x

Russell, H., O'Connell, P. J., & McGinnity, F. (2009). The impact of flexible working arrangements on work-life conflict and work pressure in Ireland. *Gender, Work and Organizations*, *16*(1), 73–97. doi:10.1111/j.1468-0432.2008.00431.x

Seibert S. E., & Kraimer M. L. (2001). The five-factor model of personality and career success. *Journal of Vocational Behavior*, *58*, 1–21. doi:10.1006/jvbe.2000.1757

Sturges, J. (1999). What it means to succeed: Personal conceptions of career success held by male and female managers at different ages. *British Journal of Management*, *10*, 239–252. doi:10.1111/1467-8551.00130

Tiedje, L. B. (2004). Processes of change in work/home incompatibilities: Employed mothers 1986–1999. *Journal of Social Issues*, *60*(4), 787–800. doi:10.1111/j.0022-4537.2004.00386.x

Valcour, M., Bailyn, L. & Quijada, M. A. (2007). Customized careers. In H. Gunz & M. Peiperl (Eds.) *Handbook of career studies* (pp. 188–210). Los Angeles: Sage.

Van Veldhoven, M. J. P. M., & Beijer, S. E. (2012). Workload, work-to-family conflict, and health: Gender differences and the influence of private life context. *Journal of Social Issues*, *68*(4), 665–683.

Vinkenburg, C. J., van Engen, M. L., Coffeng, J., & Dikkers, J. S. E. (2012). Bias in employment decisions about mothers and fathers: The (dis)advantages of sharing care responsibilities. *Journal of Social Issues*, *68*(4), 725–741.

Voydanoff, P. (2002). Linkages between the work-family interface and work, family, and individual outcomes: An integrative model. *Journal of Family Issues*, *23*(1), 138–164. doi:10.1177/0192513×02023001007

DOUGLAS T. (TIM) HALL is the Morton H. and Charlotte Friedman Professor of Management in the School of Management at Boston University and Faculty Director of the MBA Program. He was recently a Visiting Professor at IESE Business School in Barcelona, as well as the H. Smith Richardson, Jr., Visiting Fellow at the Center for Creative Leadership. He is the (co-) author of several books on careers and work–life issues, including *Careers in Organizations, The Two Career Couple, The Career is Dead–Long Live the Career, Career Management and Work-Life Integration,* and *Extraordinary Leadership.* His research and consulting deal with careers, work-life integration, and leadership development.

MARY DEAN LEE is Professor of Organizational Behavior and Human Resource Management in the Desautels Faculty of Management at McGill University, where she has spent most of her career since completing her PhD from Yale University. Her research interests include professional and managerial careers, the changing nature of work, work and family, alternative work arrangements, and work and aging. She has published articles in *Journal of Organizational Behavior, Academy of Management Journal, Human Relations,* and *Human Resource Management,* among others, and was co-author of the book *Management of Work and Personal Life* with Rabindra Kanungo.

ELLEN ERNST KOSSEK is University Distinguished Professor at Michigan State University's School of Human Resources & Labor Relations with a joint courtesy appointment in the Management Department. Dr. Kossek is Associate Director of the Center for Work, Family Health and Stress and is a founding co-PI and member of the U.S. National Institutes of Health National Work, Family and Health Network. Dr. Kossek thrives in conducting research and teaching students and managers on how to transform organizations to positively address HR and work–life challenges. Her educational degrees are from Yale University (PhD in organizational behavior); University of Michigan (MBA); and Mount Holyoke College (BA with honors in psychology). She has won many awards including the Academy of Management Divisions' Gender and Diversity in Organizations' Sage Scholarly Achievement award recognizing research to advance gender and diversity in organizations. She has authored eight books including *CEO of Me: Creating a Life that Works in the Flexible Job Age,* and over 60 chapters or articles.

MIREIA LAS HERAS is an Assistant Professor at IESE Business School—University of Navarra, Spain—where she serves as the Research Director of the International Center for Work and Family. She earned her degree in Industrial Engineering at the Polytechnic School of Catalonia, specializing on Industrial Organization, and she holds an MBA from IESE Business School, and a Doctorate in Business Administration from Boston University. In 2009 she co-edited a book (*"A Practical Guide for Implementing Effective Work Family Policies Across Countries"*) and she has published other articles and book chapters on work–family integration, career development, and leadership. Dr. Las Heras is also an active consultant and coach in the area of Work–Family Balance and Career Development for NCH & Partners.

Entitled to a Sustainable Career? Motherhood in Science, Engineering, and Technology

Clem Herman* and Suzan Lewis
The Open University and Middlesex University

Sustaining careers and motherhood are particularly challenging in highly masculinized science, engineering, and technology (SET) sectors. We explore this issue using a social comparison theory perspective, drawing on interviews with professional engineers and scientists from four companies, located in Italy, France, and the Netherlands. We examine how decisions to reduce working hours are influenced by perceived ideological, normative, and policy contexts. Despite contextual differences in opportunities and perceived entitlements and supports for family-friendly working hours, we found that sense of entitlement to do so without forfeiting career progression is limited across all the contexts. This attests to the enduring power of gendered organizational assumptions about ideal SET careers. Nevertheless we present examples of three women who achieved senior roles despite working reduced hours and discuss combinations of conditions which may facilitate sustainable careers and caring roles.

The challenges of sustaining motherhood and careers tend to be difficult in male-dominated occupations and organizations. This is particularly so in science, engineering, and technology (SET) companies where women are underrepresented, especially at more senior levels (European Commission, 2006). Many women leave after having children or remain in employment but fail to progress; part of the SET "leaky pipeline" from which girls and women drop out at different stages of their education and careers (Blickenstaff, 2005). Masculine values and work cultures are often entrenched in SET (Barnard, Powell, Bagilhole, & Dainty, 2010). Women scientists and engineers often conform to cultural expectations of constant availability and periods of time working abroad in order to manage the additional burden of maintaining both their identity as women and their own

---

*Correspondence regarding this manuscript should be addressed to Clem Herman, Department of Communication and Systems, The Open University, Milton Keynes MK7 6AA, UK [e-mail: c.herman@open.ac.uk].

professional identity as scientists, engineers and technologists—an in/visibility paradox (Faulkner, 2009). However, this often becomes unsustainable once they become mothers (Ranson, 2005). Indeed it is motherhood rather than gender per se that tends to be a key barrier, perceived as incompatible with normative SET professional careers (Herman, 2009; Herman, Lewis, & Humbert, 2012; Lewis & Humbert, 2010). This reflects wider evidence of a motherhood wage penalty (Budig & Hodges, 2010; Correll, Benard, & Paik, 2007).

Work–family policies to support parents (mostly mothers) by providing shorter or more flexible hours exist as national entitlements, to various degrees, across Europe and are also initiated within organizations. However, while these policies can help women to sustain employment and conform to normative beliefs about mothering, there are often negative career consequences (Webber & Williams, 2008). Work–family policies, especially nonstatutory initiatives, are often regarded as concessions and hence many women accept trade-offs between flexibility to deviate from normative (male) working patterns and career outcomes (Kelliher & Anderson, 2010). This raises questions about how and under what conditions women (and men) in SET can sustain careers as well as care for children. There has been some discussion of what might be considered to be socially sustainable work (Lewis, Gambles, & Rapoport, 2007), usually defined as work that enables social reproduction and care for future generations. However, in this article we consider sustainable careers, not just in terms of being able to continue in employment, but also to achieve career advancement commensurate with human capital, as SET professionals. This article focuses on women's career-related decisions in diverse contexts and explores some conditions under which mothers in SET may be able to deviate from male career patterns without forfeiting developmental careers. It does so by drawing on a qualitative study of SET professionals in four organizations in three European countries (France, Italy, and the Netherlands), undertaken via a European Union Expert Group on Women in SET, involving collaboration between SET employers and researchers.

Theoretical Background

Career-related decisions at the transition to parenthood, particularly whether to work reduced hours, are often discussed within a discourse of choice and preference (Hakim, 2002), taking an *individual* approach. Indeed mothers often rationalize their decision to work fewer hours as a personal choice, knowing that it will disadvantage their careers (Lewis & Humbert, 2010; Webber & Williams, 2008). However, this neglects the role of structural and relational factors and the importance of embedding individual agency and choice in specific institutional and cultural settings (Hobson & Fahlén, 2009). As Hantrais and Ackers (2005, p. 210) note, "Choice is something complex and elusive that emerges from the constraints, opportunities and ideologies of a particular time and place." The individual approach, with its neglect of context, fails to explain why cutting back on work during early motherhood has negative career outcomes.

A more *contextual* approach focuses on workplace policies, cultures, and practices including discrimination against mothers on the basis of motherhood as a status characteristic distinct from gender alone (Correll et al., 2007; Ridgeway & Corell, 2004) and particularly gendered organization theory (Acker, 1990). Many European SET employers now offer a range of work–family policies, usually targeted at least implicitly at mothers. These include reduced hours arrangements negotiated to enhance retention of highly qualified women in posts that are usually full-time. These policies are often presented as offering mothers choices to be able to sustain their careers. However there is abundant evidence that part-time work even in occupations requiring high levels of human capital tends to be career limiting, both in SET and more broadly (Webber & Williams, 2008), particularly in highly competitive career contexts (Cross & Linehan, 2006). Although some writers have argued that part-time jobs in other elite occupations may challenge ideal worker norms, transforming workplaces for women and men (Blair-Loy, 2003), most research suggests that entrenched and gendered ideology of the importance of availability and visibility can obscure what is often the greater efficiency of those achieving their outputs in shorter hours (Lewis, 2010; Lewis & Humbert, 2010).

Research on the gendered nature of SET and gendered organizational assumptions sheds some light on the processes whereby working shorter hours during the early years of motherhood compromises careers. There are a number of common gender-related cultural practices in SET industries, including language, informal banter, and social networking patterns which signal that women are outside the norm (Faulkner, 2009) and mysterious career paths and systems of risk and reward often reflected in professional women's stalled progress at mid career (Hewlett et al., 2008), attesting that these workplaces are far from gender neutral. More broadly, gendered organizational theory highlights widespread gendered assumptions about ideal workers, particularly professionals, who work full time and often excessive hours, are constantly available and visible and do not allow family to interfere with their working time (Acker, 1990; Holt & Lewis, 2010). This conflation of ideal workers with hegemonic masculinity (Bailyn, 2006) is particularly strong in the highly masculinized world of SET (Miller, 2004) and especially in industries where there is an expectation of mobility and frequent international travel (Ackers, 2004). The ideal worker norm is antithetical to the way the ideal mother is socially constructed in many contexts (Lewis, 1991; Ridgeway & Correll, 2004). Gendered organizational theory contributes crucially to an understanding of organizational processes that systematically disadvantage women, especially mothers and undermines capacity to sustain career and care. However although this approach highlights processes for working toward systemic workplace change (Rapoport, Bailyn, Fletcher, & Pruitt, 2002), it does not clarify how individual women trailblazers might deviate from traditional SET career patterns without forfeiting developmental careers. Moreover, research on motherhood as a status characteristic and on the impact of workplace culture and practice often neglects the impact of national context, implicitly assuming universalism, despite variations in national policies and normative beliefs about parental roles. Some recent research highlights the importance of layers of context, including both workplace and wider national contexts for understanding tensions relating to parenthood and careers (Hobson & Fahlén, 2009) and there are calls for wider contextualization of research in this area (Powell, Francesco, & Ling, 2009).

A third approach that specifically takes account of both *individual cognitions and context* is based on social comparison theory and especially the concept of sense of entitlement. Drawing on social justice theory a distinction can be made between supports which are expected and regarded as entitlements or rights, and those which are regarded as favors which have to be negotiated and/or reciprocated. Sense of entitlement, which differs from objective entitlements, denotes a set of beliefs and feelings about rights, entitlements, or legitimate expectations, based on what is perceived to be fair and equitable (Bylsma & Major, 1994; Major, 1993). In the case of working parents, this shapes outcomes that mothers and also fathers feel entitled to expect in the workplace and elsewhere (Lewis & Smithson, 2001). In the context of gendered ideal worker assumptions, mothers often view work–family policies that enable them to deviate from full-time work, as favors. This shapes and is shaped by a low sense of entitlement and can explain why mothers are often willing to trade-off time with family for career progress (Webber & Williams, 2008).

Sense of entitlement is theorized as determined by social comparison processes (Lerner, 1987), and constructed on the basis of social, normative, and feasibility comparisons (Lewis & Smithson, 2001; Lewis & Haas, 2005). Judgments about what is fair or equitable are made on the basis of normative comparisons with social comparators, that is, those who are assumed to be similar to oneself (Bylsma & Major, 1994; Major, 1993). Gender appears to be particularly significant in influencing what is perceived as normative, appropriate, and feasible. Research has consistently shown that men and women tend to feel entitled to different outcomes in employment, where, for example, women may feel entitled to lower rates of pay or other rewards (Bylsma & Major, 1994). If motherhood is socially constructed as a woman's primary role then employment is often viewed as something that women undertake for their own satisfaction and independence, even if their income is essential for the family (Lewis, Kagan, & Heaton, 2000). Ideologies of motherhood embedded in workplace and in national cultures are therefore likely to impact on mothers' sense of entitlement to employer support that will enable them to work when they have family responsibilities, and also to men's (lower) sense of entitlement to employer support for involvement in caring. There is some evidence that sense of entitlement is also influenced by aspects of national contexts including social policies and the cultural values that they reflect (Lewis & Smithson 2001; Lewis & Haas, 2005). However, previous research exploring sense of entitlements has not examined sense of entitlement to both flexible/part time work and career progression. Nor has it looked specifically at traditionally masculine workplace cultures such as the SET industries.

Role models are important in providing social comparisons. If there are few, if any, organizational role models of women who modify working patterns for family and sustain career progression, social comparisons result in perceptions that this would be neither normative nor feasible. Thus fewer mothers are likely to feel entitled to deviate from ideal career patterns without career disadvantage. However, this still does not explain why or under what conditions women trailblazers can become social comparative referents for achieving career progression without conforming to normative male career patterns.

Thus previous research has explained women's lack of career progression in SET in terms of individual decisions about using work–family arrangements at the transition to parenthood, and also in terms of contextual factors including the disadvantaging role of social perceptions of motherhood status itself and gendered organizational cultures which marginalize and penalize those who deviate from traditional linear careers. The impact of wider national policy and normative contexts has received less attention, although there is some indication that this influences sense of entitlement to use work–family arrangements. However, much less is known about sense of entitlement to use work–family arrangements without career detriment, and about the conditions under which mothers in highly gendered organizations can forge trailblazing careers without forfeiting time for care, even without obvious social referents. This article addresses these gaps, using sense of entitlement as a conceptual lens for exploring individual, contextualized experiences of motherhood and careers in four SET organizations in three national contexts. As the transition to motherhood is a key turning point, with the impact of decisions made at this time often manifested in stalled progression by mid career, we therefore look at SET professionals' accounts of both career/life course phases. The main objective is to further understand mothers' lack of progression in SET. Specifically the aims are:

(1) To examine the ways in which mothers (and some fathers) talk about decisions concerning working hours at the transition to parenthood. We explore (a) how SET professionals define their situations in terms of their perceived sense of entitlement to modify work for family and at the same time develop sustainable careers, and (b) how perceptions of national contexts, including social policy and normative parenting beliefs, contribute to shaping their sense of entitlement to sustainable careers.

(2) To examine, as careers unfold in diverse national contexts, the conditions under which some women scientists and engineers are able to make use of

work–family arrangements without accruing career penalties, and may thus increase the pool of social comparators for SET careers that deviate from the male norm.

Method

Background

The study derives from a project carried out in 2007–2009 as part of the EU Women in Science and Technology project: WIST2 (European Commission, 2009). An earlier EU research program identified the "leaky pipeline" and "work–life balance" as areas for further investigation into the reasons for women's under representation and limited progression in SET employment in Europe (European Commission, 2006). WIST2 brought together a panel of researchers with representatives of European SET companies, all of whom had identified an organizational need to retain and develop more highly qualified women SET professionals. The remit of the group was to identify relevant research areas and to carry out investigations to support companies in addressing the problems of attrition and women's stalled career progression in this sector within their own organizations. The companies provided access to existing data and/or suitable research participants. This article brings together the results of two linked studies carried out within the overall WIST2 project.

Design and Methods

A qualitative approach was adopted, using semistructured interviews to explore the lived experiences of parents as they negotiated motherhood and in some cases fatherhood, in the context of their professional lives as engineers and scientists. Thus our focus is on situated meanings and how these are constructed by participants (Gephart, 2004). A process of negotiation between the researchers and the company representatives led to a commitment by seven of the companies to provide study participants. As there were only one or two interviews in three of the companies, we focus here on the four remaining organizations with 8–13 interviews in each. Although the two interlinked studies used aspects of the same, collaboratively developed, interview schedule, the priorities of the companies involved resulted in slightly different foci. Both projects addressed career issues, but one focused on the impact of the transition to motherhood and the other on experiences of work–family policies and practices (European Commission, 2009). Consequently, one sample was all women while the other included some men. Companies were asked to recruit professionally qualified scientists or engineers with children ranging from under a year old to secondary school age.

Table 1. Participant Nationalities and Working Time Patterns

	Country	No of cases	Women	Men	Full-time[a]	Part-time
Company1	NL	8	8	0	3	5
Company2	Italy	8	8	0	7	1
Company3	France	13	9	4	5	8
Company4	France	9	5	4	6	3

[a]These figures reflect contracted working patterns at the time of interview but many of now working full time had periods of working part time in the past.

The interview schedule took a life course approach, focusing on career history, decisions, and turning points in working lives and expectations and actual experiences of support to sustain career and family. Discussion covered use and experiences of work–family practices including periods of leave, flexible working, and reduced hours work within the company or of working full-time. The interviews lasted about 1 hour and were recorded, transcribed, and translated as appropriate. Most interviews were conducted in English although some were carried out in French. In this article, we analyze the experiences of 30 mothers in three countries, as well as eight men from two French companies (see Table 1).

Procedures Used for Coding and Analyzing

A coding scheme was developed between the two authors with general headings. These included professional identity (career history, ambitions and aspirations, work patterns) discourses of expectations and choice, organizational culture (progression/stagnation, attitude to motherhood, gender biases, ideal workers, flexible work options, leave arrangements, in/visibility paradox), motherhood (motherhood ideologies, childcare arrangements, domestic arrangements), and national cultural practices. The transcripts were then coded using Nvivo8 software, a qualitative data analysis tool that enables coding, linking, modeling, and annotation of rich textual data. An inductive approach was used to identify further emerging themes and we exchanged Nvivo coded files and discussed our coding at regular intervals to ensure intercoder reliability.

Setting

All the organizations are large multinationals in the highly masculinized SET sector, including one pharmaceutical, one energy, and two oil and gas companies. All four had concerns about the lack of progression of their women employees and two had already instituted well-developed training and development initiatives to address these issues. However, in only one of the companies were there any highly visible senior women. The two French companies were alike in many ways but also diverged in some respects which allowed us to explore and compare experiences within workplace as well as national layers of context.

All the companies are subject to EU Directives including those on parental leave and on equal treatment for part time workers, which set parameters for policy at the nation state level. However, although the principle of equal treatment of part-time and full-time workers is accepted in terms of working conditions in European law, it is more difficult to enforce equal career progression. Moreover, the ways in which directives are implemented and subsequent opportunity structures vary considerably across Europe (Den Dulk & van Doorne-Huiskes, 2007), influenced by factors such as labor market conditions, availability of day care, attitudes toward parents' involvement in work and care, and partner support (Kangas & Rostaard, 2007). In each of the three national contexts there were subtle differences in normative ideologies of motherhood, but all resulted in gendered patterns of part-time work where this was available.

Among the countries in which the participating organizations are located, French mothers have the fewest objective external constraints to integration of work and family. French social policy is designed to provide parents (mostly mothers in practice) with formal entitlements to and support for combining family responsibilities and employment, including childcare support, the right to work part-time and generous family leaves. Policy is based on a dual-earner family model, but with mothers as the main carers (Fagnani, 2009). The ideal French mother expects and is expected to work and be the principle carer, with supporting resources such as childcare. There is no stigma in delegating childcare to the state (Hantrais & Ackers, 2005). Furthermore full-time working hours tend to be shorter in France than elsewhere and reduced hours working is common, mostly for mothers.

In the Netherlands, a one and a half earner family is the norm for parents of young children and part-time employment has long been promoted by the state as a work–family strategy. However, normative beliefs about parenting are strongly gendered. While mothers who combine work with family care are viewed positively, fathers who do so often suffer career penalties (Vinkenburg, Van Engen, Coffeng, & Dikkers, 2012). Most mothers (and some fathers) work part-time during their children's early years, supported by a mix of private and state childcare provisions (Cousins & Tang, 2004). This reflects the strong preference for care at home for young children (Den Dulk & Van Doorne-Huiskes, 2007). In Italy, by contrast, the norm is for full-time work for men and women. Although maternity leave is generous with some flexibility available in working hours during the first 3 years, there are few part-time work opportunities for professionals and public childcare is limited. Instead there is a tradition of extended family especially grandmothers, providing considerable support (Del Boca, Locatelli, & Vuri, 2005).

Results

For professional scientists and engineers in these companies, there were no existing part-time posts or career routes, rather these were negotiated on an individual basis. In the French companies this was a formal entitlement and in one company a collective agreement allowed a reduction from full-time (35 hours) to 32 hours over 4 days, with favorable conditions. In the Italian company part-time work was a concession that only one participant had negotiated. Other Italian mothers relied on extended family members to provide childcare support in order to sustain full-time careers. In France and the Netherlands, reduced hours contracts comprised options for working 3 or 4 days per week although some worked reduced hours over 5 days. In addition, most of the mothers on full-time contracts in the four sites limited the amount of time they worked beyond their contracted hours, although extra hours were expected to a greater or lesser degree across all the companies. These mothers were thus regarded and also regarded themselves as working reduced hours compared with the norm and so they are also included in our analysis.

Below we first explore parents' accounts of decisions about working hours and their explanation, in terms of social comparisons, norms, and feasibility, within the context of national and workplace policies and norms. This qualitative study does not, of course, aim to make cross-national generalizations, but rather to explore how parents used their own perceptions of normative values and cultures to understand and make sense of their particular life and career choices and the consequences. Details about the participants we have quoted are in Table 2. Their citations were chosen as representative illustrations of themes identified across the whole sample. We then explore the experiences of three mothers who progressed in their careers, focusing on some conditions under which it is possible to sustain career progress without working full time during early motherhood.

Working Hours, Sense of Entitlement, and National Context

Mothers' working time decisions after maternity leave, whether formally working reduced hours or continuing full-time but limiting their extra availability, were usually framed as *choices*, but it was clear that these were not unfettered compromises. Their explanations often included discourses about national contexts. In particular, they drew on normative gender and parenting roles as well as availability of childcare and extended family support.

Among the French mothers support for continued employment was taken for granted, although those who had worked on assignments elsewhere were more sensitive to the impact of national context. Sabine, who had worked in both Germany and France, was able to locate her sense of entitlement to work–family support in social comparisons based on cultural ideological difference. Similarly

Table 2. Details about Cases Quoted in the Text

Identifier	Occupation	Country	Current working hours[a]	Career length (years)	Age	No of children	Age of youngest
Tineke	Senior Manager	NL	3.5 days	20	43	2	10
Pierre	Research Chemist	France	Full time	15	38	2	2
Marie	Project Manager	France	3 days	12	38	3	1.5
Soraya	Devt Manager	Italy	Full time	15	41	1	5
Sabine	Research Manager	France	4 days	9	35	2	<1
Isabella	Engineer	Italy	On leave	10	34	1	<1
Helene	Deputy Director	France	Full time	15	38	3	4
Els	Senior Manager	NL	Full time	20	42	3	8
Sophia	Engineer	Italy	On leave	5	33	1	<1
Anna	Research Engineer	France	4 days	13	37	3	1
Carlotta	Engineer	Italy	Full time	18	46	1	8

[a] These figures reflect contracted working patterns at the time of interview but many of those working full time had periods of working part time in the past.

to perceptions of mothers in Okimoto and Heilman's (2012) study, she faced additional stress by having to combat assumptions about her parenting role. In this extract she notes the disapproving voice of normative German motherhood ideology (which labels women who "neglect" their children as Rabenmutter or "raven mothers").

> I've been living for six years in Germany and have recently moved back to France because the border is very nearby – I have experienced that other women (in Germany) who are not working and looking after their children until they are at least three, they would look at me as a very bad mother – how can you leave your child with a nanny at three months old?[. . .] That was fine by me because since you have the French culture from the beginning I was self confident to do it but I can understand the pressure for German women.

However, this did not mean that French mothers wanted to or felt entitled to conform to the male model of work. Rather, the strong ideology of mothers as the main carers underpinned decisions to reduce contracted hours or limit extra hours. There was a frequent discourse among the French mothers, and also some of the Dutch mothers, of "choices" made to avoid "sacrificing" children, albeit alongside recognition that not all mothers are the same in this respect, as Anna describes.

> I know that some people come back from work when their children are in bed. I don't want to do that. I want to see them, to give them dinner, to bath them, to put them to bed every night. It's inconceivable not to do so. I would never sacrifice my children. It's a choice. There are a lot of people who come home too late in the evening. But that's their choice.

Social comparison discourses were also used by mothers working full-time to justify their decision making, for example, discussing the extra material benefits of having two working parents, redefining traditional notions of the good mother.

Mothers in the Dutch company also had a strong sense of entitlement to work part-time which was viewed as normative and feasible, despite a less well established infrastructure of support than in France. Some had considerable partner support. Fathers were involved in childcare to a greater or lesser degree in all the companies but there were only a few cases where mothers talked of partners actually working part-time in order to be involved in childcare. For example, Els' husband worked 4 days a week when they first had children 15 years ago, which was still quite exceptional within their social circles at the time. Now she believed that Dutch fathers see it as more feasible, if not yet normative to reduce their working hours, suggesting an emerging sense of entitlement for men to do so and mothers to expect this support. Here she describes how other people have reacted to her husband's childcare role:

> *Now everyone's used to it, but before it was 'are you ill?', 'are you taking a day off?', 'has your wife asked to look after the kids for the day?'...... [Now] it's changing a lot. [There are] many men at the school nowadays, or more men*

In Italy where the choice for a mother is mainly between full-time or no employment there were few opportunities and little sense of entitlement to work reduced hours. For Carlotta, for example, despite a strong ideology of motherhood this meant she was able to make a very positive social comparison.

> *If I do a comparison between me and other mothers who are completely dedicated to their children – I don't see that my son or their son is any different. He seems to be happy to have this type of family because he has the opportunity to travel with us and he understands that at home there is a lot of opportunity and me and my husband we speak about our jobs and our work and this is also good for my son*

This may be possible because of the involvement of wider family in childcare. There are few expectations of nonfamilial support, but those who had worked abroad made social comparisons between national cultural norms. For example, Isabella, an Italian engineer, had spent 2 years working in Norway.

> *When I stayed these two years in Norway I saw a totally different reality, I'm not surprised that they have so many children compared to an Italian family because really the possibilities and the support that you have is completely different*

This experience challenged her feasibility beliefs and raised her sense of entitlement to support from the company, although she was not optimistic about this actually materializing, in the Italian context.

Sense of Entitlement to Reduce Working Hours without Forfeiting Careers

Despite differences in national normative and policy contexts and childcare support, few of the women interviewed appeared to have a strong sense of entitlement to work shorter hours without giving something back in exchange; working harder or forfeiting career progression. Given the pervasive ideology of ideal SET careers with constant availability, most still regarded reduced hours as favors to be reciprocated, rarely associated with a sense of entitlement to career progression. This was usually viewed as neither normative nor feasible, although we discuss some exception in the next section. Social comparators were both real and ideological, that is, other mothers and the ideal SET professional. Low sense of entitlement was often reflected in willingness to condense a full-time workload in shorter hours, working at home or in the evenings to maintain productivity and for less pay, particularly in the French companies. This work intensification and financial penalty was understood as normative and an acceptable compromise, as Marie, for example, describes:

> *I asked to work three days a week and my boss asked me "are you sure you can make it?", so it was a bit of a challenge. Working three days a week, they could have given me a different job with less responsibilities, less autonomy. So I said "I work three days a week, I keep the project and I'll manage to make things work"*

Yet despite greater efficiency in managing her workload, she, like most participants, believed that her part-time status would stall her career.

> *I want to do some management...., but I know I can't ask for [promotion] while working three days a week.*

The men in the two French companies were also entitled to reduce working hours. However, while some men worked 4 days a week in one company all reported that this was for reasons other than childcare and men interviewed in the other company did not feel entitled to take this option. For example, Pierre, although describing himself as a very involved father, explained:

> *It's not in the culture. There are two women in my team who work four days a week, but I don't know any man who does the same....[...] it's also possible to work at home one day a week but men just don't. But it's not even discussed..... If I had the opportunity to work one day at home, I could be ok, but if I had the possibility to work only four days I wouldn't do it. [...] Because I don't have the time in five days to do everything I have to do. I'm not sure if I'm fully efficient.... and working four days would be even more complicated for me.*

Pierre considered it neither normative for fathers to reduce working hours, nor feasible given his workload. He compared himself with other fathers and not with the mothers in his team, who, he acknowledged, organized their work differently.

Even mothers working full-time largely accepted that their reduced visibility relative to male colleagues' would limit their progression potential, as Lisette a French engineer explains:

> It's true that if you work like a man, with the same hours and the same commitment, you can be promoted. But when you have a family, you can choose to spend more time with them, and when I say more time it's not a lot of time, it just means that you don't go back home at 8pm, which is quite late for me. In this case, I don't think you can get the same position that men get. [I leave work] between 7 pm and 7.30 pm, and I start here at 8.30 am

While there were a number of women managers at mid management level in all of the companies, there were few visible as role models in senior management, limiting social comparators for sustainable part time careers. This was most acute in the Italian company with no visible senior women to challenge the established male culture. Nevertheless, awareness of how this is culturally constructed offers the possibility for social comparisons and change, as Sophia an engineer at the Italian company observes:

> at the higher positions there are only men. It's true that also [women] started to be a considerable number just in recent years so maybe it's for the future generation, now there are more women in the company. There are older women in the company but they didn't get into management. It will start to be a common problem, someone needs to break through. In other companies (not in Italy) there are women higher up

Sustainable Careers after Motherhood

All the participating companies were motivated by the wish to gain competitive edge by improving retention and development of talented women scientists and engineers. Yet we have seen that it can be difficult to maintain a sense of entitlement to both a sustainable career and culturally acceptable models of motherhood in these companies. Below we discuss three mothers at mid career who despite a period of part-time work progressed into senior management, exceptionally sustaining both career and family life, and we explore some conditions under which this can occur even without other successful women as social comparators. These critical cases are selected because they appeared to be less likely than others to accept trade-offs. However, they also illustrate the complex and dynamic processes involved.

Tineke, one of the first woman engineers in the Dutch company 20 years ago, and now in a senior role, was proud of her achievements. In the absence of female senior role models, she cited her social comparators as male colleagues

> I think you have to be realistic, if I compare myself to male colleagues who joined at the same time, I've done pretty well. A lot of them haven't and never will reach the level that I've got.

Tineke worked part-time since her children were born and her husband also worked reduced hours. In the Dutch context with widespread part-time work she had a clear sense of entitlement to work reduced hours, although in her company she was among the first engineers to do so. The national cultural context provided a counterbalance to the predominant organizational culture. Rather than trading-off career for reduced hours she believed her part-time status had a positive effect on her image within the company. Although she achieved that through being highly organized and with some work intensification, the possibility of a sustained career gradually appeared more feasible.

> *I saw [that] people admired me a lot because they couldn't understand how I could cope with the work and the kids. And I think that it also had like a positive effect on my career progression because people were quite surprised with what I was still able to do in three days a week. And also I became more effective, more selective, not attending meetings where my presence was not really necessary. So I think it helped me to get promotions.*

Later she became a single parent and she had to rethink the feasibility of a sustained career. However, the company's supportive attitude and willingness to offer flexible work solutions continued and she was able to negotiate a change in career direction in order to secure a job closer to home. Yet despite company support and her strong track record and esteem within the company Tineke seemed ambivalent about her entitlement to modify work for childcare and she endeavored to keep her childcare commitments as invisible as possible.

> *I just have recurring appointments at a certain time and I'm not going to put in that I have to collect my children. I refused a meeting, I've got an appointment, not everybody has to see that I'm leaving at that time because of my children.*

Although Tineke viewed her career experience and progression as successful she still framed it as exceptional and fortunate given the prevailing belief within the company that career success requires continuous full-time work. It seems that a combination of the perception of reduced hours as normative in the national, although not the workplace context, support from her husband in the early years of parenting, and her determination to demonstrate that her ability and commitment were not compromised by part-time hours, which in turn elicited support from management, helped her to maintain a view that career progression, though not normative, was feasible even given difficult life circumstances.

Soraya, originally from North Africa but working in Italy, also viewed her trajectory as exceptional. She became a mother at the age of 37 when her career was already well established. This may have accounted for the strong support she experienced after maternity leave.

> *when I came back from the leave after a few months I had a salary increase to give me the power and to restart again. They told me that this was not common*

The company helped her accommodate her family commitments by enabling flexible working, reducing the need for travel, and facilitating remote working.

> *In a year and a half I travelled only 3 times and my boss he understands this and he told me that if it's not strictly necessary we can manage with video conferences I can manage everything. . . . . So I can work also two hours today and ten hours tomorrow. . . . we use a lot of video conferences and teleconferences and online meetings – I stay till 7 o'clock when its needed but when it is not then no. I have the mobile PC at home so I can work at home. On Sunday I worked at home when my son was sleeping and when I am sick [if] we have something to do I will still work at home.*

These arrangements contributed to her ability to progress to a senior level. She and her manager displayed mutual flexibility and like Tineke she also worked hard to communicate her dedication. Thus she was able to work reduced hours and flexibly until her son started school. Her line manager, in enabling her flexible and remote work, gave her a strong message about her continued value to the company and boosted her own sense of entitlement to her career success. Nevertheless, there were contradictory messages about her potential to continue to rise to senior management, signaled by the total lack of senior women role models in the company, which caused her to adopt self-limiting beliefs.

Helene, a French mother of three also managed to demonstrate her efficiency while working reduced hours, earning the support of her manager. Her recent promotion to Deputy Director of her large research department led her to return to full-time work after many years working on a part-time contract. She explained that prior to her change of job:

> *I worked less, very much less. I never worked at home, or perhaps one evening in the week only . . . . and my manager at this time was a man, and he always said that I was very efficient and he encouraged me take the job of Deputy Director because he said that you are efficient and you will manage to do that job with your family*

The attitude of her manager before she was promoted was important, as it was clear from other participants that not all line managers recognized the greater efficiency of mothers condensing their work into 4 days. Also, she worked in research and development and the nature of the work may have lent itself more easily to flexible working than other SET jobs. This together with the fact that her new manager was a woman contributed to her belief that a sustainable career after reduced hours work was feasible and might even become normative. In her case the challenge was to convince senior colleagues of her ability, again by demonstrating commitment in ways congruent with the ideal worker model.

> *I had to work with the director of [the company], who is very likely to set the meeting early in the morning, and at the beginning I said to my husband I have to be available for this meeting. It's the first time I work with this man, I had to be available . . . .he wanted me to be at the meeting at 8 o'clock and I tried to say, not possible for me, and he said, no you have to be, you have to be. So I make a big effort to be at the meeting. And after two or three weeks, he saw that I was answering all his questions and I was doing the job he asked*

me and I begin to say 'I can't be here on the next morning', 'ok no problem'....... When people are confident in your job, they accept that you are less available

In all three of the above cases, career success (indicated by ability to progress to senior levels) was achieved with strong intervention and encouragement from the company, in providing reduced hours and flexible working options where necessary in response to changing family circumstances over time. Mothers' sense of entitlement was facilitated and fostered by supportive managers, while individual solutions were framed within national contextual norms. Thus for Helene and Tineke, working part-time for a number of years was congruent with normative expectations of motherhood within French and Dutch national cultures, yet did not hamper their own career motivation and aspirations for promotion and career sustainability. They were able to intensify or decrease their working hours at different periods of their lives to accommodate changed circumstances. In Soraya's case where part-time working was less nationally acceptable, her career sustainability was achieved through technologically facilitated work flexibility. However, all had to work hard to prove they could "do it all."

Discussion

This article extends previous research on motherhood and SET and work–family issues more broadly, in three ways. First, while previous research tended to take either an individual or a contextual approach to understanding the leaky pipeline in SET, we combine the two by using sense of entitlement as a conceptual lens, based on social comparison theory to understand the career decisions and trade-offs made by these mothers (but rarely fathers) in diverse SET contexts. Second, we extend the body of contextual research by examining accounts of mothers (and some fathers) in SET in four organizations in three European national contexts varying in social policy and cultural norms. We do not make claims about how representative participants' perspectives are of broader national opinions and beliefs. Rather, the qualitative approach illustrates how individuals used their own perceptions of normative values and cultures to understand and make sense of their particular life and career choices and their consequences. Third, we address one of the potential limitations of a social comparison theory approach, that is the neglect of trailblazers who can provide new social comparators, by exploring the conditions under which some women were able to advance in their careers without adopting traditional male career trajectories or feeling they have compromised their time for care.

The findings show that career decisions after becoming a mother, and sense of entitlement to support for career and family roles, are strongly influenced by intersecting layers of national and workplace policy and normative context that shape what individual mothers perceive to be normative, feasible, and acceptable.

However, despite contextual differences our main overall finding is that the evolution of mothers' perceived entitlements to be able to modify work for family reasons is rarely combined with a sense of entitlement to sustain career progression. This is a major stumbling block to mothers' career progression across the national contexts. Nevertheless, a minority of women scientists and engineers are able to modify work for family reasons without accruing career penalties. This seems to be facilitated by interrelated contextual and individual factors, as discussed later.

Entitlements and Norms Shaping Career Decisions

Research on work and family and organizational processes are increasingly criticized for the neglect of context (Bamberger, 2008; Powell et al., 2009), particularly cultural workplace and national beliefs and norms and national institutional factors. In this article we demonstrate that scientists and engineers in European companies, who are also mothers, make career-related decisions on the basis of both objective and subjective entitlements and cultural norms and that there are both similarities and differences across contexts.

The most fundamental influence on new mothers' decision making are norms of motherhood which both reflect ideology of the good mother and also underpin national social policy relating to employed mothers. Our data show that all the mothers engage with these norms whether they decide to reject or conform to them in some way. Gendered assumptions about mothers as the main carers and conflicting assumptions about ideal workers who are constantly available at work prevailed in all the companies, albeit with some differences in dynamics. For example, although the notion of the employed mother is embedded in French social policy and the French mothers have an infrastructure of support to enable them to sustain jobs, they are also aware of strong pressures to be the main carers in most cases. The same is true of mothers in the Dutch and Italian companies, although the Dutch women interviewed appeared to have more sense of entitlement to partner support which could influence their career decisions.

Contextual factors and subjective, individual processes influence the ways in which mothers make sense of and reconcile competing social directives regarding ideal SET professionals and mothers and consequent career decisions. Contextual factors include the nature of work. Mothers' decisions to reduce working hours were somewhat easier in desk or laboratory based jobs than in roles requiring frequent overseas travel. Structural support include the availability of childcare (public or, in Italy, family based) for part time or full time work, family leaves, and especially the availability of part time work. Where part-time or reduced hours work is available and normative (in the Netherlands and the French companies) this enabled women to adopt a social practice that satisfies personal and societal ideologies of the good mother, albeit not the ideal worker. Other mothers in these contexts and in the Italian context, where the part time route was not available, redefined this ideal by working full time but reducing the expected extra hours.

These contextual factors influence sense of entitlement to support and yet there are individual differences in career-related decisions and trajectories which can be related to social comparison processes. Social comparators feeding into sense of entitlement to work less and/or progress in careers are both actual and ideological. Mothers usually compared themselves with other mothers in their company and/or country in terms of hours worked which reproduced normative patterns. However, SET professionals in international companies are often required to undertake overseas assignments. Those who have worked in other countries observed variations in ideologies of motherhood and work and the feasibility of different support available to employed mothers. Thus wider social comparisons helped them to articulate the socially constructed nature of work and family ideals and contributed to enhanced sense of entitlement to support for career and motherhood. However in terms of entitlement to career progression, available social comparators were those who advanced in their careers; predominantly men who conformed to the male ideal worker norm. With few if any role models of men or women who progressed in their careers despite reducing working hours when children are young, this was widely perceived as neither normative nor feasible. Supports that enable mothers to work in ways that are compatible with family life continue to be largely regarded as favors that must be reciprocated by tradeoffs in career terms. It is clear that gendered organizational assumptions about the need for continuous full-time career trajectories, visibility and availability and a career-primary focus which inherently conflicts with motherhood ideology are the major barriers to mothers' sense of entitlement to modify working hours and sustain careers. This is often so even when workloads are condensed rather than reduced, so it is visibility and availability rather than work output that are decisive. Furthermore, given the limited progression of mothers who worked full-time but without excess time beyond contracted hours, part-time work per se cannot fully account for mothers' stalled careers across the contexts and the possibility of motherhood status (Ridgeway & Correll, 2004) contributing to the leaky pipeline cannot be ruled out.

Conditions under Which Some Women Are Able to Advance Their Careers

While differentiation can be made between objective and subjective definitions of career success (see, for example, Hall, Lee, Kossek, & Las Heras, 2012), this study has focused on objective criteria associated with career progression such as promotions. No simple recipe emerged for enhancing mothers' sense of entitlement to and actual career advancement after part-time work. However, various combinations of contextual and personal factors emerged from the cases of trailblazing mothers. In terms of individual processes these women were more likely than others to use male social comparators and expect similar career progression or to compare themselves with other women but focus on the (financial) benefits of mothers' careers to families, redefining good mothering. Partner support was also important both practically and also symbolically in the rejection of the norm of mother as main carer. Strategic approaches to "proving themselves" also helped, for example, becoming a mother later or demonstrating efficiency by traditional work patterns before asking to work less. This usually resulted in an intensification of work, but was regarded as an acceptable trade off. Nevertheless women's agency is limited by contextual factors. Other mothers also worked intensively to accomplish more in less time but their efficiency was not recognized by managers. The most important contextual factor appeared to be support and encouragement from management in communicating confidence in individual mothers and the feasibility of combining reduced hours and career progress. The availability of flexible or part time hours is important, but not sufficient without management supportiveness. In Italy where the option of part time work was not available, extended family plays a substantial role in childcare reducing the guilt sometimes associated elsewhere with substitute childcare.

Sense of entitlement is not static but reflects shifting contexts that provide new social comparators as illustrated by the evolving expectations of father involvement in care described by Dutch participants. As more mothers in SET organizations achieve career advancement despite periods of reduced working hours this could be reflected in a greater sense of entitlement for women scientists and engineers and perhaps also more men to sustain parenthood and developmental careers. However, the evidence from this study suggests that women who are able to do this tend to be regarded as exceptional rather than normative. In that case other mothers who compare themselves with high achieving women and do not define themselves as exceptional may feel less entitled to try to for similar outcomes.

Limitations and Implications for Further Research

While the study was qualitative and therefore seeking theory developments rather than generalizations, it is limited to some extent by the range of participants in terms of gender, sector and nationality. First, the number of fathers interviewed was very small. Although findings are congruent with other research on fathers' careers (Hobson & Fahlén, 2009) this restricts understanding of how mothers and fathers' sense of entitlement varies and informs decision making. There were some indications of changes in men's decisions on working hours, largely through accounts of partners' behaviors. Future research focusing specifically on the minority of men who reduce working hours in SET either formally or informally would help to understand whether there are shifts and if so how this comes about. Second, further research in other countries could help to understand the relationship between national contexts such as welfare systems, normative gender assumptions about parenthood, and career progression and potential in SET occupations. Finally, more in-depth research highlighting the differences between different SET sectors, occupations, and indeed departments and functions within individual companies would add valuable understanding of how gendered cultures are perpetuated despite the good intentions of many SET employers.

Implications for Practice

Employer recognition of the need to develop and retain talented women has become increasingly important, supported by the so-called business case for diversity. All the participating organizations in this study were concerned to retain talented women and remove barriers to their advancement, but gendered assumptions about ideal workers that conflict with parenting commitments and expectations still prevailed.

The mothers in this study valued both the careers for which they were highly trained and also motherhood. Strong attachment to their professional identities is not surprising given their considerable investment in their human capital to reach their current positions as professional scientists and engineers, and often having had to fight entrenched gender stereotypes to prove that women could do these jobs well. However the parents are actors in social contexts where, to varying degrees, flourishing in family roles is constructed as being at the expense of career roles and vice versa. This has implications for the sustainability of SET companies and of families. Organizations must recognize that well-intentioned work–life policies are not in themselves sufficient to change entrenched values. We have seen the vital role of sensitive and creative approaches by line managers in our three examples of sustainable careers. Companies should ensure that training is given to those decision makers who are in a position to challenge stereotypical views and assumptions about mothers. Furthermore, senior role models working part time and progressing (both men and women) should be made more visible to foster a greater sense of entitlement to sustainability of careers and caring roles.

References

Acker, J. (1990). Hierarchies, jobs, bodies: A theory of gendered organizations. *Gender & Society*, 4, 139–158. doi:10.1177/089124390004002002.
Ackers, L. (2004). Managing relationships in peripatetic careers: Scientific mobility in the European Union. *Women's Studies International Forum*, 27, 189–201. doi:10.1016/j.wsif.2004.03.001.
Bailyn, L. (2006). *Breaking the mold: Redesigning work for productive and satisfying lives.* Ithaca and London: ILR Press.
Bamberger, P. (2008). Beyond contextualization: Using context theories to narrow the micro-macro gap in management research. *Academy of Management Journal*, 51, 839–846.

Barnard, S., Powell, A., Bagilhole, B., & Dainty, A. (2010). Researching UK women professionals in SET: A critical review of current approaches. *International Journal of Gender Science and Technology*, 2, 361–381. Retrieved February 14, 2011, from http://genderandset.open.ac.uk/index.php/genderandset/article/view/65/175.

Blair-Loy, M (2003). *Competing devotions: Career and family among women executives.* Cambridge, MA: Harvard University Press.

Blickenstaff, J. C. (2005). Women and science careers: Leaky pipeline or gender filter? *Gender and Education*, 17, 369–386. doi:10.1080/09540250500145072.

Budig, M. J., & Hodges, M. J. (2010). Differences in disadvantage. Variation in the motherhood penalty across white women's earnings distribution. *American Sociological Review*, 75, 705–728. doi:10.1177/0003122410381593.

Bylsma, W. H., & Major, B. (1994). Social comparisons and contentment: Exploring the psychological costs of the gender wage gap. *Psychology of Women Quarterly*, 18, 241–249.

Correll, S. J., Benard, B., & Paik, I. (2007). Getting a job. Is there a motherhood penalty? *American Journal of Sociology*, 112(5), 1297–1338. doi:10.1086/511799.

Cousins, C., & Tang, N. (2004). Working time and work and family conflict in the Netherlands, Sweden and the UK. *Work Employment & Society*, 18, 531–549. doi:10.1177/0950017004045549.

Cross, C., & Linehan, M. (2006). Barriers to advancing female careers in the high-tech sector: Empirical evidence from Ireland. *Women in Management Review*, 21, 28–39. doi:10.1108/09649420610643394.

Del Boca, D., Locatelli, M., & Vuri, D. (2005). Child-care choices by working mothers: The case of Italy. *Review of Economics of the Household*, 3, 453–477. doi:10.1007/s11150-005-4944-y.

Den Dulk, L., & Van Doorne-Huiskes, A. (2007). Social policy in Europe: Its impact on work and family. In R. Crompton, S. Lewis, & C. Lyonette (Eds.), *Women, men, work and family in Europe*. Houndmills: Palgrave Macmillan.

European Commission (2006). *Women in science and technology–The business perspective*. Luxembourg: European Commission–Office for Official Publications of the European Communities. Retrieved February 14, 2011, from http://ec.europa.eu/research/science-society/pdf/wist_report_final_en.pdf.

European Commission (2009). *Women in science and technology: Creating sustainable careers*. Brussels: European Commission, DG Science, Economy and Society. doi:10.2777/57428. Retrieved October 10, 2012, from http://ec.europa.eu/research/science-society/document_library/pdf_06/wist2_sustainable-careers-report_en.pdf.

Fagnani, J. (2009). Childcare policies in France: The influence of organizational changes in the workplace. In S. Kamerman, S. Phipps, & A. Ben-Arieh (Eds.), *From child welfare to child well-being: An international perspective on knowledge in the service of making policy* (pp. 385–402). Child Indicators Research book series, Vol. 1, Dordrecht, Netherlands: Springer.

Faulkner, W. (2009). Doing gender in engineering workplace cultures: Part II–Gender in/authenticity and the in/visibility paradox. *Engineering Studies*, 1, 169–189. doi:10.1080/19378620903225059.

Gephart, R. (2004). Qualitative research and the Academy of Management Journal. *Academy of Management Journal*, 47, 454–462.

Hakim C. (2002). Lifestyle preferences as determinants of women's differentiated labour market careers. *Work and Occupations*, 29, 428–459. doi:10.1177/0730888402029004003.

Hall, D. T., Lee, M. D., Kossek, E. E., & Las Heras, M. (2012). Pursuing career success while sustaining personal and family well-being: A study of reduced-load professionals over time. *Journal of Social Issues*, 68(4), 742–766.

Hantrais, L., & Ackers, P. (2005). Women's choices in Europe: Striking the work-life balance. *European Journal of Industrial Relations*, 11, 197–212. doi:10.1177/0959680105053963.

Herman, C. (2009). Paying the price: The impact of maternity on career progression of women scientists and engineers in Europe. In S. Ihsen, J. Klumpers, S. Pageler, R. Ulrich, & B. Wieneke-Toutaoui. (Eds.), *Gender and diversity in engineering and science* (Report 39) VDI, Dusseldorf.

Herman C., Lewis, S., & Humbert A. L. (2012). Women scientists and engineers in European companies: Putting motherhood under the microscope. *Gender, Work and Organization*, doi:10.1111/j.1468-0432.2012.00596.x.

Hewlett, S., Buck Luce, C., Servon, L., Sherbin, L., Shiller, P., Sosnovich, E., & Sumberg K. (2008). The Athena factor: Reversing the brain drain in science, engineering, and technology. *Harvard Business Review Research Report*. Boston: Harvard Business Publishing.

Hobson, B., & Fahlén, T. (2009). Competing scenarios for European fathers. Applying Sen's capabilities and agency framework to work-family balance. *The ANNALS of the American Academy Political and Social Sciences, 624*, 214–233.

Holt, H., & Lewis, S. (2011). You can stand on your head and you still end up with lower pay: Gliding segregation and gendered work practices in Danish 'Family-friendly' workplaces. *Gender, Work & Organisation, 18*, e202–e221. doi: 10.1111/j.1468-0432.2009.00501.x.

Kangas, O., & Rostaard, T. (2007). Preferences or institutions? Work-family life opportunities in seven European countries. *Journal of European Social Policy, 17*, 240–256. doi:10.1177/0958928707078367.

Kelliher, C., & Anderson, D. (2010). Doing more with less? Flexible working practices and the intensification of work. *Human Relations, 63*, 83–106. doi:10.1177/0018726709349199.

Lerner, M. J. (1987). Integrating societal and psychological rules of entitlement: The basic task of each social actor and fundamental problem for the social sciences. *Social Justice Research, 1*, 107–125. doi:10.1007/BF01049386.

Lewis, S. (1991). Motherhood and/or employment. In A. Phoenix, A. Woollett, & E. Lloyd (Eds.), *Motherhood: Meanings, practices and ideologies*. London: Sage.

Lewis, S. (2010). Reflecting on impact, changes and continuities. Restructuring workplace cultures: The ultimate work-family challenge? *Gender in Management, 25*, 348–354. doi:10.1108/17542411011056859.

Lewis, S., Gambles, R., & Rapoport, R. (2007). The constraints of a 'work-life balance' approach: An international perspective. *International Journal of Human Resource Management, 18*(3), 360–373, doi:10.1080/09585190601165577.

Lewis, S., & Haas, L. (2005). Work-life integration and social policy: A social justice theory and gender equity approach to work and family. In E. Kossek & S. Lambert (Eds.), *Work and life integration: Organizational, cultural and individual perspectives* (pp. 349–374). Mahwah, NJ: LEA.

Lewis, S., & Humbert, A. (2010). Discourse or reality? "Work-life balance", flexible working policies and gendered organisations. *Equal Opportunities International, 29*, 239–254. doi:10.1108/02610151011028840.

Lewis, S., Kagan, C., & Heaton, P. (2000). Dual earner parents with disabled children. Patterns for working and caring. *Journal of Family Issues, 21*, 1031–1060. doi:10.1177/019251300021008005.

Lewis, S., & Smithson, J. (2001). Sense of entitlement to support for the reconciliation of employment and family life. *Human Relations, 54*, 1455–1481 doi:10.1177/00187267015411003.

Major, B. (1993). Gender, entitlement, and the distribution of family labor. *Journal of Social Issues, 49*(3), 141–159. doi:10.1111/j.1540-4560.1993.tb01173.x.

Miller, G. (2004). Frontier masculinity in the oil industry: The experience of women engineers. *Gender, Work & Organization, 11*, 47–73. doi:10.1111/j.1468-0432.2004.00220.x.

Okimoto, T. G., & Heilman, M. E. (2012). The "bad parent" assumption: How gender stereotypes affect reactions to working mothers. *Journal of Social Issues, 68*(4), 704–724.

Powell, G. N., Francesco, A. M., & Ling, Y. (2009). Towards culture sensitive theories of the work-family interface. *Journal of Organizational Behavior, 30*, 597–616.

Ranson, G. (2005). No longer "one of the boys": Negotiations with motherhood, as prospect or reality, among women in engineering. *Canadian Review of Sociology & Anthropology, 42*, 145–166.

Rapoport, R., Bailyn, L., Fletcher, J. K., & Pruitt, B. H. (2002). *Beyond work-family balance: Advancing gender equity and workplace performance*. San Francisco, CA: Jossey-Bass.

Ridgeway, C. L., & Correll, S. J. (2004). Motherhood as a status characteristic. *Journal of Social Issues, 60*(4), 683–700. doi:10.1111/j.0022-4537.2004.00380.x.

Vinkenburg, C. J., Van Engen, M. L., Coffeng, J., & Dikkers, J. S. E. (2012). Bias in employment decisions about mothers and fathers: The (dis)advantages of sharing care responsibilities. *Journal of Social Issues, 68*(4), 725–741.

Webber, C., & Williams, C. (2008). Mothers in "good" and "bad" part time jobs. *Gender and Society, 22*, 752–777. doi:10.1177/0891243208325698.

CLEM HERMAN is Senior Lecturer in Communication and Systems at *The Open University*. She has worked for over 25 years as an educator, practitioner, and researcher to support women in ICT and other science, engineering, and technology sectors. She is the founding editor of the *International Journal of Gender Science and Technology*.

SUZAN LEWIS is Professor of Organisational Psychology at Middlesex University Business School. Her research focuses on work–personal life issues and workplace practice, culture and change, in diverse national contexts. She is a founding editor of the international journal *Community, Work and Family*.

Work–Family Conflict in Sri Lanka: Negotiations of Exchange Relationships in Family and at Work

Pavithra Kailasapathy[*]
University of Colombo

Isabel Metz
Melbourne Business School

This study's aim is to understand how individuals who are part of dual-earner couples experience and deal with work–family conflict in Sri Lanka. Twenty-five interviews were conducted to identify if and how couples negotiated within their marital relationships, and between themselves and their supervisors, to reduce or cope with work–family conflict. The interviews indicated that negotiations at home and at work concerned contributions to the exchange relationship and were unlikely to adversely affect the (home or work) exchange relationships. Negotiations at home were more likely to be initiated by women than men. Further, the interviews revealed an influence of spouse's gender role ideology on the success of the negotiation at home. Negotiations at work were more likely to be initiated by the interviewees than by their supervisors. The results suggest that individuals in cultures with high power distance should still initiate negotiations when they feel it is possible to obtain favorable outcomes.

Introduction

With the increase in dual-earner couples, conflict and balance between family and work lives have become important issues for families and organizations. Using social exchange and conflict theories, we explored in this study if and how individuals reorganized two exchange relationships, leader-member exchange and partner exchange, to reduce or cope with work–family conflict (WFC). Manageable WFC

---

[*]Correspondence concerning this article should be addressed to Department of Human Resources Management, Faculty of Management & Finance, University of Colombo, Colombo 03, Sri Lanka [e-mail: pavithra@fmf.cmb.ac.lk].

allows individuals to combine work and care. Leader–member exchange is defined as the quality of the relationship shared by a supervisor and a subordinate (Dienesch & Liden, 1986). Based on the leader–member exchange literature and definition, we defined a parallel concept in the family sphere—"partner exchange"—as the quality of the exchange relationship between spouses/partners. Exchange relationship can be defined as the relationship between two people where one expects rewards or profits, in the form of resources, proportional to costs or investment. Such relationships evolve over time into trusting, loyal and mutual commitments. An individual's relationship with important others, such as a partner/spouse, is argued to be essential for understanding WFC (e.g., Parasuraman & Greenhaus, 2002). The relationship with the supervisor can also be an important factor in this understanding (Casper, Eby, Bordeaux, Lockwood, & Lambert, 2007). Further, most WFC research has been conducted in Western cultures. However, due to globalization and workforce mobility there is a growing need to understand WFC in non-Western cultures.

This study's overarching aim, therefore, is to understand how dual-earner couples experience and deal with WFC in a non-Western culture, such as Sri Lanka. As a result, one contribution of this study to the WFC literature is the extension of WFC research and social exchange theory to a non-Western culture. A second contribution is a more fine-grained understanding of dual-earner couples' experiences of WFC and their negotiation of exchange relationships to reduce that conflict. A third contribution of this study is the finding that the extended family serves as a "work–family arrangement" for Sri Lankan dual-earner couples, something not found in most Western cultures.

Reorganization of Exchange Relationships

Individuals utilize various strategies to cope with or reduce the conflict and stress derived from their work and family lives (Fogarty, Machin, Albion, Sutherland, Lalor, & Revitt, 1999; Moore & Gobi, 1995; Quick, Henley, & Quick, 2004). Negotiation is one such strategy. Negotiations of relationships at home and at work are forms of structural role redefinition (Hall, 1972). Structural role redefinition is "to confront one's role senders and come to mutual agreement on a revised set of expectations" (Hall, 1972, p. 474). An example is a woman who negotiates with her employer to finish work early so that she can be home when her children arrive from school. Other examples are rescheduling home activities that clash with work activities (Powell & Greenhaus, 2006) and the reallocation and sharing of one's role tasks, such as cleaning, washing, and child care, with one's spouse. According to Hall (1972), the critical feature of these structural redefinition approaches is that they all involve dealing directly with environmental transmitters of the structurally imposed demands, actively attempting to alter (reduce, reallocate, reschedule, and so forth) these demands and coming to an agreement with the role senders on a new set of expectations (p. 474).

Reorganization of an exchange relationship can occur within the exchange relationship or by leaving the exchange (Rank & LeCroy, 1983; Sprey, 1979). It is reasonable to assume that individuals will attempt to reorganize relationships in order to cope with or reduce their WFC before deciding to leave the exchange relationship (e.g., separation or divorce). Reorganization of the exchange relationships requires that individuals negotiate with the other party (in this case, the spouse or the supervisor). Negotiation facilitates the solving of problems by people. The negotiation process is invoked by two or more people attempting to make joint decisions when their initial preferences differ (Kossek, Noe, & DeMarr, 1999). It is assumed that the people involved in the dispute best know the facts, so the eventual resolution of the dispute will reflect the parties' actual needs and priorities (Roberson, 2006). When there is commitment toward the exchange relationship, the two parties are most likely to resort to negotiation to solve the problem and arrive at a win-win solution (Lin & Miller, 2003). Thus, reorganization of exchange relationships is expected to be a characteristic of whatever strategy dual-earner couples use to reduce their WFC (Rank & LeCroy, 1983).

To reduce WFC, individuals may negotiate their roles within exchange relationships at either home or at work. At home, one aspect that individuals may negotiate in the partner exchange is the allocation of household responsibilities. Research has shown that women's full-time employment and higher income have an effect on the division of household work, such that there is a trend toward an egalitarian gender division of household work (bargaining power theory or resource theory) (Strober & Chan, 1998). This effect on the division of family responsibilities is due to women's greater bargaining power in negotiating the sharing of household work with their spouses (Fuwa & Cohen, 2007; Mannino & Deutsch, 2007; Standh & Nordenmark, 2006). A country's social policies with regard to gender equality at work (such as affirmative action, antidiscrimination policy, parental leave, and child care facilities) also influence women's bargaining power to negotiate household work with their spouses and gender equality at home (Fuwa & Cohen, 2007). For example, the provision of child care facilities by the State reduces the child care burden of women and the use of parental leave by both parents encourages sharing of household and child care work. Similarly at work, employees may negotiate the relationships with their supervisors (leader–member exchange). For example, an employee might negotiate working hours (e.g., start time and/or finish time), responsibilities, and working conditions.

With regard to social exchange relationships, Liden and Maslyn (1998) define leader–member exchange in terms of four dimensions: affect, loyalty, contribution and professional respect. In a high quality exchange relationship, leaders and members show mutual affection, express public support for one another, contribute efforts to help one another achieve work goals, and demonstrate respect for each other's professional accomplishments (Liden & Maslyn, 1998). According to leader–member exchange theory, supervisors treat their employees differently in line with the quality of their relationship (Dienesch & Liden, 1986). This differential treatment might include flexible work schedules or other changes to work priorities to help balance work and family (Carlson & Perrewé, 1999; Dienesch & Liden, 1986). Following the leader–member exchange construct, we further define partner exchange in terms of affect, loyalty, contribution, and respect within the dyad. In partner exchange relationships, "affect" can be seen as the mutual affection spouses have for each other based primarily on interpersonal attraction. "Loyalty" can be seen as the expression of public support for one's partner. It also requires faithfulness to the partner. "Contribution" is proposed to be the perception of the current level of household-oriented activity each partner puts forth toward the (explicit or implicit) mutual goals of the family. "Respect" is proposed to be admiration of one's partner as a good human being, for the qualities and characteristics she or he possesses (that is, the positive perception of the total person). These four dimensions combined constitute partner exchange.

Finally, a person who values a traditional gender role ideology will abide by cultural traditions and expectations of family and gender roles. The traditional gender role ideology identifies specific and distinct roles for men and women in marriage, such that the husband should be the head of the family and the wife should be submissive (Denton, 2004). The male partner who values traditional gender roles will expect the female to follow traditional wife and mother roles. In contrast, when male partners do not value a traditional gender role ideology, they provide domestic support to their female partners. Our theoretical rationale is supported by past research. Research shows that husbands with a nontraditional gender role ideology are more supportive of their wives' employment than are husbands with a traditional gender role ideology. Such husbands do somewhat more housework and child care, and share decision-making power more readily (Amato & Booth, 1995; Scanzoni & Szinovacz, 1980). Therefore, the male spouse's gender role ideology is likely to influence the negotiation of domestic duties between a dual-earner couple.

To our knowledge, no studies have been conducted to examine the reorganization of the exchange relationships between a focal person and his/her spouse (partner exchange), and between a focal person and his/her supervisor (leader–member exchange) in an Eastern culture. All studies to date on the division of work and care use Western samples or participants (e.g., Mannino & Deutsch, 2007). Further, some of the existing literature is based on experimental design (e.g., Kluwer, Heesink, & van de Vliert, 2000). Hence, this study is exploratory and aims to understand the ways in which individuals in an Eastern culture reorganized their exchange relationships (with partners and supervisors) in an attempt to reduce WFC.

In the next section, we describe the research methodology, data source, interview sample and results of this study. We conclude with a discussion of the results, practical implications, this study's limitations, and recommendations for future research.

Method

Research Site: Sri Lanka

Sri Lanka is rich in its diversity of culture, race, language and religion. It has a recorded history spanning over 2,500 years, which explains how Sri Lankan society and culture have been influenced by the traditional Indian civilization and culture, by the British and European colonial heritage and development policies, and by the strategies of post-independence governments. Sri Lankans display many Eastern characteristics in their family and social interactions (Chandrakumara, 2007), but are starting to demonstrate some Western influence (Nanayakkara, 1992). For example, Sri Lankan society is slowly changing in relation to attitudes toward women. It is becoming acceptable for married women to work outside their homes, but women are still expected to have the full or primary responsibility for child care and housework even if they undertake paid work outside their homes (Jawahir, 1992). Further, "culture-bound assumptions about the sanctity of marriage and the woman's responsibility to her family are nourished and sustained by religious ethics, moral codes and traditions which help promote an ideology of male dominance" (Dias, 1990, p. 220). Although Sri Lankans exhibit many Eastern traits in family and other social interactions, at work these traits tend to be mixed with Western philosophies and practices. For example, Nanayakkara (1992) noted that many Sri Lankan managers maintain high power distance and individualistic cultural traits (compared to many Western countries). Power distance is "the extent to which the less powerful members of institutions and organizations within a country expect and accept that power is distributed unequally" (Hofstede, 2001, p. 98). However, they tend to exhibit collective traits in familial and other social interactions (Chandrakumara & Budhwar, 2005). Thus, there is variance in values, beliefs and behavior, especially among Sri Lankans living in urban areas.

There is also variance in the country's legislative approach to women's rights and work practices. Sri Lanka's constitution guarantees equal rights to women. However, Sri Lanka has not ratified the International Labour Organization's (ILO) Convention 156 regarding equal opportunity and equal treatment in employment for men and women workers with family responsibilities (ILO, 2005). As a result, Sri Lankan organizations do not have policies to help reduce WFC. In particular, Sri Lankan labor laws and company policies are not family-friendly. For example, companies do not provide flexi-time and part-time options, or on-site child care or crèche facilities. Labor laws provide for paid maternity leave of only 84 working days for the first two childbirths and unpaid maternity leave is not available (Maternity Benefits Act of 1985). Further, discrimination, the "glass ceiling" and sexual harassment prevail (Wickramasinghe & Jayatilaka, 2006).

Data Source

This study was conducted as part of a larger study on WFC. Data were collected in the Spring of 2007 by surveying a large sample of dual-earner heterosexual couples who were employed full-time in Sri Lanka. Homosexual couples were excluded from the sample so as not to confound WFC issues with stressors associated with being a homosexual couple, such as coping with being treated differently and/or experiencing discrimination (Button, 2001; Hunt, 2002; Ragins & Cornwell, 2001). The sample of dual-earner couples is appropriate for the study of sustainability in combining career and care for three reasons. First, couples in which both partners work outside the home are increasingly common. Second, as van Veldhoven and Beijer's study (2012) show, men and women in dual-earner families experience higher levels of WFC than individuals in many other private life contexts (e.g., single men and women without children). Third, dual-earner couples allowed us to hear from individuals in a type of family unit that should incentivize both spouses/partners to work together toward combining dual careers and care in a sustainable manner. A total of 709 survey packets containing two questionnaires (one for the focal person and the other for her/his spouse) were distributed among managerial level employees and professionals in 42 private sector organizations in and around Colombo, Sri Lanka. Each organization's HR manager distributed the questionnaire among the managerial and professional staff through internal mail. Surveys were distributed only to individuals with a working spouse/partner. Each participant was asked to provide his/her spouse with the spousal questionnaire. Spouses were instructed to complete their questionnaire independently of the focal person. Gender role orientation was obtained from the spouse's survey; all other variables were measured on the focal employee's survey. The surveys were precoded to help match the focal person's and his/her spouse's surveys upon return.

Of the 709 surveys packets delivered, 226 (or 32%) were completed and returned. Of these 226 respondents, we obtained the matched spouse survey for 205 of them. The final sample size was 185 (for a 26.1% final response rate) employee–spouse dyads after deleting cases with missing data in relevant variables. The interviews were conducted with a subsample of the 185 dual-earner couples who participated in our larger study. Eighty-one (81) focal persons and 56 spouses volunteered to be interviewed. Among these volunteers, there were 38 matched couples. From these matched dual-earner couples, 13 (34%) couples met the selection criteria which was that both parties in the relationship (1) had to agree to be interviewed and (2) were among the dual-earner couples with the highest scores on the Carlson, Kacmar, and William's (2000) WFC scale. The cutoff point for selection of interviewees was at least one spouse should have work interference with family conflict (WIF; e.g., a meeting at work prevents an individual from picking up her/his child from school) and family interference with work conflict (FIW; e.g., a child's sickness prevents an individual from attending work) scores of 3 each (out of a maximum of 5). The second selection criterion was required to explore if and how individuals in such "couple" situations (i.e., individuals in dual-earner couples with conflict scores of at least 3 in a 5-point Likert scale) were reorganizing their relationships in an attempt to reduce WFC. In conclusion, we selected the couples that reported most WFC, because couples low on WFC are less likely to need to engage in renegotiations of the exchange. Therefore, the sampling technique was purposive, as recommended by Kuzel (1999).

Instrument and Procedure for Data Capture

We were unable to interview the spouse (the husband, as he had gone abroad on work) of one of the 13 dual-earner couples selected for this study. Hence, 25 interviews were conducted instead of 26. The first author conducted all 25 interviews in 2007 in Colombo, Sri Lanka. Nineteen interviews were done in person and six were conducted by telephone. We obtained written consent from the interviewees prior to the interviews. Twenty interviewees gave permission to digitally record their interviews. For the remaining five interviews, the interviewer noted the main points of the conversation during the meeting and wrote additional notes immediately after it. Interviews were conducted in a place convenient to the participants: at their workplace, in a public place (e.g., KFC), or in an office at the University of Colombo.

The interviews lasted on average half an hour; six interviews lasted between 45 minutes and 1 hour. A semistructured format was used to interview the participants. Each spouse was interviewed separately so that one spouse did not influence the other's answers. All interviews were conducted in English except for one, which was conducted in Sinhala. The first author was able to conduct this interview because she is sufficiently fluent in Sinhala. Furthermore, as the interviewee understood English (she was able to read and answer the survey), the first author was able to ask her questions in English. In turn, the interviewee answered the questions in Sinhala. The majority of the interviewees appeared to be candid in stating their opinions and experiences during the interviews. The interview commenced with four structured questions, two of which were identical to questions asked on the survey. The identical questions were "how long have you been married to your spouse?" and "how long have you been working under the current supervisor/manager?" The other two questions were about the individual's daily routine and whether she/he experienced stress as a result of combining work and family responsibilities. These four questions served two purposes: one as an ice-breaker and the other to check the answers obtained in the survey. There was 100% agreement in the answers for the two identical questions in the survey and the interview.

In the second part of the interview, the interviewer asked participants about the sources of stress at home and at work, the relationships with the spouse and the supervisor, any negotiations regarding workload at home and at work, and the consequence of such negotiations on their relationships. We focused on stress as an outcome or as an antecedent of WFC because past studies have found relationships between stress and WFC. For example, family role stressors and work role stressors, such as work–role conflict, have been found to be causes of WFC (Boyar, Maertz Jr., Pearson, & Keough, 2003; Kopelman, Greenhaus, & Connolly, 1983). Further, job stress is an antecedent to WIF conflict (Fox & Dwyer, 1999). Similarly, individuals have reported conflict between work and family roles because they experienced extensive stress in the work and family domains (Stoeva, Chiu, & Greenhaus, 2002). Judge, Boudreau, and Bretz Jr. (1994) found that conflict between work and family roles led to job stress. Some researchers consider WFC as a source of stress that influences an individual's well-being (e.g., Frone, Russell, & Cooper, 1992).

All interviews were transcribed verbatim in English, including the "ers," "uhs," and pauses (Miles & Huberman, 1994, p. 51). Word emphasis, incomplete sentences and grammatical errors as spoken by the interviewees were also included in the transcriptions. As the interviews were transcribed verbatim, the interview quotes reflect the fact that English was a second language for all the interviewees, as well as illustrating the prevalence of "Sri Lankan English" (Mendis, 2007). The "ers," "uhs," and pauses were omitted from the interview quotes included in this manuscript.

Sample Description

Of the 25 Sri Lankans interviewed, 13 were female and 12 were male. The average age of interviewees was 34.4 years (ranging from 26 to 51 years). The interviewees had been married for an average of 7.24 years (ranging from 6 months to 25 years) and they had been working for their current manager for an average of 39.15 months (ranging from 1.5 months to 16 years). Four of the 13 couples had no children.

The above descriptive data were obtained from the interviewees' surveys and interview data. Specifically, information on the interviewee (i.e., whether the interviewee is the focal person or the spouse) and on age were obtained from the surveys. Data on the number of years the respondents had been married for and the number of months under the current supervisor were obtained from the interview data (and cross-checked against the survey data).

Method of Analysis

All 25 text files of the transcriptions were imported into QSR NVivo 7 software package for analysis (Bazeley, 2007). After coding the main themes using the software, we manually coded the subthemes, given the manageable volume of data.

The qualitative data obtained through interviews were analyzed using an inductive approach (Braun & Clarke, 2006; Langley, 1999) and thematic analysis method (Braun & Clarke, 2006). Prior knowledge and theoretical concepts informed the interview protocol, but the themes and codes used to code the data were data-driven. Initially, we used themes based on the interview questions to code each interview. Then, transcripts were constantly compared to arrive at new themes and categories that reflected recurrent patterns (Braun & Clarke, 2006; Loscocco, 1997; Miles & Huberman, 1994). This is also known as the template organizing style of analysis (Crabtree & Miller, 1999). Thus, in the second stage of the analysis, new codes/themes were created to fit the themes that emerged. At each stage of coding we calculated the number of responses for the themes and subthemes.

With regard to the calculation of number of responses for subthemes, if an interviewee gave more than one example for a subtheme, we counted those examples as one response. However, if interviewees gave examples while elaborating on their experiences that fitted more than one subtheme, we counted each example as a separate response.

This research was conducted from a positivistic paradigm (Hatch, 2006). As a result, frequency counts and tabulations were employed in the analysis (Denzin & Lincoln, 2008). The analysis was performed at the *individual level* (regardless of whether the individual was a focal person or spouse), not at the couple level.

Reliability

We addressed the issue of reliability by using multiple coders (Duriau, Reger, & Pfarrer, 2007) and by calculating inter-coder reliability. Inter-coder reliability addresses the consistency of implementation of a rating system (Stemler, 2001). A doctoral candidate, who was proficient in qualitative research, was the second rater. We gave a list of the themes and subthemes to the second rater who then independently content-coded a subsample of 19 interviews. The results of the content-coding of the transcripts by the two independent raters (the first author and the doctoral student) were compared. We then calculated two indices of inter-coder reliability: the percentage agreement and Cohen's kappa. Cohen's kappa is the proportion of agreement between the raters after accounting for chance agreement. The percentage agreement was 80.89%, and Cohen's kappa was 0.37. Percentage agreement of 80% or greater is acceptable and Cohen's kappa between

0.21 and 0.40 is considered a fair strength of agreement (Stemler, 2001). We were able to resolve the discrepancies in coding and, therefore, the coding of the transcripts (i.e., content analysis) can be regarded as reliable.

Results

The results of the qualitative analysis are grouped into the codes/themes that emerged. As can be seen from Table 1, we identified four themes on the topic of negotiation. The themes were: negotiation at home, the consequence of negotiation on the relationship with one's spouse, negotiation at work, and the consequence of negotiation on the relationship with one's supervisor. As previously explained, coding in more than one subtheme was possible; when interviewees mentioned more than one subtheme, each was counted as a separate response.

Negotiation at Home

The objective of the study was to examine if negotiation of the exchange relationship occurred at home and/or at work due to WFC. The majority of the interviewees (84%) reported that they engaged in formal negotiation of the exchange relationships at home. However, the perceptions differed among husbands and wives with regard to who took the initiative to negotiate the exchange relationships at home. Of the 13 women who stated that there was negotiation at home, nine said that they were likely to be the ones to initiate the negotiation. As this female interviewee explained,

> I ask . . . . . otherwise he prefers reading or watching TV.
> (Interviewee 16, spouse, female, 32 years)

In contrast, of the eight men who reported negotiating at home, five perceived the negotiations to be jointly initiated by them and their wives. The other three (14%) male interviewees reported that they initiated the negotiation. It can be concluded, therefore, that in most cases the woman initiated the negotiation at home. She did so possibly because she had the primary responsibility for household and child care work and found it difficult to manage those responsibilities together with paid work and, hence, needed her spouse's assistance. This result is in line with research conducted in Western contexts (e.g., Kluwer et al., 2000).

Negotiations at home are likely to evolve in many ways. For example, one interviewee explained that when she got married she was too young to know about discussing the sharing of household work with her husband, but now she does after realizing the benefits of discussing such matters with her husband to sort them out. Another interviewee said,

Table 1. Themes, Subthemes, Frequencies, and Sample Quotes

Themes and subthemes	Frequency (%) (number of responses)[1]	Sample quotes (Interviewee number)
1. Negotiation at home[2]		
1.1 Yes	84 (21)	After about 2 months after marriage I told him that it is difficult for me to do and he very willingly took over all the cleaning in the house. (Interviewee 1)
		My husband is a very cooperative person. There is no separation, like you are the woman you wash and do everything. If I even say today I am tired can you cook, he is ready to cook. (Interviewee 9)
1.2 No	12 (3)	As per my experience dialogue [with my wife] doesn't work. (Interviewee 11)
		My wife, my mother is there. With that we have two domestics. Most of the work is taken care of. (Interviewee 23)
1.3 Gradual/voluntary	16 (4)	He on his own actually by looking at my … behaviors. That's how he has adjusted. (Interviewee 10)
		Actually I don't know if we discussed but it gradually happened … maybe like after 4 years after marriage. (Interviewee 14)
		Actually spontaneously we settled in. We didn't even talk [about sharing housework]. (Interviewee 21)
2. The consequence of negotiation on the relationship with one's spouse[3]		
2.1 Positive	49 (10)	Positive, positive. We try to give our best effort when we contribute to each other and try to support. So it is positive effect. (Interviewee 25)
		It has got better. Because my wife has understood that I am doing everything to enhance the standard of the family. (Interviewee 5)
2.2 Negative	14 (3)	It has affected the degree of relationship I think. Because those days … we had a very close relationship. I think that kind of behavior [of mine of not sharing work when my wife asked] has affected the relationship. (Interviewee 11)
		He … orders that I have to do certain things. (Interviewee 19)
2.3 No consequence	38 (8)	Actually there is no bad effect [on the relationship] as most of the time we understand each other and do the work. (Interviewee 12)
		Asking for contribution at home did not affect the relationship with my husband. (Interviewee 6)

Continued

Table 1. Continued

Themes and subthemes	Frequency (%) (number of responses)[1]	Sample quotes (Interviewee number)
3. Negotiation work		
3.1 Yes	68 (17)	Yes I have talked to my manager about work. (Interviewee 6)
		My boss knows my situation. I have spoken to him. (Interviewee 7)
3.2 No	32 (8)	I have not spoken to my boss about it. Because I feel there will be no positive outcome even if I take up this matter. (Interviewee 18)
		Actually no. I feel if I tell such things [negotiation] to him [boss] then it will show my inabilities. (Interviewee 11)
4. The consequence of negotiation on the relationship with one's supervisor [4,5]		
4.1 Positive	35 (6)	He understood me. He understood that I really have problems. (Interviewee 12)
		They [directors] were happy about the changes. (Interviewee 5)
4.2 Negative	18 (3)	I feel he would have perceived it in a negative way. I feel it... he never openly said anything bad. But I feel it would have affected negatively to some extent. (Interviewee 15)
		Yes they did initially [perceive it negatively]. I mean when you try to change something which has been going on for a long time. (Interviewee 24)
4.3 No consequence	53 (9)	No, no. I don't see it has affected. (Interviewee 13)
		I consider my boss as a very nice man. So, it hasn't affected the relationship. (Interviewee 17)

[1] When interviewees mentioned more than one subtheme, each was counted as a separate response. However, if an interviewee gave more than one example for the same subtheme, his/her responses were counted only once. $n = 25$ was used to calculate percentage/frequency except when stated otherwise.
[2] One interviewee provided examples for "no negotiation" and "voluntary contribution." Two interviewees provided examples for "negotiation" and "gradual contribution."
[3] Percentage/frequency based on $n = 21$; those who answered "yes" to negotiation at home.
[4] Percentage/frequency based on $n = 17$; those who answered "yes" to negotiation at work.
[5] One interviewee provided example of "negative" and "positive consequence of negotiation with one's supervisor."

> *Since February we are discussing it out and we are trying to work out things, these are the activities which he will be doing and these are the activities that I will be doing. So it's a very recent development which has happened in our lives.*
> (Interviewee 25, spouse, female, 32 years)

A further 16% of the interviewees reported to engage in gradual or voluntary negotiation of the exchange relationship at home. That is, they did not verbally or formally negotiate their exchange relationship, but changes were nonetheless made to the exchange relationship with the spouse because male spouses were sufficiently sensitive to their wives' family workload.

> *I will help her and I personally believe in that. When it comes to marriage both husband and wife should help each other.*
> (Interviewee 21, focal, male, 38 years)

One interviewee said that her husband voluntarily shared the housework and, therefore, there was no need to initiate negotiation.

> *Changes actually come from my husband's side. He gives good support and adjusts. Looking at me sometimes he comes and asks "Can I help you?".... He on his own, actually by looking at my way, my behaviors sometimes I get angry, mad. Because I need clean environment also. But I don't have time to do it. When I see my house messed up so I get mad with him. Now he knows and he cleans. That's how he has adjusted.*
> (Interviewee 10, spouse, female, 27 years)

The above comments and quotes illustrate the objective of negotiations in the spousal exchange relationship. Negotiations with the spouse seemed to focus on the spouse's contribution toward household and child care work. The above quotes also demonstrate that these husbands do not hold a traditional gender role ideology. They seem to view marriage as equal partnerships where both spouses should contribute toward household responsibilities (i.e., belief in egalitarian gender roles).

Apart from the interviewees who formally negotiated and gradually negotiated the exchange relationship, 12% of the interviewees, all of whom were men, reported that there was no need to negotiate with the spouse. Specifically, the interviewees said there was no need to negotiate household work, as they had their mother/mother-in-law/domestic help to assist their wives with the home responsibilities. Therefore, these male interviewees saw no role for themselves in household and child care work as they believed home responsibilities were women's domain. These sentiments reflect a belief in traditional gender roles in the family.

> *We are living with my parents. There is no difficulty for us.*
> (Interviewee 4, focal, male, 26 years)

It should be noted that of the 13 couples interviewed, only three couples had no help from either their parents or paid domestic with the household and/or child care work. Of the remaining 10 couples, three couples had parents and/or in-laws' help, another three couples had paid help at home, and four couples had both parents/in-laws and paid help. This finding, together with van Veldhoven and Beijer's study (2012), highlights the need to examine private life context in WFC research as it influences the level of conflict experienced by the individual.

In summary, some negotiation of the exchange relationship between spouses took place within the dual-earner couples interviewed. The objective of the negotiation was to adjust each of the spouse's contribution toward household and/or child care responsibility. For example, help was sought in household tasks such as cooking, cleaning and washing clothes. Further, these negotiations took place as and when workload was high or was negotiated in advance. Therefore, the negotiation was in terms of the contribution dimension of the social exchange rather than in terms of the affect, respect or loyalty dimensions. In addition, a male spouse's value of traditional gender roles seemed to have an influence on whether negotiations took place or not. The above two results are similar to past research conducted in Western contexts (e.g., Mannino & Deutsch, 2007). Finally, the fact that 84% reported engaging in formal negotiations and 16% experienced gradual negotiations or voluntary contributions indicate that redistributions of domestic labor among Sri Lankan dual earner couples were, by and large, achieved.

The Consequence of Negotiation on the Relationship with One's Spouse

It is said that every action has a reaction. Therefore, we investigated whether the negotiation with the spouse (and the supervisor) had a consequence on the relationships with the spouse (and the supervisor). Of the interviewees who reported engaging in negotiation at home, the majority (86%) said that the negotiations had a positive consequence or had no consequence on the relationships with their spouses. In fact, 49% of the interviewees felt that such negotiations strengthened their relationships, because discussions gave them an opportunity to understand each other. The remaining interviewees said that the negotiations had no consequence on their spousal relationships.

> *Because we have been married for 6 years we have an understanding of each other.*
> (Interviewee 12, spouse, female, 29 years)

> *Then we started talking. Now things are OK, both of us are able to discuss and talk among each other and rectify matters which didn't happen initially. I think it all depends on how mature you are in life.*
> (Interviewee 24, spouse, female, 38 years)

Only three interviewees reported a negative consequence on the relationship with the spouse because of attempts to negotiate the exchange relationship at home.

> *And what he says is [that] bringing home the food and dropping me to transport is sort of enough for a man to do.*
> (Interviewee 19, spouse, female, 27 years)

> *I have asked my husband [to share household and child care work] but he said it is a woman's job. He has never touched a broom.... He watches TV after work.... I did all the work myself. Even kids I looked after. I did not depend on my parents for that. At one point I thought of leaving the relationship as he never helped.*
> (Interviewee 2, focal, female, 46 years)

The above two quotes highlight the fact that when husbands believe in a traditional gender role ideology, the wives might not be successful in negotiating at home.

In summary, negotiations with spouses had predominantly positive effects for this sample of dual-earner Sri Lankan couples. However, the success of the negotiations depended on the male spouse's degree of belief in traditional gender roles.

Negotiation at Work

The majority of the interviewees (68%) reported that they engaged in formal negotiation of the exchange relationships at work. Of the 17 interviewees who reported negotiation at work, 13 of them (77%; five men and eight women) reported initiating the negotiations themselves. The remaining four interviewees (23%) reported that either their supervisors or they initiated the negotiations. Men and women were similarly likely to initiate negotiations at work.

Most formal negotiations involved negotiating heavy workloads that interfered with their family responsibilities (i.e., WIF conflict). There were a few reasons why the interviewees did not negotiate with their supervisors. One reason was that the interviewee perceived the supervisor not to be in a position to do anything about heavy workloads due to lack of resources.

> *But this is the normal thing [high workload]. All the people in our department work like that. So this is not only for me. [So I did not negotiate with my boss.]*
> (Interviewee 4, focal, male, 26 years)

Another reason was that the interviewees perceived work in the private sector to be hard and stressful, and that they had to learn to deal with this workload and stress. For example, two interviewees said that although they had no problem talking or negotiating with their supervisors they did not do so, as no positive outcome was expected. The third reason was that interviewees thought their supervisors might view attempts to negotiate work matters as a sign of weakness or lack of ability on the part of the individual. Interestingly, the length of the work relationship does not appear to be a reason for non-negotiation. There was no significant difference in the average length of time under one's supervisor between those who reported engaging in formal negotiation and those who did not (38.73 months vs. 39.93 months, respectively).

However, interviewees who took the initiative to negotiate with their supervisors enjoyed successful outcomes.

> *At the beginning of the year when we prepare duty list we talk a lot. . . . Compared to others' work load if mine is more I have spoken to him. If I cannot do all the allocated work I tell him. Because after undertaking to do the tasks I cannot neglect them, right?*
> (Interviewee 12, spouse, female, 29 years)

A few interviewees felt the need to return the kindness and understanding shown by their supervisors by, for example, working hard, putting in more hours or doing extra work. In one particular instance, the interviewee was quite emotional and sounded deeply touched by the supervisor's behavior when she was describing her supervisor's kindness and understanding, and the need to reciprocate him. This behavior is similar to Morgan and King's (2012) finding that individuals who experience family-to-work guilt respond by engaging in prosocial work behavior, although in our study the prosocial work behavior was toward the supervisor rather than a colleague. Such appreciation and reciprocation of a supervisor's understanding of FIW conflict reflect the high-power distance characteristic of an Eastern culture.

> *My father met with an accident. . . . I always want to see my father every day after the accident, and to be with him at least for one hour. So, I asked her [the executive] whether the manager could give me around 2 to 3 hours for me to see my father and then come back to work . . . . my manager called me to his office and said you can always use my driver and the car if you have a problem, not to worry about that. . . . . I couldn't express my happiness in words . . . . Now, if he asks me to come on Sunday to work I can't, I can't tell no. Because I feel that I am dedicated. I also have a responsibility to respect him, to show my gratitude. I always feel that I should . . . if he is in a difficult situation if **he** [interviewee's emphasis] asks help I think that I **must** [interviewee's emphasis] do it.*
> (Interviewee 19, spouse, female, 27 years)

In summary, most of the Sri Lankan men and women in this study's sample were able to discuss work-related problems (WIF conflict) with their supervisors and sort them out. A few interviewees were also able to discuss home-related problems (FIW conflict) with their supervisors, such as having a sick parent. In line with past research on the impact of supervisor support on WFC (e.g., Beutell & Wittig-Berman, 2008), the interviewees in this study said that having an understanding supervisor helped deal with their stress and, thus, reduce their WFC. Peculiar to this study, and reflecting its Eastern cultural context, is the interviewees' profound appreciation of their supervisors' approachability and understanding.

The Consequence of Negotiation on the Relationship with One's Supervisor

Of the 17 interviewees (68%) who reported negotiating the exchange relationship at work, 15 interviewees (88%) felt that the negotiations had either a positive consequence or no consequence on the relationships with their supervisors.

> *Actually he appreciated. Because I told him I don't want to make mistake just because I am overloaded. So, he actually appreciated before I have done something wrong I am telling him ahead.*
>
> (Interviewee 14, focal, female, 34 years)

More specifically, most of the interviewees (53%) stated that negotiations had no consequence on their relationships with the supervisor. We consider negotiations at work not having any consequence on the relationship with one's supervisor as a good outcome, because the interviewees described their relationships with their supervisors as quite open and friendly. Only three interviewees (18%) felt that their supervisors did not appreciate their attempts to negotiate or discuss the workload. For example, one interviewee perceived some negative feelings in the relationship with her supervisor postnegotiation.

In summary, regardless of gender, it was mostly the interviewees who initiated the negotiations with their supervisors. In most cases, negotiations of exchange relationships at work were successful in that the supervisors were able to address the interviewees' requests and the negotiations did not change the quality of the relationships between the interviewees and their supervisors.

Discussion

The aim of the interviews was to identify whether and how dual-earner couples negotiated their exchange relationships to reduce WFC. To achieve this aim, we interviewed a sample of 25 individuals likely to have high family and work demands (i.e., those living in dual-earner couple situations) in Sri Lanka. The semistructured interview method was chosen to obtain in-depth descriptions of the work and family lives of dual-earner couples in Sri Lanka. As both individuals (in a couple) worked outside the home, we expected that both would experience some WFC and at least one would explore ways to reduce it, to enable the couple to combine work and care in a sustainable manner.

The majority of the individuals in this sample engaged in formal or informal negotiation of the exchange relationships at home and at work to alleviate family- or work-derived conflict. Whether at home or at work, it was the individual who experienced the inequality in the exchange relationship who was likely to initiate the negotiation. As a result, negotiations at home were more likely to be initiated by the women than the men, and negotiations at work were initiated by the interviewees rather than by their supervisors. Further, negotiations with one's spouse and supervisor were about contributions. Negotiations regarding other aspects of the social exchange such as trust, respect, and affect were not reported. In addition, the quality of the relationship with one's spouse and supervisor remained intact or improved postnegotiations. While the success of negotiations at home depended on the husband's gender role ideology, successful negotiations at work depended on supervisor characteristics (such as approachability and empathy) and on resources available. As a result of having an understanding and supportive spouse and/or supervisor and successful negotiations, individuals reported experiencing increased commitment, affection and loyalty toward the other party (i.e., spouse and/or supervisor). This indicates that, even in Eastern cultures with very strong gender roles, dual-earner couples benefit from talking to each other to sort out matters such as the sharing of household and child care responsibilities. In particular, women who work outside the home benefit from initiating the negotiation of the division of labor with their spouses. Further, our study shows that gender role ideology can influence an individual's behavior, which is in contrast to the findings of Franco, Sabattini, and Crosby (2004). The discrepancy in results may be due to differences between the two studies' samples. In Franco et al.'s (2004) study the sample consisted of undergraduate students and the perception of the link between their parents' ideology and behavior.

Despite the Eastern cultural values of high power distance, individuals' negotiations with their supervisors yielded positive outcomes. Further, such negotiations did not have negative consequences on the relationships between the individuals and their supervisors. Hence, we have one recommendation for individuals and another for supervisors. Individuals living in Eastern countries, such as Sri Lanka, are encouraged to initiate negotiations with their supervisors when they feel it is possible to obtain favorable outcomes. Such negotiations involve, for example, the implementation of family-friendly programs, such as flexible work practices (e.g., compressed work week, flexi-hours) and control over work hours. In contrast to many Western countries, such family-friendly policies and practices are not officially offered by many Sri Lankan organizations.

In turn, we encourage supervisors to be supportive of their employees by being open to suggestions that minimize WFC. Past research has shown that family-supportive supervisor behavior is linked to positive employee outcomes, such as job satisfaction (e.g., Hammer, Kossek, Yragui, Bodner, & Hanson, 2009). In contrast, nonfamily-supportive supervisors might exacerbate WFC and negative employee outcomes. For example, Morgan and King (2012) show how individuals who experience work-to-family guilt might respond by shirking work responsibilities. Therefore, we recommend that supervisors be open to negotiations aimed at minimizing WFC to avoid antisocial behavior directed at the organization (e.g., absenteeism).

The negotiations between the spouses, and between the interviewees and their supervisors, in this study were similar to Hall's (1972) coping strategy of structural role redefinition (role bargains). The stress/conflict coping strategies used by the interviewees such as sharing of household and child care work at home with one's spouse can be considered examples of structural role redefinition. Overall, these strategies are problem-focused strategies. In addition, our study extends Tiedje's (2004) findings on coping strategies (superwoman strategy, planning and time management, cognitive reinterpretation of roles, and divesting unimportant activities) by identifying two more coping strategies; namely, negotiating with the spouse at home and negotiating with the supervisor at work.

Two additional cultural characteristics emerged from the interviews. First, dual-earner couples in Sri Lanka rely heavily on their parents and/or in-laws for help with household and child care responsibilities. This family-based arrangement is not found in most Western countries, and yet it helps dual-earner couples, especially the women, reduce or cope with their WFC. Second, dual-earner couples in Sri Lanka might be embracing a combination of Eastern and Western values that help them cope with WFC. For example, possibly as a result of high education and urban living, most of the Sri Lankan individuals in dual-earner couple situations exhibit less traditional gender ideologies than what would be expected in an Eastern society. Yet, they still use the typically Oriental extended social network of parents/family to assist them in taking care of children.

Limitations of the Methodology

One of the major limitations of qualitative research is the inability to generalize interview findings to other settings. However, the aim of the interviews was not to obtain generalizable data but to gain an understanding of how individuals in dual-earner couple situations coped with or reduced their WFC by negotiating their exchange relationships.

A second limitation is the subjectivity involved in qualitative research. However, this drawback was minimized in this study as the interviewer (the first author) had had prior training and experience in interviewing. Second, as all interviews were conducted by one interviewer a high level of consistency was maintained in capturing interview data. Third, as we used an interview protocol and a semistructured interview method we were able to obtain comparable information from all interviewees. Finally, we calculated two inter-coder reliability measures, the percentage agreement and Cohen's kappa. The results of these measures suggested that the analysis was reliable.

Suggestion for Future Research

We now have new insights regarding negotiations among dual-earner couples and between individuals and supervisors to reduce or cope with WFC. These insights were gained from the qualitative data. Such detailed descriptions from interviewees about their work and family lives could not be obtained from a quantitative survey. However, given that this study was exploratory, more nuanced and in-depth research is required in this area. For example, future qualitative research can investigate if negotiation with regard to affect, loyalty and respect take place within dual-earner couples to reduce WFC and if these dimensions influence WFC.

Conclusion

Overall, an important contribution of this study is its (indirect) test of the cross-cultural robustness of "Western" work–family and social exchange theories. More specifically, "Western" work–family and social exchange theories were used in this study to gain insights on the WFC experienced by dual-earner couples in an Eastern society. The notion that women are responsible for household and child care work seems to be universal. In the case of Sri Lankan women, they are undoubtedly socialized to feel and be responsible for household and child care work (Gunawardena et al., 2004; Wickramasinghe & Jayatilaka, 2006). It is possible that because of this socialization, some Sri Lankan men are slow to adapt to having a working spouse, and to being requested to help with the household and child care responsibilities. It is also possible that because of socialization, women accept the fact that they will spend more hours in household and child care work than their husbands (even though both are in paid employment).

Furthermore, this study provides a fine-grained understanding of the negotiations in the exchange relationships (with spouses and supervisors) of Sri Lankan dual-earner couples to reduce or cope with WFC. For example, insights from the interviews revealed an influence of male spouse's gender role ideology on the negotiation of the exchange relationship at home. Previous research in Western countries has found a relationship between division of labor and marital satisfaction (Stevens, Kiger, & Riley, 2001; Strober & Chan, 1998; Wilkie, Ferree, & Ratcliff, 1998). Similarly, this study's interviews indicate that Sri Lankan women who work outside the home report marital unhappiness when their husbands do not share household and child care work, and report marital happiness when they do. Hence, this study's results suggest that gender role ideology might be an especially important factor to consider in research on WFC in Eastern cultures.

Negotiating exchange relationships at home and at work is a stress and conflict management strategy. Further, negotiations of exchange relationships at home and at work are forms of structural role redefinition (Hall, 1972), which include the reallocation and sharing of role tasks such as cleaning, washing, and child care with one's spouse. Such a direct approach to coping with stress is possible only if the situation or environment is changeable by the individual (Quick et al., 2004; Somech & Drach-Zahavy, 2007). Therefore, the interviews indicate that Sri Lankan individuals identify the sources of stress that are changeable by them (or under their control) and attempt to change the root causes of the stress or conflict. Thus, the negotiation strategy adopted by the individuals in this study was used to manage as well as resolve WFC and stress.

In addition to negotiating with the spouse and/or supervisor, this study found that the extended family serves as a "work–family arrangement" for Sri Lankan dual-earner couples, something not found in most Western cultures. This arrangement helps individuals in dual-earner couple situations, especially the women, to reduce or cope with their WFC. This "work–family" arrangement in combination with gradual negotiations or voluntary contributions (that enable redistributions of domestic labor) facilitate the sustainable combination of career and care for both spouses in an Eastern culture.

References

Amato, P. R., & Booth, A. (1995). Changes in gender role attitudes and perceived marital quality. *American Sociological Review*, 60(1), 58–66.
Bazeley, P. (2007). *Qualitative data analysis with NVivo*. Los Angeles: Sage Publications.
Beutell, N. J., & Wittig-Berman, U. (2008). Work-family conflict and work-family synergy for generation X, baby boomers, and matures. *Journal of Managerial Psychology*, 23(5), 507–523. doi: 10.1108/02683940810884513.
Boyar, S. L., Maertz , C. P., Jr, Pearson, A. W., & Keough, S. (2003). Work-family conflict: A model of linkages between work and family domain variables and turnover intentions. *Journal of Managerial Issues*, 15(2), 175–190.
Braun, V., & Clarke, V. (2006). Using thematic analysis in psychology. *Qualitative Research in Psychology*, 3, 77–101. doi: 10.1191/1478088706qp063oa.
Button, S. B. (2001). Organizational efforts to affirm sexual diversity: A cross-level examination. *Journal of Applied Psychology*, 86, 17–28. doi: 10.1037//0021-9010.86.1.17.
Carlson, D. S., Kacmar, K. M., & Williams, L. J. (2000). Construction and initial validation of a multidimensional measure of work-family conflict. *Journal of Vocational Behavior*, 56, 249–276. doi: 10.1006/jvbe.1999.1713.
Carlson, D. S., & Perrewé, P. L. (1999). The role of social support in the stressor-strain relationship: An examination of work-family conflict. *Journal of Management*, 25(4), 513–540.
Casper, W. J., Eby, L. T., Bordeaux, C., Lockwood, A., & Lambert, D. (2007). A review of research methods in IO/OB work-family research. *Journal of Applied Psychology*, 92, 28–43. doi: 10.1037/0021-9010.92.1.28.
Chandrakumara, A. (2007). Does HRM fit really matter to citizenship and task performance? Sri Lankan manufacturing sector experience. *Employee Relations*, 29, 611–639. doi: 10.1108/01425450710826113.
Chandrakumara, A. & Budhwar, P.S. (2005). Doing business in Sri Lanka. *Thunderbird International Business Review*, 47(1), 95–120.
Crabtree, B. F., & Miller, W. L. (1999). Using codes and code manuals: A template organising style of interpretation. In B. F. Crabtree & W. L. Miller (Eds.), *Doing qualitative research* (2nd ed., pp. 163–177). Thousand Oaks, CA: Sage Publications, Inc.
Denton, M. L. (2004). Gender and marital decision making: Negotiating religious ideology and practice. *Social Forces*, 82(3), 1151–1180.
Denzin, N. K., & Lincoln, Y. S. (2008). Introduction: The discipline and practice of qualitative research. In N. K. Denzin & Y. S. Lincoln (Eds.), *Collecting and interpreting qualitative materials* (3rd ed., pp. 1–43). Los Angeles: Sage Publications.
Dias, M. (1990). Marriage, motherhood and employment. In S. Kiribamune & V. Samarasinghe (Eds.), *Women at crossroads: A Sri Lankan perspective* (pp. 216–227). New Delhi: Vikas Publishing House Pvt. Ltd.

Dienesch, R. M., & Liden, R. C. (1986). Leader-member exchange model of leadership: A critique and further development. *Academy of Management Review, 11*, 618–634.

Duriau, V. J., Reger, R. K., & Pfarrer, M. D. (2007). A content analysis of the content analysis literature in organization studies. *Organizational Research Methods, 10*(1), 5–34. doi: 10.1177/1094428106289252

Fogarty, G. J., Machin, M. A., Albion, M. J., Sutherland, L. F., Lalor, G. I., & Revitt, S. (1999). Predicting occupational strain and job satisfaction: The role of stress, coping, personality, and affective variables. *Journal of Vocational Behavior, 54*, 429–452.

Fox, M. L., & Dwyer, D. J. (1999). An investigation of the effects of time and involvement in the relationship between stressors and work-family conflict. *Journal of Occupational Health Psychology, 4*, 164–174.

Franco, J. L., Sabattini, L., & Crosby, F. J. (2004). Anticipating work and family: Exploring the associations among gender-related ideologies, values, and behaviors in Latino and White families in the United States. *Journal of Social Issues, 60*(4), 755–766.

Frone, M. R., Russell, M., & Cooper, M. L. (1992). Antecedents and outcomes of work-family conflict: Testing a model of the work-family interface. *Journal of Applied Psychology, 77*, 65–78.

Fuwa, M., & Cohen, P. N. (2007). Housework and social policy. *Social Science Research, 36*, 512–530. doi: 10.1016/j.ssreseach.2006.04.005

Gunawardena, C., Lekamge, D., Bulumulle, K., & Dissanayake, S. (2004). *A study of child rearing practices and gender role socialization prevalent in selected communities in Sri Lanka–A pilot study*. Paper presented at the Ninth National Convention on Women's Studies, CENWOR, Colombo.

Hall, D. T. (1972). A model of coping with role conflict: The role behavior of college educated women. *Administrative Science Quarterly, 17*(4), 471–486.

Hammer, L. B., Kossek, E. E., Yragui, N. L., Bodner, T. E., & Hanson, G. C. (2009). Development and validation of a multidimensional measure of family supportive supervisor behaviors (FSSB). *Journal of Management, 35*, 837–856.

Hatch, M. J. (with Cunliffe, A. L.). (2006). *Organization theory: Modern, symbolic, and postmodern perspectives* (2nd ed.). Oxford: Oxford University Press.

Hofstede, G. (2001). *Culture's consequences: Comparing values, behaviors, institutions, and organizations across nations* (2nd ed.). Thousand Oaks, CA: Sage Publications.

Hunt, G. C. (2002). The continuing challenge of sexual diversity at work. In C. Harvey & M. J. Allard (Eds.), *Understanding and managing diversity* (2nd ed., pp. 130–140). Upper Saddle River, NJ: Prentice Hall.

International Labour Organization. (2005). C156 Workers with family responsibilities convention, 1981. Retrieved October 6, 2005, from http://www.ilo.org/ilolex/ english/convdisp2.htm

Jawahir, K. (1992). Women in the administrative and allied services. In S. Kiribamune (Ed.), *Reconciliation of roles: Women, work and family in Sri Lanka* (pp. 220–239). New Delhi: Navrang.

Judge, T. A., Boudreau, J. W., & Bretz , R. D., Jr. (1994). Job and life attitudes of male executives. *Journal of Applied Psychology, 79*, 767–782.

Kluwer, E. S., Heesink, J. A. S., & Van de Vliert, E. (2000). The division of labor in close relationships: An asymmetrical conflict issue. *Personal Relationships, 7*(3), 263–282.

Kopelman, R. E., Greenhaus, J. H., & Connolly, T. F. (1983). A model of work, family, and interrole conflict: A construct validation study. *Organizational Behavior and Human Performance, 32*, 198–215.

Kossek, E. E., Noe, R. A., & DeMarr, B. J. (1999). Work-family role synthesis: Individual and organizational determinants. *International Journal of Conflict Management, 10*, 102–129.

Kuzel, A. J. (1999). Sampling in qualitative inquiry. In B. F. Crabtree & W. L. Miller (Eds.), *Doing qualitative research* (2nd ed., pp. 33–45). Thousand Oaks, CA: Sage Publications, Inc.

Langley, A. (1999). Strategies for theorizing from process data. *Academy of Management Review, 24*(4), 691–710.

Liden, R. C., & Maslyn, J. M. (1998). Multidimensionality of leader-member exchange: An empirical assessment through scale development. *Journal of Management, 24*(1), 43–72.

Lin, X., & Miller, S. J. (2003). Negotiation approaches: Direct and indirect effect of national culture. *International Marketing Review, 20*(3), 286–303. doi: 10.1108/02651330310477 602.

Loscocco, K. A. (1997). Work-family linkages among self-employed women and men. *Journal of Vocational Behavior, 50,* 204–226.

Mannino, C. A., & Deutsch, F. M. (2007). Changing the division of household labor: A negotiated process between partners. *Sex Roles, 56*(5–6), 309–324. doi: 10.1007/s11199-006-9181-1.

Mendis, D. (2007). Speech at the launch of A Dictionary of Sri Lankan English. Retrieved June 13, 2008, from http://www.mirisgala.net/Dushyanthi_Mendis_speech.html

Miles, M. B., & Huberman, A. M. (1994). *Qualitative data analysis: An expanded sourcebook* (2nd ed.). Thousand Oaks, CA: Sage Publications.

Moore, D., & Gobi, A. (1995). Role conflict and perceptions of gender roles (The case of Israel). *Sex Roles, 32,* 251–270.

Morgan, W. B., & King, E. B. (2012). The association between work-family guilt and pro- and anti-social work behavior. *Journal of Social Issues, 68*(4), 684–703.

Nanayakkara, G. (1992). *Culture and management in Sri Lanka.* Colombo, Sri Lanka: Postgraduate Institute of Management.

Parasuraman, S., & Greenhaus, J. H. (2002). Toward reducing some critical gaps in work-family research. *Human Resource Management Review, 12,* 299–312.

Powell, G. N., & Greenhaus, J. H. (2006). Managing incidents of work-family conflict: A decision-making perspective. *Human Relations, 59*(9), 1179–1212. doi: 10.1177/0018726706069765.

Quick, J. D., Henley, A. B., & Quick, J. C. (2004). The balancing act–At work and at home. *Organizational Dynamics, 33*(4), 426–437. doi: 10.1016/j.orgdyn.2004.09.008.

Ragins, B. R., & Cornwell, J. M. (2001). Pink triangles: Antecedents and consequences of perceived workplace discrimination against gay and lesbian employees. *Journal of Applied Psychology, 86,* 1244–1261. doi: 10.1037//0021-9010.86.6.1244.

Rank, M. R., & LeCroy, C. W. (1983). Toward a multiple perspective in family theory and practice: The case of social exchange, symbolic interactionism, and conflict theory. *Family Relations, 32,* 441–448.

Roberson, L. (2006). Negotiation strategies: Civility and cooperation without compromising advocacy. *American Journal of Family Law, 20,* 7–20.

Scanzoni, J., & Szinovacz, M. (1980). *Family decision-making: A developmental sex role model.* Beverly Hills: Sage Publications.

Somech, A., & Drach-Zahavy, A. (2007). Strategies for coping with work-family conflict: The distinctive relationships of gender role ideology. *Journal of Occupational Health Psychology, 12*(1), 1–19. doi: 10.1037/1076-8998.12.1.1

Sprey, J. (1979). Conflict theory and the study of marriage and the family. In W. R. Burr, R. Hill, F. I. Nye & I. L. Reiss (Eds.), *Contemporary theories about the family* (Vol. II, pp. 130–159). New York: The Free Press.

Standh, M., & Nordenmark, M. (2006). The interference of paid work with household demands in different social policy contexts: Perceived work-household conflict in Sweden, the UK, the Netherlands, Hungary, and the Czech Republic. *The British Journal of Sociology, 57,* 597–617. doi: 10.1111/j.1468-4446.2006.00127.x

Stemler, S. (2001). An overview of content analysis [Electronic Version]. *Practical Assessment, Research & Evaluation, 7,* 1–7. Retrieved August 25, 2008 from http://PAREonline.net/getvn.asp?v=7&n=17.

Stevens, D., Kiger, G., & Riley, P. J. (2001). Working hard and hardly working: Domestic labor and marital satisfaction among dual-earner couples. *Journal of Marriage and the Family, 63,* 514–526.

Stoeva, A. Z., Chiu, R., & Greenhaus, J. H. (2002). Negative affectivity, role stress, and work-family conflict. *Journal of Vocational Behavior, 60,* 1–16.

Strober, M. H., & Chan, A. M. K. (1998). Husbands, wives, and housework: Graduates of Stanford and Tokyo Universities. *Feminist Economics, 4*(3), 97–127.

Tiedje, L. B. (2004). Processes of change in work/home incompatibilities: Employed mothers 1986–1999. *Journal of Social Issues, 60*(4), 787–800.

Van Veldhoven, M. J. P. M., & Beijer, S. E. (2012). Workload, work-to-family conflict, and health: Gender differences and the influence of private life context. *Journal of Social Issues, 68*(4), 665–683.

Wickramasinghe, M., & Jayatilaka, W. (2006). *Beyond glass ceilings and brick walls: Gender at the workplace*. Sri Lanka: International Labour Organisation.

Wilkie, J. R., Ferree, M. M., & Ratcliff, K. S. (1998). Gender and fairness: Marital satisfaction in two-earner couples. *Journal of Marriage and the Family, 60*, 577–594.

PAVITHRA KAILASAPATHY is a Senior Lecturer and currently the Head of the Department of Human Resources Management at the Faculty of Management & Finance, University of Colombo, Sri Lanka. She has a PhD from the University of Melbourne, Australia. Her research interests are in the areas of work–family conflict and gender issues in organizations. Pavithra lectures in areas such as HRM, Research Methodology, Organizational Behavior, and Gender Issues. Pavithra is an Associate member of Institute of Personnel Management (IPM) Sri Lanka and was a member of the IPM Council in 2002/3. She was a Director of the Board of Women's Education and Research Centre, Colombo, Sri Lanka. Pavithra has conducted training for nongovernmental organizations leaders and staff on personal development, organization development, and leadership development.

ISABEL METZ (PhD, Monash University) is an Associate Professor of Organizational Behavior at the Melbourne Business School, University of Melbourne. Her research interests are in the areas of gender and careers, diversity management, work and family, and employment relationships. She has been awarded multiple research grants and several best paper awards. Isabel lectures in areas such as Diversity Management, Human Resource Management, and Management in Organizations. Isabel is a member of the Academy of Management (AOM), Australia and New Zealand Academy of Management, the Australian Human Resources Institute (AHRI), and a Senior Associate of the Financial Services Institute of Australasia. She serves on the AOM's Diversity & Inclusion Theme Committee, and on the editorial boards of *Human Resource Management*, *Journal of Organizational Behavior*, and *Group and Organization Management*.

The More Things Change, the More They Stay the Same: Gender, Culture, and College Students' Views about Work and Family

Wendy A. Goldberg,* Erin Kelly, Nicole L. Matthews, Hannah Kang, Weilin Li, and Mariya Sumaroka
University of California, Irvine

A culturally/ethnically diverse sample of 955 students (M = 20.2 years old) at a large U.S. university completed online surveys about their parents' division of labor, trajectories of their mothers' employment, gender role ideology, and beliefs about the costs and benefits of maternal employment for children. Differences in these work–care domains were examined by student gender, culture/ethnicity, acculturation status, and own employment. Generational differences in beliefs about maternal employment also were examined. Propensity score matching reduced selection bias. Asian American students, especially male students and those less acculturated, were more likely to endorse gender role segregation and maternal nonemployment when children are young. Their mothers' employment and own employment status were associated with more positive views about maternal employment. However, students' work–care beliefs have held fairly constant since the 1980s. The views of young adults about career and care may impinge on their success in attaining work–family goals. The more things change, the more they stay the same: Gender, culture, and college students' views about work and family

Around the globe, recent decades have witnessed a rise in women's labor force participation and an increase in dual-earner and single-parent families (Korabik, Lero, & Whitehead, 2008). Establishing a favorable work–family balance is a challenge for women and men in many countries around the world (Aryee, Srinivas, & Tan, 2005; Yang, Chen, Choi, & Zou, 2000). The current study focuses on the United States, for which the latter decades of the 20th century were marked by a

---

*Correspondence concerning this article should be addressed to Wendy A. Goldberg, Department of Psychology and Social Behavior, University of California, Irvine, 4201 Social and Behavioral Sciences Gateway, Irvine, CA 92697-7085 [e-mail: wendy.goldberg@uci.edu].

steady increase in the number of mothers of minor children who participated in the labor force in response to prevailing social and economic issues (Juhn & Potter, 2006). By the late 1970s, close to half of mothers of children under the age of 18 in the United States were labor force participants. By the 1980s, the pace of women's employment in the United States had accelerated and the majority of mothers with children under the age of 18 were employed (Hoffman & Youngblade, 1999). The shift toward greater maternal labor force participation has continued, and the rate has hovered between 71% and 73% since 2000 (U.S. Department of Labor, Bureau of Labor Statistics, 2010).

While maternal employment was becoming normative, concerns regarding the effects of maternal employment on children's development surfaced in academia and in public arenas (Greenberger, Goldberg, Crawford, & Granger, 1988). These concerns centered on the possible negative outcomes for young children due to employed mothers' absence from the home (e.g., the belief that children of employed mothers "suffer more" than other children). However, the empirical data indicate that these concerns have been overstated. A recent meta-analytic review of 50 years of research on maternal employment during early childhood revealed few effects on children's achievement and behavior overall; whether small negative or positive consequences were supported depended upon contextual variables such as family structure and socioeconomic status (Lucas-Thompson, Goldberg, & Prause, 2010).

Despite women's meaningful inroads into the labor force, their representation in a wide array of occupations, their ascendancy to positions of authority, and the narrowing of the wage gap in recent years (U.S. Department of Labor, Bureau of Labor Statistics, 2010), employed women and mothers continue to shoulder the majority of household labor in comparison to employed men and fathers, with evidence of a "leisure gap" between men and women (U.S. Department of Labor, Bureau of Labor Statistics, 2010). The domestic labor gap is narrowing in the sense that men have begun assuming more child care responsibilities (Hook, 2006), but men have been slow to take on an equal amount of household chores (Bianchi, Milkie, Sayer, & Robinson, 2000; Craig, 2006; Pailhe & Solaz, 2006) or elder care responsibilities (National Alliance for Caregiving, 2009).

A positive association between parents' and children's egalitarian gender ideologies has been regularly observed, and such intergenerational transmission has been attributed in part to the structure of children's home environments (Davis & Greenstein, 2009). Children of employed mothers are often found to have less traditional (i.e., less gender-stereotyped) views on work and family related issues (Davis & Greenstein, 2009). Parents' gender-typed views and behavior regarding household division of labor and employment may play an important role in shaping family outcomes and children's attitudes regarding work and family issues.

Gender Ideology

Gender ideologies, or individuals' attitudes about appropriate roles for men and women, have been shown to be affected by a number of socializing agents including, but not limited to, culture, mother's gender ideology, and parents' household division of labor (see Kroska & Elman, 2009). Additionally, gender role ideology has become less rigid over the decades. Galinsky and colleagues reported that both male and female employees who participated in the 2008 Families and Work Institute National Study of the Changing Work force were less likely than participants in the 1977 U.S. Department of Labor Quality of Employment Survey to agree with the statement "It is much better for everyone if the man earns the money and the woman takes care of the home and children" (Galinsky, Aumann, & Bond, 2008). This change was more pronounced among men than women; women were less likely than men to agree with the statement at both time points.

Researchers have also studied generational differences in regard to domestic and employment roles. In comparison to a cohort studied in 1975, a younger generation assessed in the year 2000 demonstrated differing attitudes toward work-related issues as a consequence of changing home, educational and workplace environments (NiDitale & Boraas, 2000). The young women of the recent generation were more likely to be employed and more likely to receive more favorable pay as the wage gap between men and women had narrowed (but not closed) over the years. In general, the direction of generational change has been toward greater similarity and equality between the sexes when it comes to work and family roles and attitudes. Despite some generational differences in work values, both young and older American workers place a premium on balancing work and personal goals (Smola & Sutton, 2002).

Beliefs about Maternal Employment

Concerns remain about the looming negative effects of maternal employment on children's social and academic well-being despite research evidence to the contrary (Goldberg, Prause, Lucas-Thompson, & Himsel, 2008; Lucas-Thompson et al., 2010). Young adults today face mixed messages of maternal employment as normative (based on population data) alongside normative beliefs that mothers will work around their children's schedules and shoulder most of the hands-on child care (Garey, 1999). It is typically mothers who cut back on employment to care for young children; only 3% of families with children under 15 have "stay-at-home" fathers (Kreider & Elliott, 2009). Understanding emerging adults' (Arnett, 2007) beliefs about the desirability of mothers in the work force may help us forecast sustainability in combining career and care.

Mothers' employment history also is relevant. College students whose mothers were not employed during the pre-school and elementary school years perceived higher costs of maternal employment for children (Cochran & Chambliss, 2009; D'Olio, 2009; Filipokowski & Chambliss, 2009). In contrast, students whose mothers were employed full-time during the pre-school and elementary school years perceived higher benefits of maternal employment (D'Olio, 2009; Filipokowski & Chambliss, 2009) and reported professional career aspirations (Cochran & Chambliss, 2009). These findings indicate college students' beliefs about maternal employment are consistent with the labor force status of their mothers during their upbringing and suggest an important role for socialization processes.

In 1988, Greenberger and colleagues developed the Beliefs about the Consequences of Maternal Employment for Children scale (BACMEC) to capture beliefs about the costs and benefits of maternal employment for children among college students and adults (Greenberger et al., 1988). In one of the 1980s college student samples, male students saw more costs to children when mothers worked outside of the home and female students saw more benefits. College students of both sexes who believed that maternal employment was problematic for children also scored higher on a measure of gender role traditionalism (Greenberger et al., 1988). This finding suggests that beliefs about the consequences of maternal employment for children are linked to a larger set of beliefs and attitudes about gender roles and raises questions about how we can move beyond traditional beliefs about expected costs of mothers' employment.

Cultural Differences Associated with Beliefs about Gender Roles and Maternal Employment

Cultures with collectivistic orientations (e.g., Asian and Latino) often emphasize family members' obligations to one another. Unlike individualistic cultures (i.e., Western cultures) where individuality is encouraged, members of collectivistic cultures are expected to support the goals and interests of the group over the individual (Triandis, 1995). Furthermore, familial duty and devotion are imperative (Chilman, 1993) and children are socialized to practice these cultural norms. Collectivistic cultures typically support a gender-segregated division of labor, wherein women are responsible for the domestic realm and men for the work realm. For example, regardless of wives' employment statuses, Japanese husbands are involved in little or no household chores (Gender Equality Bureau, 2004). In Latin American countries, women spend substantially more time on domestic duties than their husbands (Treas & Drobnič, 2010). However, one study found that Latino men who hold traditional views about the division of labor perform more household and childcare tasks compared to White men, especially when they are not employed full-time (McLoyd, Cauce, Takeuchi, & Wilson, 2000). Gender-related attitudes and behaviors are not always consistent; only weak-to-moderate correspondence was reported in a study that included both Latino and White samples (Franco, Sabattini, & Crosby, 2004).

Acculturation, or the process of adapting to the norms of another culture, also influences gender role behavior (Chen, 1992; Golding, 1990). Research on acculturation among Latin American and Asian American families indicates a shift toward greater male involvement; however, Latin American and Asian American women are still responsible for a disproportionate amount of household responsibilities compared to their husbands (Chen, 1992; Golding, 1990; Stohs, 2000). Moreover, more acculturated Mexican American and Asian American women report more dissatisfaction and higher levels of conflict with their spouses over unequal divisions of household labor ("unfair share") compared to less acculturated Mexican American and Asian American women (Stohs, 2000). Indeed, women who are more acculturated to Western values are less likely to hold traditional gender role beliefs than women who are less acculturated (Park & Liao, 2000; Kranau, Green, & Valencia-Weber, 1982), suggesting that acculturation may be a means to make gender ideology and gender role behavior more egalitarian. Perceived fairness about the division of labor seems to reflect in part the level of gender equity at the national level (Greenstein, 2009).

With more relaxed gender norms reported among college students compared to older adults (Galinsky et al., 2008), it is important to examine how experiences and beliefs regarding household division of labor, gender roles, and maternal employment might differ by respondents' cultural heritage. The college years are a time marked by increasing individuality (Arnett, 2007), and students from collectivist cultures may face acculturative stressors associated with fulfilling traditional familial roles while living in an individualistic society. In turn, this conflict could influence their perceptions of gender roles and beliefs about the consequences of maternal employment, and these associations may differ for young men and women.

The Current Study

Taken together, the previous literature suggests that the current work–care climate is one of diminished (but not abolished) gender barriers in occupational realms and stalled progress in domestic spheres. How likely is the next generation to create greater opportunities for sustaining dual commitments to career and family? The current study examines the reported childhood experiences and current beliefs of young adults regarding gender roles and maternal employment. Data were gathered from a contemporary, culturally/ethnically diverse sample of college students regarding household division of labor and maternal labor force participation during their formative years, along with their current gender ideology and beliefs about maternal employment. A unique feature was the over time comparison of college students' beliefs about the consequences of maternal employment for children.

The primary hypotheses of the present study were: (1) College students who reported a more traditional (gender segregated) parental household division of labor during childhood were expected to espouse a more traditional gender ideology and see more costs and fewer benefits of maternal employment for children than students whose parents divided chores more equitably; (2) College students whose mothers participated in the workforce when they were growing up, or who themselves were employed, were expected to express less traditional gender ideologies and be more likely to see fewer costs and more benefits of maternal employment than college students whose mothers were not employed for pay and who did not themselves work for pay; (3) Male students, students who were less acculturated (i.e., at least one parent not born in the United States), and students whose cultural backgrounds were non-Western were expected to have more traditional gender role ideologies and beliefs about the consequences of maternal employment for children, and (4) Current college students were expected to hold less traditional beliefs about the consequences of maternal employment for children than students who attended the very same university in the 1980s and completed the same scale at that time (see Greenberger et al., 1988).

Method

Participants

Participants in the focal sample were 955 undergraduate students at a large public university in the western United States. Students represented a wide range of majors, with most (61%, $n = 584$) clustered in psychology and the social sciences. Students were mostly female (80%) and the mean age of the participants was 20.2 years, ($SD = 1.5$; range $= 17-25$ years). Over one-third (39.3%; $n = 375$) of the students were employed while in college. Few students were married (8.3%, $n = 80$) or had children (3.6%, $n = 34$).

Cultural/ethnic background was diverse and representative of the geographical area. The cultural/ethnic distribution of the sample was 52.5% Asian American, 19.5% European American, 12.5% Hispanic, 4% Middle Eastern, 1.3% African American, 7.2% other/mixed background. The majority of the sample was native to the United States (82.9%). Of those who were non-native to the U.S., the average age of arrival was 8.78 years old ($SD = 5.78$). Parents of students were primarily non-native to the United States; 69% of students had two parents who were non-native to the United States and another 10% of students had one parent who was non-native.

For comparative analyses, we used data collected from two samples of students who attended the same university in the mid-late 1980s as reported in Greenberger et al. (1988). We randomly selected participants from the 2010 sample that matched the first 1988 subsample in terms of the culture/ethnic proportions and gender ($N = 75$). Majors were similar in both samples; students in sample 1 ($N = 75$) had been enrolled in an introductory course in human development and those in sample 2 ($N = 66$) were enrolled in summer session courses in the social sciences. Gender was distributed similarly in both samples: 75% of students in sample 1 and 67% of those in sample 2 were female. The mean ages were 21.6 years for sample 1 and 23.8 years for sample 2. The two 1980s samples were less culturally diverse than the 2010 sample, but they accurately reflected the larger demographics of the county during that era. The 1980s samples were majority European American (64.0% sample 1; 77.4% sample 2), then Asian American (21.3% sample 1; 16.1% sample 2), Hispanic (9.3% sample 1; 6.5% sample 2), African American (2.7% sample 1; 0.9% sample 2), and other/mixed (2.7% sample 1; 0% sample 2).

Measures

Demographic questionnaire. Participants provided demographic information about themselves and their parents. This information included age, gender, culture/ethnicity, country of birth, acculturation status (at least one parent not born in the United States or both parents born in the United States), current paid employment, parental marital status, and length of parental marriage.

Division of labor during childhood. Participants reported the division of responsibilities for eight common household tasks (e.g., meal preparation, laundry, doing house repairs) between their parents. Students were asked to indicate the division of the tasks when they were growing up and currently. The items for this scale were similar to those used in prior studies (e.g., Blair, 1998; Himsel & Goldberg, 2003; Hochschild & Machung, 1989; Lennon & Rosenfield, 1994). Two count scores were created for students' parents. The primary score indicated the total number of tasks that a parent did (range $= 0$ to 9). The second score, used descriptively, indicated participation in same-sex-typed tasks. Mothers' count of female-typed tasks could range from 0 to 5 ($M = 3.34$, $SD = 1.37$); fathers' count of male-typed tasks could range from 0 to 3 ($M = 1.67$, $SD = 0.97$, range $=$ 1 to 3).

Mothers' employment. Students responded to questions about their mothers' current employment and employment history during successive periods of their childhood. Full-time employment was defined as 35 hours/week or more. To address maternal work history, students indicated their mothers' primary employment status (full-time, part-time, not employed) during their infancy (birth–2 years), preschool period (3–5 years), and formal school years (elementary through high school).

Across infancy, preschool, and grade school, 35% of college students' mothers consistently worked full-time, 6% worked part-time, and 15% never worked.

Among the remaining 54% of the sample, 30% had mothers who were initially unemployed or part-time employed and over time increased their labor force participation, 7% began full-time or part-time employment but gradually decreased their labor force participation, 13% were employed variably, and 4% could not accurately recall their mother's employment status during their upbringing (and were subsequently dropped from analyses).

Gender ideology. Students completed a Gender Ideology Scale (see Wenzel & Lucas-Thompson, 2012 for an abbreviated version of the scale). Participants rated on a 5-point Likert-type scale their agreement with 33 statements about roles of men and women. The scale brought together single items and short scales used in prior national surveys and empirical studies of gender equality at work and in the home (e.g., Blankenhorn, 1995; Bureau of Labor Statistics, National Longitudinal Study of Youth 1979; Ferree, 1991; General Social Surveys, 1977; Moen, Erikson, & Dempster-McClain, 1997). Sample items are, "men and women should have an equal chance for any job" and "regardless of who earns more money, husbands and wives should make decisions about the family together." The alpha for the scale was .89.

Beliefs about the consequences of maternal employment for children (BACMEC; Greenberger et al., 1988). Students indicated the extent of their agreement with statements concerning the costs and benefits of maternal employment for children. The 24 items had a 6-point Likert-type response scale. Previous research demonstrated that the BACMEC is a reliable and valid scale with two subscales, a Benefits and a Costs subscale (alphas = .93 for both scales; Greenberger et al., 1988). In the current sample, the reliability coefficients were alpha = .93 for costs, alpha = .93 for benefits, and alpha = .93 for the total scale. A sample Benefits item is, "children whose mothers work are more independent and able to do things for themselves"; an example of a Costs item is, *"children are less likely to form a warm and secure relationship with a mother who is working full-time."*

Procedures

Consent and recruitment. Participants in the 2010 study came from the subject pool at a large public university in the western United States. Students voluntarily participated via the Experimetrix website in exchange for one unit of extra credit. Participants were provided with a link directing them to the Survey Monkey website for the study. The survey took approximately 45 minutes to complete online. The first page included a study information sheet, description of the study, and consent procedures.

For the 1980s sample, the procedures are detailed in Greenberger et al., (1988). To summarize, data were collected in the mid-late 1980s from two samples of students who attended the same university as those participants in the 2010 study. Data from one sample were obtained during the regular academic year and another during the summer session. Students who agreed to participate in the study completed hard copies of the questionnaires.

Data Analysis

Data were screened for outliers, skewness, and collinearity. The main study hypotheses were tested using chi square, paired and unpaired t-tests, ANOVAs, and hierarchical linear regression. For the analyses of main effects, culture/ethnicity was coded into 4 groups: European American, Asian American, Hispanic, and other ethnicities. For the testing of interaction terms, due to the small number of male students who identified as Hispanic or who were in the "Other" category, Hispanic and other cultures/ethnicities were recoded into one group to increase statistical power.

Part of the data analysis included examining how college students' gender ideology and beliefs vary by different maternal employment trajectories. Because mothers self-select into their respective maternal employment trajectories, students whose mothers had different employment trajectories might not have been comparable. To avoid this source of bias, we used propensity score matching such that groups of students whose mothers had different employment trajectories were matched according to demographic and parental factors (e.g., student gender, culture/ethnicity, whether born in the United States, parents' marriage status and length of parents' marriage). In this way, students with similar demographic statuses but contrasting maternal employment trajectories formed matched pairs for the purpose of comparisons. The matching procedure balanced the distribution of the relevant covariates in both targeted and comparison groups.

Results

Propensity scoring procedures were implemented to reduce selection bias. Propensity scores were computed by entering the dummy coded covariates into a stepwise logistic regression analyses to predict treatment group membership using an inclusion criterion of .10 (Rubin, 1997). As can be seen in Tables 1 and 2, before propensity score matching, all of the variables used to match students had significant associations with outcomes, except length of parental marriage. The propensity score match reduced bias below .10 for all covariates except for the likelihood of U.S. birth, which retained a high bias of -0.61 (more students had one parent who was not born in the United States).

Table 1. Differences across Gender, Acculturation, and Marital Status for Gender Ideology and Beliefs about Maternal Employment

	Gender ($N = 921$)						Acculturation ($N = 915$)						Parental marital status ($N = 915$)					
	Male		Female				Parent not born in the United States		Parent born in the United States				Not married		Married		
Outcomes	M	SD	M	SD		t	M	SD	M	SD		t	M	SD	M	SD		t
Gender ideology	2.30	0.47	1.97	0.44		8.47***	2.07	0.47	1.92	0.44		3.87***	2.01	0.49	2.05	0.46		−1.13
Costs	3.19	1.02	2.98	1.01		2.51*	3.10	0.04	2.71	0.08		4.25***	2.88	1.02	3.07	1.01		−2.38*
Benefits	4.26	0.87	3.97	0.79		−4.44***	4.20	0.03	4.22	0.07		−0.34	4.24	0.89	4.19	0.80		0.78

Note. $*p < .05$, $***p < .001$.

Table 2. Gender Ideology, Costs, and Benefits of Maternal Employment Ratings across Cultural Groups

Outcomes	European American M	Asian American M	Hispanic M	Other M	df	Simple effects F	η^2
Gender ideology	1.93$_a$	2.10$_{ab}$	1.96$_b$	2.01	(3, 916)	7.72***	0.02
	(0.45)	(0.47)	(0.40)	(0.44)			
Costs	2.72$_a$	3.18$_{ab}$	2.88$_b$	2.92	(3, 910)	11.03***	0.04
	(1.10)	(0.92)	(1.09)	(1.03)			
Benefits	4.22	4.15	4.29	2.93	(3, 910)	1.48	0.00
	(0.86)	(0.79)	(0.92)	(1.03)			

Note. ***$p < .001$. Standard deviations appear in parentheses below means.
Means with differing subscripts within rows are significantly different at $p < .05$ based on Games-Howell post hoc paired comparisons.

Division of Labor during Childhood

We examined division of household labor between parents as reported by their college-aged children. On average, mothers performed more household tasks ($M = 4.08$, $SD = 1.98$) than fathers ($M = 2.31$, $SD = 1.44$; paired $t(955) = 18.87$, $p < .001$). Tasks were divided along stereotyped lines: Mothers completed more meal preparation, clean up after meals, house cleaning, grocery shopping, and laundry tasks and fathers handled more of the car and house repairs; no differences were found for bill payment. After correcting for the unequal possible range for female and male tasks, we calculated proportional scores: Mothers completed 66% of the female-typed tasks and fathers completed 51% of the male-typed tasks. Married fathers completed more chores ($M = 2.55$, $SD = 1.34$) than did single fathers ($M = 1.61$, $SD = 1.46$, $t(357) = 8.68$, $p < .001$), and married mothers completed significantly fewer chores ($M = 3.93$, $SD = 1.79$) than did single mothers ($M = 4.67$, $SD = 2.34$, $t(313) = 4.41$, $p < .001$). Mothers' and fathers' reported contributions to the division of household labor were negatively associated ($r = -.40$, $p < .001$).

In order to test whether college students' parents' division of labor during childhood was associated with their ideology about gender roles and beliefs about maternal employment, we conducted a series of hierarchical linear regressions. Indices of multicollinearity, Tolerance and Variance Inflation Factor were well within normal ranges, indicating that multicollinearity was not a significant concern in these analyses. After controlling for student gender ($\beta = -.22$, $p < .001$, $R^2 = 5\%$), the greater the number of household tasks that mothers ($\beta = .11$, $p = .002$, $R^2 = .6\%$) and fathers ($\beta = .08$, $p = .04$, $R^2 = .5\%$) completed, the more likely the students were to espouse traditional ideology about gender roles. Associations between parents' division of labor and students' beliefs about the consequences of maternal employment for children were not significant.

Mothers' Employment and Own Employment

Married mothers of the college students reportedly returned to full-time work later than single mothers. A larger proportion of single mothers (70%) compared to married mothers (60%) returned to full-time or part-time work while their child was still an infant ($\chi^2(1, 914) = 6.89, p = .009$). This workforce pattern continued for preschool-age (76% single mothers; 66% married mothers) ($\chi^2(1, 922) = 7.28, p = .008$) and grade school (85% single mothers; 76% married mothers ($\chi^2(1, 937) = 8.13, p = .004$). Labor force participation of mothers dropped for both groups once students reached college-age, but the single/married distinction continued (single, 80%; married, 68%; $\chi^2(1, 940) = 11.99, p = .001$).

After propensity score matching, students whose mothers had worked full-time their entire lives believed that maternal employment had fewer costs for children than did students whose mothers were in the other employment groups (see Table 3). Conversely, compared to the other groups, students whose mothers had never been employed or who had inconsistent labor force participation believed that there were fewer benefits of maternal employment for children.

Following propensity score matching on major covariates, there were no differences in beliefs about the costs of maternal employment for children among students who were employed ($M = 2.98, SD = 1.03$) and students who were not employed ($M = 3.05, SD = 1.00; t(939) = -1.16, p = .25$). However, employed students reported perceiving significantly greater benefits of maternal employment ($M = 4.29, SD = 0.82$) compared to students who were not employed ($M = 4.14, SD = 0.81; t(939) = 2.73\ p < .01$).

Students' Gender Ideology

There were significant differences between male and female college students regarding the proper gender role behavior for men and women. Female students ($M = 2.30, SD = 0.47$) were significantly less likely to endorse traditional gender roles than were male students ($M = 1.97, SD = 0.44; t(268) = 8.47, p < .001$). After propensity score matching, there were no significant differences in gender role attitudes by trajectory of maternal employment (see Table 3). There was, however, a borderline significant finding, such that students whose mothers never worked had more traditional beliefs.

As a group, Asian American students held significantly more traditional gender attitudes than did European American and Hispanic students (see Table 2). Examining the gender by culture interaction, female students of all cultures/

Table 3. Differences across Propensity Score Matched Maternal Employment Trajectories for Gender Ideology and Beliefs about Maternal Employment

	Maternal employment trajectories																		
	Steady full time				Steady part time				Steady not work				Low to high				High to low				Unstable		
	FT	Other			PT	Other			Not work	Other			L-H	Other			H-L	Other			Unstable	Other	
Outcomes	M	M		t	M	M		t	M	M		t	M	M		t	M	M		t	M	M		t
Gender ideology	1.95	2.08		−0.93	2.20	2.08		0.80	2.18	1.96		1.91	2.00	2.11		−0.78	2.16	2.02		0.93	2.11	1.93		1.25
	(0.44)	(0.46)			(0.48)	(0.46)			(0.50)	(0.45)			(0.41)	(0.48)			(0.49)	(0.46)			(0.50)	(0.46)		
Costs	2.64	3.32		−2.49*	3.21	3.53		−0.87	3.46	3.42		0.12	3.01	3.38		−1.44	3.24	3.06		−0.56	3.12	2.74		1.34
	(0.98)	(0.98)			(0.86)	(1.02)			(0.98)	(1.00)			(0.96)	(1.02)			(0.97)	(1.01)			(1.05)	(1.01)		
Benefits	4.34	4.50		−0.79	4.17	4.47		−1.02	4.03	4.55		−2.60*	4.15	4.54		−1.89	4.24	3.93		1.36	4.18	4.70		−2.44*
	(0.83)	(0.80)			(0.54)	(0.83)			(0.83)	(0.81)			(0.84)	(0.81)			(0.74)	(0.83)			(0.80)	(0.82)		

Note. $*p < .05$. Standard deviations appear in parentheses below means.
For the *t*-tests, comparisons were made across two propensity score matched groups. Each analysis compared the reference group to all others in the sample that were selected for matching ($n = 877$). The group sizes for inclusion in analyses were as follows: $n = 313$ Steady Full Time employment, $n = 51$ Steady Part Time employment, $n = 136$ Steady Not Work, $n = 269$ Low to High, $n = 63$ High to Low, and $n = 45$ Unstable.

ethnicities were significantly less likely than Asian American male students ($M = 2.33$, $SD = 0.46$) to report traditional views of gender roles ($F(5, 909) = 21.60$, $p < .001$, $\eta^2 = .11$; Games–Howell post hoc comparisons).

European American ($M = 1.83$, $SD = 0.38$) and Hispanic/Other female students ($M = 1.94$, $SD = 0.40$) also reported significantly less traditional beliefs about gender roles than European American male students ($M = 2.29$, $SD = 0.52$). European American female students reported significantly less traditional beliefs than Asian American female students ($M = 2.03$, $SD = 0.46$) or Hispanic/Other male students ($M = 2.22$, $SD = 0.45$).

In terms of acculturation status, students who had at least one parent born outside of the United States expressed significantly more traditional gender ideology (see Table 1). From post hoc contrasts we saw that Asian American students with at least one non-native parent ($M = 2.10$, $SD = 0.47$) held significantly more traditional views about gender roles than European American students who had two U.S. born parents ($M = 1.88$, $SD = 0.41$; $F(5, 911) = 5.62, p = .01$, $\eta^2 = .03$). Other contrasts were not significant.

Students' Beliefs about Maternal Employment

There were significant differences between genders in perceived costs and benefits of mothers' employment for children. Male students ($M = 3.19$, $SD = 1.02$) saw more costs of maternal employment than did female students ($M = 2.98$, $SD = 1.01$; $t(915) = 2.51$, $p = .01$), and female students saw more benefits ($M = 4.26$, $SD = 0.79$) than did male students ($M = 3.97$, $SD = 0.87$; $t(915) = -4.44$, $p < .001$).

On average, Asian American male and female students thought that there were significantly more costs of maternal employment for children than did European American and Hispanic/Other female students ($F(5,903) = 8.76, p < .001$, $\eta^2 = .05$). Asian American and European American male students believed that there were significantly fewer benefits of maternal employment than did European American and Hispanic/Other female students ($F(5,903) = 4.98, p = .001$, $\eta^2 = .03$).

Students who had at least one parent born outside of the United States perceived more costs for children than students whose parents were both born in the United States when their mothers were employed, but perceived benefits did not differ between these groups (see Table 1). Post hoc contrasts indicated that Asian American students with at least one non-native parent ($M = 3.19$, $SD = 0.92$) saw significantly more costs to children due to maternal employment than did European American students with two native U.S. parents ($M = 2.64$, $SD = 1.09$; $F(5, 905) = 7.59, p < .001$, $\eta^2 = .04$).

Changes over Time in Students' Beliefs about Maternal Employment

Changes over time in students' beliefs about the consequences of maternal employment for children were compared using independent sample t-tests. Compared to male and female students in both 1988 subsamples, contemporary male and female students did not differ on average in their views of either the costs or benefits of maternal employment.

Comparing the matched 2010 sample to the 1988 samples, there were no differences in the costs seen by male or female students. The comparison over time of benefits scores between the college women in the 1988 and 2010 samples almost reached significance in the direction of the 2010 women perceiving more benefits of maternal employment ($M = 4.48$, $SD = 0.75$) than their counterparts in 1988 ($M = 4.23$, $SD = 0.68$; $t(104) = 1.80$, $p = .07$). Male students did not differ over time in seeing benefits of maternal employment, even after matching the culture/ethnic distribution of the original sample.

Discussion

The current study addresses this special issue's topic of sustainability in combining work and family care by examining gender role attitudes and normative beliefs about maternal employment among young adults in the United States. We examined how reported childhood experiences of parental division of labor and maternal employment were related to college students' gender role attitudes and beliefs about the consequences of maternal employment for children. The views of male and female students were contrasted, as were the attitudes and beliefs of students from different cultural backgrounds. A unique feature of this study was a "then and now" comparison between contemporary students' beliefs about maternal employment and the views of college students who attended the same university a generation ago.

Examination of the trajectories of the students' mothers' employment indicated that their mothers participated in the labor force in larger numbers as the students aged during childhood. The subsample of college students reared by single mothers was more likely to have experienced their mothers working outside the home when they were younger than students whose mothers were married. Despite social changes that have made men's and women's employment behavior more comparable for the current generation, concerns about maternal employment posing risks for children persist among today's young adults, particularly among male students and Asian American students. In the data, there was evidence both for changes and stability over time.

The More Things Change

Mirroring national trends in the United States, the majority of the college students in this study had mothers who had returned to paid work when they were very young. Students who experienced their mothers' full-time employment from an early age or their increased labor force participation during their childhood were most likely to perceive fewer costs to maternal employment. Conversely, students whose mothers did not work and/or had an unstable employment history were less likely to see benefits of maternal employment. This association suggests that "change begets change": Students who were raised in a less gendered household in terms of maternal work patterns, perhaps through direct teaching or role modeling, held beliefs about maternal employment that also were less conventional.

Students who experienced their mothers' full-time labor force participation saw fewer costs of maternal employment for children. This finding is similar to past research that revealed higher perceived benefits among college students whose mothers worked full-time when they were young (D'Olio, 2009; Filipokowski & Chambliss, 2009). Being raised by full-time employed mothers may help children see first-hand that maternal employment does not have negative consequences for their development, a perception that is consistent with the effect sizes for the associations between maternal employment and children's functioning (Goldberg et al., 2008; Lucas-Thompson et al., 2010). The significance for the costs, but not the benefits, subscale in these analyses may indicate a cultural lag with students recognizing that maternal employment, while not harmful to children, may not overtly benefit them.

Students who themselves had the experience of working during college were more likely than nonemployed students to see benefits of maternal employment. First-hand experience with the economic benefits of paid employment during the college years may predispose young men and women to expect that employment while engaged in family care can benefit children.

The More Things Stay the Same

Several lines of data indicate that parental domestic and paid work activities during the childhood of the college students and the students' beliefs about maternal employment have not changed greatly from decades' old patterns. As reported by the college students, parents' division of household labor was segregated along gender lines: mothers, especially single mothers, reportedly performed a disproportionate amount of household chores in comparison to fathers, and mothers did more female-typed tasks and fathers did more of the male-typed tasks. This profile is consistent with prior studies of men and women (Bianchi et al. 2000; Craig, 2006). However, students did not differ in their gender ideologies based on when and to what extent their mothers had been employed during their childhoods.

Parental division of labor was related to students' conceptions of male and female roles. Students who endorsed more traditional beliefs about gender roles also reported that their parents engaged in more household tasks. Because parents tended to do more of the chores associated with their own gender, the college students likely were observing gendered household task behavior during their childhood. Given the significant association between parental division of labor and students' attitudes about gender roles, mechanisms of role modeling and/or overt verbal expressions of attitudes by parents might be responsible for maintaining the status quo.

Results of the "then and now" comparisons between the BACMEC scale scores were surprising. By and large, the 2010 students did not differ significantly from students who attended the same university 25 years ago in their perceptions of the costs and benefits of maternal employment for children despite the fact that maternal employment was less normative in the 1980s. The only exception was the borderline significant finding for college women on the benefits subscale: modern young women tended to see slightly more benefits to maternal employment than did the students a generation ago. However, women who work outside the home still may need to contend with stereotypes that they are less effective parents (Okimoto & Heilman, 2012)—and less agentic and committed workers (Fuegen, Biernat, Haines, & Deaux, 2004).

When it came to gender differences, college-aged men saw more costs to maternal employment and women perceived more benefits. Social trends indicate that today's college students can expect to spend their twenties building careers, finding partners and coordinating dual careers (Barnett, Gareis, James, & Steele, 2003). However, the lack of convergence between the sexes about whether maternal employment is desirable suggests that this emerging generation of young (heterosexual) couples will have to resolve their differing views about whether mothers should be employed and balance those views against economic pressures and personal ambitions. Whether or not those negotiations are successful may reflect the couple's gender ideology and the larger socio-cultural context (Kailasapathy & Metz, 2012). In the United States, lingering outdated images of what it means to be a good worker and good mother are compounded by meager support from the federal level for adults who are combining work and family responsibilities (Williams & Cooper, 2004).

Students who themselves were working for pay perceived greater benefits to children when mothers were employed, which suggests that students who were already involved in the labor force also were better acquainted with one tangible benefit of employment, namely that of greater economic resources in the home. Perhaps as more of the young adults become employed, their attitudes toward the potential economic benefits of maternal employment will become even more favorable. However, students' employment status was not significantly related to beliefs about the costs of maternal employment for children. Future research might be directed toward exploring what actions or policies would mitigate young adults' concerns about the costs of maternal employment for children.

Importance of Culture/Ethnicity

The current study illuminated the role of culture/ethnicity as related to attitudes and beliefs about gender roles and maternal employment. Asian American students were the most traditional and European American students the least traditional in their gender role attitudes. Male Asian American students were particularly likely to believe that maternal employment engenders adverse effects for children. European American and Hispanic female students were least likely to see costs of maternal employment for children. These findings about beliefs run counter to cultural/ethnic variation in U.S. women's employment: Asian American women have higher-level jobs and lower rates of unemployment than European American, African American, or Hispanic women (U.S. Department of Labor, Bureau of Labor Statistics, 2010). The discrepancy between Asian American students' traditional beliefs and the nontraditional employment behavior may be a source of stress for these educated young adults if they feel that they need to excel simultaneously in both domestic and employment spheres. Practical constraints (Deutsch, 1999) and opportunities, as well as socioeconomic factors (Franco et al., 2004) may partially explain the lack of correspondence between gender-related beliefs and behaviors.

The current study examined the role of acculturation as defined by having at least one parent born outside the United States. Students who had at least one non-native parent held more traditional gender ideologies and perceived more costs to maternal employment. Tests of interactions between cultural group and acculturation status indicated that Asian American students with at least one non-native parent held more traditional gender role attitudes and saw more costs to maternal employment than the contrast group of European American students with two native-born parents. These findings suggest that having even one parent born outside the United States exposes children from Asian backgrounds to views that value gender segregated roles for men and women—values that are echoed in the self-reports of these children when they reach college-age. Future research could examine whether it is of consequence to have been raised by two versus one non-native parent. It also would be useful to include other measures of acculturation such as language usage and cultural identities and social affiliations.

Limitations

Although this study had a large, culturally diverse sample of college students, several limitations should be noted. First, the sample was one of convenience and was drawn from one university, which limits generalizability. Second, most students were majors in psychology or other social sciences, which also limits generalizability and which produced an unequal gender distribution favoring women. Also, bias due to acculturation status persisted: a disproportionate number of students had at least one non-U.S. born parent. Finally, all measures were obtained from one source, the college students themselves. The self-report measures introduce the problem of common method variance, which can inflate correlations among measures; however, current perspectives suggest that the connection between common method variance and an upward bias in correlations may be overstated (Meade, Watson, & Kroustalis, 2007).

Conclusions

Although the context of work and family roles has changed dramatically over the past few decades, the current generation of college students does not differ much from students decades ago in their beliefs about the consequences of maternal employment for children. Gender differences persisted in the 2010 sample, with women holding less traditional beliefs and attitudes than men, which suggest that as they enter adulthood and long-term relationships, these young men and women will have to negotiate who-does-what because they hold conflicting views. Findings also support the utility of distinguishing beliefs about the costs and from beliefs about the benefits of maternal employment for children because some differences by gender, culture/ethnicity, across time held for one subscale but not the other.

Before the current economic recession, there was a plateau in the labor force participation of mothers with minor children; debate ensued about whether there was an "opting out" trend among married mothers of young children, especially those with high levels of education and income (Day & Downs, 2009; Hoffman, 2009). Beliefs about the expected costs and benefits of maternal employment for children may affect these trends by influencing young adults' decision-making about career sustainability—the type of job and the extent of labor force attachment—while rearing young children. After insuring that the items are meaningful cross-culturally (Gibbons, Hamby, & Dennis, 1997), the importance of beliefs about maternal employment could be examined among young adults in other countries that have experienced increases in the number of employed mothers with young children.

The subsample of students whose childhoods showed evidence of social role change in terms of their mothers working full-time held less traditional views about the impact of maternal employment on children. Although causal links cannot be derived from the current study, the findings are consistent with the position that childhood experiences shape later attitudes and beliefs through processes such as role modeling. Findings also are consistent with the position that national contexts and cultural backgrounds are influential in establishing what is normative regarding work and care roles. We can expect that if, as the current generation of male and female college students assumes their adult roles of worker, partner, and parent and model more gender-equal arrangements both inside and outside the home, their children will see fewer costs of maternal employment and hold views about gender that are consistent with the larger social landscape. However, if the students' ambivalence about mothers' working when their children are young persists, we may continue to see delays in starting families, smaller family size, more part-time paid work for mothers, and more pressure on men to be breadwinners. Perhaps as these college students start accumulating their own work and care experiences, their views about career and care will become more egalitarian. Taken together, the results of this study showcase the importance of ascertaining the work-life views and expectations of young adults within a framework that includes gender, culture/ethnicity, and childhood experiences.

References

Arnett, J. J. (2007). Emerging adulthood: What is it, and what is it good for? *Child Development Perspectives*, *1*, 68–72. doi: 10.1111/j.1750-8606.2007.00016.x.

Aryee, S., Srinivas, E. S., & Tan, H. H. (2005). Rhythms of life: Antecedents and outcomes of work-family balance in employed parents. *Journal of Applied Psychology*, *90*, 132–146.

Barnett, R. C., Gareis, K. C., James, J. B., & Steele, J. (2003). Planning ahead: College seniors' concerns about career-marriage conflict. *Journal of Vocational Behavior*, *62*, 305–319.

Bianchi, S. M., Milkie, M. A., Sayer, L. C., & Robinson, J. P. (2000). Is anyone doing the housework? Trends in the gender division of household labor. *Social Forces*, *79*, 191–228.

Blair, S. L. (1998). Work roles, domestic roles, and marital quality: Perceptions of fairness among dual-earner couples. *Social Justice Research*, *11*, 313–336. doi: 10.1023/A:1023290917535.

Blankenhorn, D. (1995). *Fatherless America: Confronting our most urgent social problem*. New York: Basic Books.

Bureau of Labor Statistics, U.S. Department of Labor. National Longitudinal Survey of Youth 1979 cohort, 1979–2002 (rounds 1–20) [computer file]. *Produced and distributed by the Center for Human Resource Research, The Ohio State University*. Columbus, OH, 2002.

Chen, H. (1992). *Chinatown no more: Taiwan immigrants in contemporary New York*. Ithaca, NY: Cornell University Press.

Chilman, C. S. (1993). Hispanic families in the United States: Research perspectives. In H. P. McAdoo (Ed.), *Family ethnicity: Strength in diversity* (pp. 141–163). Newbury Park, CA: Sage.

Cochran S., & Chambliss, C. (2009). The relationship between full-time and part-time maternal employment during the preschool years and young adults' attitudes about maternal work status and career aspirations. In C. Chambliss (Ed.), *Maternal employment: Marvel or menace* (pp. 25–60). New York, NY: Nova Science Publishers, Inc.

Craig, L. (2006). Does father care mean fathers share? A comparison of how mothers and fathers in intact families spend time with children. *Gender and Society*, *20*, 259–281.

Davis, S. N., & Greenstein, T. N. (2009). Gender ideology: Components, predictors and consequences. *Annual Review of Sociology*, *35*, 87–105. doi: 10.1146/annurev-soc-070308-115920.

Day, J. C., & Downs, B. (2009). *Opting-out: An exploration of labor force participation of new mothers.* Presented at the Population Association of America, 2009 Annual Meeting, Detroit, Michigan.

D'Olio, C. M. (2009). Male and female college students' perception of the costs and benefits associated with maternal employment during the preschool versus elementary school years. In C. Chambliss (Ed.), *Maternal employment: Marvel or menace* (pp. 25–60). New York: Nova Science Publishers, Inc.

Ferree, M. (1991). The gender division of labor in two-earner families. *Journal of Family Issues, 12*, 158–180.

Filipokowski, J. N., & Chambliss, C. (2009). College students' perceptions of the costs andbenefits associated with maternal employment during preschool and their expectations for future spouse, self and family. In C. Chambliss (Ed.), *Maternal employment: Marvel or menace* (pp. 25–60). New York, NY: Nova Science Publishers, Inc.

Franco, J. L., Sabattini, L., & Crosby, F. J. (2004). Anticipating work and family: Exploring the associations among gender-related ideologies, values, and behaviors in Latino and White families in the United States. *Journal of Social Issues, 60*, 755–766.

Fuegen, K., Biernat, M., Haines, E., & Deaux, K. (2004). Mothers and fathers in the workplace: How gender and parental status influence judgments of job-related competence. *Journal of Social Issues, 60*, 737–754. doi:10.1111/j.0022-4537.2004.00383.x.

Galinsky, E., Aumann, K., & Bond, J. (2008). Times are changing: Gender and generation at work and at home. Retrieved from the Families and Work Institute web site: http://familiesandwork.org/site/research/reports/Times_Are_Changing.pdf.

Garey, A. I. (1999). *Weaving work and motherhood.* Philadelphia, PA: Temple University Press.

Gender Equality Bureau (2004). *Women in Japan today 2004.* Retrieved January 22, 2011 http://www.gender.go.jp/english_contents/women2004/index.html.

General Social Surveys 1977, 1986. NORC. University of Chicago, Chicago, IL.

Gibbons, J. L., Hamby, B. A., & Dennis, W. D. (1997). Researching gender-role ideologies internationally and cross-culturally. *Psychology of Women Quarterly, 21*, 151–170.

Goldberg, W. A., Prause, J., Lucas-Thompson, R., & Himsel, A. (2008). Maternal employment and children's achievement in context: A meta-analysis of four decades of research. *Psychological Bulletin, 134*, 77–108. doi: 10.1037/0033-2909.134.1.77.

Golding, J. M. (1990). Division of household labor, strain, and depressive symptoms among Mexican Americans and Non-Hispanic Whites. *Psychology of Women Quarterly, 14*, 103–117. doi: 10.1111/j.1471-6402.1990.tb00007.x.

Greenberger, E., Goldberg, W. A., Crawford, T. J., & Granger, J. (1988). Beliefs about the consequences of maternal employment for children. *Psychology of Women Quarterly, 12*, 35–59. doi:10.1111/j.1471-6402.1988.tb00926.x.

Greenstein, T. N. (2009). National context, family satisfaction, and fairness in the division of household labor. *Journal of Marriage and Family, 71*, 1039–1051. doi: 10.1111/j.1741-3737.2009.00651.x.

Himsel, A., & Goldberg, W. A. (2003). Social comparisons and the division of housework among dual-earner couples: Implications for satisfaction and role strain. *Journal of Family Issues, 24*, 843–866.

Hoffman, S. D. (2009). The changing impact of marriage and children on women's labor force participation *Monthly Labor Review, 132*, 3–14.

Hoffman, L., & Youngblade, L. (1999). *Mothers at work: Effects on children's well-being.* Cambridge, UK: Cambridge University Press.

Hochschild, A. R., & Machung, A. (1989). *The second shift.* New York: Viking.

Hook, J. L. (2006). Care in context: Men's unpaid work in 20 countries, 1965–2003. *American Sociological Review, 71*, 639–660.

Juhn, C., & Potter, S. (2006). Changes in labor force participation in the United States. *Journal of Economic Perspectives, 20*, 27–46.

Kailasapathy, P., & Metz, I. (2012). Work-family conflict in Sri Lanka: Negotiations of exchange relationships in family and at work. *Journal of Social Issues, 68*(4), 790–813.

Korabik, K., Lero, D. S., & Whitehead, D. L. (Eds.). (2008). *Handbook of work-family integration.* London, England: Elsevier.
Kranau, E. J., Green, V., & Valencia-Weber, G. (1982). Acculturation and the Hispanic woman: Attitudes toward women, sex-role attribution, sex-role behavior, and demographics. *Hispanic Journal of Behavioral Sciences, 4,* 21–40.
Kreider, R. M., & Elliott, D. B. (2009). America's families and living arrangements: 2007. *Current Population Reports, P20–561.* Washington, DC: U.S. Census Bureau.
Kroska, A., & Elman, C. (2009). Change in attitudes about employed mothers: Exposure,interests, andgender ideology discrepancies. *Social Science Research, 38,* 366–382. doi: 10.1016/j.ssresearch.2008.12.004.
Lennon, M. C., & Rosenfield, S. (1994). Relative fairness and the division of housework: The importance of options. *American Journal of Sociology, 100,* 506–531. doi: 10.1086/230545.
Lucas-Thompson, R. G., Goldberg, W. A., & Prause, J. (2010). Maternal work early in the lives of children and its association with achievement and behavior problems: A meta-analysis. *Psychological Bulletin, 136,* 915–942. doi: 10.1037/a0020875.
McLoyd, V., Cauce, A. M., Takeuchi, D., & Wilson, L. (2000). Marital processes and parental socialization in families of color: A decade review of research. *Journal of Marriage and the Family, 62,* 1070–1093.
Meade, A. W., Watson, A. M., & Kroustalis, C. M. (2007). *Assessing common methods bias in organizational research.* Paper presented at the 22nd Annual Meeting of the Society for Industrial and Organizational Psychology, New York.
Moen, P., Erickson, M. A., & Dempster-McClain, D. (1997). Their mothers' daughters? The intergenerational transmission of gender role orientations in a world of changing roles. *Journal of Marriage and the Family, 59,* 281–293.
National Alliance for Caregiving (2009). *Executive summary: Caregiving in the U.S.* National Alliance for Caregiving and the AARP. Retrieved from http://www.caregiving.org/data/CaregivingUSAllAgesExecSum.pdf. Accessed January 10, 2010.
NiDitale, M., & Boraas, S. (2000). The labor force experience of women from 'Generation X.' *Monthly Labor Review, 125,* 3–16.
Okimoto, T. G., & Heilman, M. E. (2012). The "bad parent" assumption: How gender stereotypes affect reactions to working mothers. *Journal of Social Issues, 68*(4), 704–724.
Pailhe, A., & Solaz, A. (2006). Time with children: Do fathers and mothers replace each other when one parent is unemployed? *European Journal of Population, 24,* 211–236. doi: 10.1007/s10680-007-9143-5.
Park, J., & Liao, T. F. (2000). The effect of multiple roles of South Korean married women professors: Role changes and the factors which influence potential role gratification and strain. *Sex Roles, 43,* 571–591.
Rubin, D. B. (1997). Estimating causal effects from large data sets using propensity scores. *Annals of Internal Medicine, 127,* 757–763.
Smola, S. W., & Sutton, C. D. (2002). Generational differences: Revisiting generational work values for the millennium. *Sex Roles, 23,* 363–382. doi: 10.1002/job.147.
Stohs, H. J. (2000). Multicultural women's experience of household labor, conflict, and equity. *Sex Roles, 42,* 339–361.
Treas, J., & Drobnic, S. (Eds.). (2010). *Dividing the domestic: Women, men and household work in cross-national perspective.* Palo Alto, CA: Stanford University Press.
Triandis, H. C. (1995). *Individualism and collectivism.* New York: Simon & Schuster.
U.S. Department of Labor, Bureau of Labor Statistics. (2010). *The editor's desk.* Retrieved from http://bls.gov/opub/ted/2010/ted_2010. Accessed May 5, 2012.
Wenzel, A. J., & Lucas-Thompson, R. G. (2012). Authenticity in college-aged males and females, how close others are perceived, and mental health outcomes. *Sex Roles, 67,* 334–350.doi: 10.1007/s11199-012-0182-y.
Williams, J. C., & Cooper, H. C. (2004). The public policy of motherhood. *Journal of Social Issues, 60,* 849–865. doi: 10.1111/j.0022-4537.2004.00390.x.

Yang, N., Chen, C. C., Choi, J., & Zou, Y. (2000). Sources of work-family conflict: A Sino-U.S. comparison of the effects of work and family demands. *Academy of Management Journal, 43,* 113–123.

WENDY A. GOLDBERG is a Professor in the Department of Psychology and Social Behavior in the School of Social Ecology at the University of California, Irvine and holds a courtesy appointment in the Department of Education. She received her PhD from the University of Michigan and did postdoctoral work at Northwestern University. She is a member of several professional societies including the *Society for Research in Child Development* and the *American Psychological Society.* Her numerous scholarly articles and several books broadly concern the family context of parenting and child development. Recent empirical articles feature meta-analytic reviews of the associations between maternal employment and child development.

ERIN KELLY is an advanced doctoral student in the Department of Psychology and Social Behavior. Her main research interests include factors related to risk and resilience for psychopathology and violence for both those working and treated in public institutions (i.e., mental hospitals, domestic violence centers, juvenile justice facilities). She has extensive experience in data collection and analysis of large datasets and collaborates with Dr. Goldberg on work–family research. She has published in several journals including the *Journal of Clinical Psychiatry.*

NICOLE MATTHEWS is a doctoral candidate in the Department of Psychology and Social Behavior at the University of California, Irvine. She earned her BA with Honors at the University of California, Santa Barbara and her MA from UC Irvine. Her dissertation research concerns factors related to theory of mind performance among children with and without Autism Spectrum Disorders. She has completed several studies of early social cognition among children with and without autism, including the examination of family factors, such as sibling relationships, and has published her work in *Developmental Science.* Nicole has collaborated with Dr. Goldberg on autism research and on projects related to work and family.

HANNAH KANG is a graduate student in the Department of Psychology and Social Behavior at the University of California, Irvine. She completed her MA degree in 2010 in Social Ecology. Her research interests broadly include culture and emotion and how parent–child attachment affects children's socio-emotional development. Currently she is working on her dissertation proposal exploring how parent factors, such as discipline and warmth, affect the academic and socio-emotional development in Caucasian, Asian, and Hispanic children from kindergarten up to eighth grade.

WEILIN LI is a doctoral student in the Department of Education at the University of California, Irvine. Her research focuses on early childhood education, maternal employment, and research methodology. She currently is working on a meta-analysis project for the National Forum on Early Childhood Policy and Programs and a research project on early childhood education and school readiness for the Institute on Education Sciences.

MARIYA SUMAROKA earned her MA from UC Irvine in the Department of Psychology and Social Behavior. Her research interests include the developmental consequences of child maltreatment and early deprivation, and physiological reactivity to stress in special needs and typically developing children. She recently completed a proposal to study how unemployment contributes to rates of child abuse.

The "Triple-N" Model: Changing Normative Beliefs about Parenting and Career Success

Steven Poelmans*
EADA Business School

In the discussion of the special issue on Sustainability in Combining Career and Care, Poelmans identifies common themes across all contributions and derives an inclusive model incorporating the insights generated by the different contributors. Using an exemplary hypothetical case, Poelmans effectively shows how the crucial influence of normative beliefs about working parents and careers is imbedded in multiple layers of context created by the spousal relationship, the occupation, the organization, and the national or ethnic culture. In order to challenge the status quo and to change multilevel normative beliefs about parenting and career success, Poelmans develops and calls for further research on the "Triple-N Model," where "Triple N" stands for (1) Nominating Norms, (2) Navigating Norms, (3) and creating New, No-nonsense Norms.

This special issue on sustainability in combining career and care of the *Journal of Social Issues* offers a wide variety of papers reporting studies (of perceptions) of parenting, work–family conflict, and career success (Van Engen, Vinkenburg, & Dikkers, 2012). The variables studied cover a broad spectrum situating individual behavior, emotion and cognition within dyadic, organizational, and socio-cultural contexts, as can be expected in a journal dedicated to the psychological study of social issues. The methods used reflect both quantitative (e.g., laboratory experiments and surveys) and qualitative research orientations (e.g., interviews), offering both large-scale comparisons and in-depth discussions. Combined, the manuscripts in this issue offer a lot of food for thought related with one of the most challenging problems in our contemporary society—the assurance of gender equity and inclusion of individuals, a condition for both individual wellbeing and organizational success.

---

*Correspondence concerning this article should be addressed to Steven Poelmans, EADA Coaching Competency Center, EADA Business School, Calle Aragón 204, 08011 Barcelona, Spain [e-mail: spoelmans@eada.edu].

As the discussant of this special issue I could submit to the academic norm of comparing and contrasting the studies reported here. Yet, this would not do justice to the rich diversity of theoretical orientations, focus variables and methods used. In order to inspire further research, practice, and agency, I believe it is more useful to look for common themes and derive an inclusive model incorporating the insights generated by the different authors regarding how to challenge the status quo. Something that struck me while reading the different pieces was the presence of a central leitmotiv throughout all papers: the influence of *normative beliefs about working parents and careers* imbedded in the multiple layers of context created by the spousal relationship, the occupation, the organization, and the national or ethnic culture. Normative beliefs are based on group norms, informal rules which groups adopt to regulate and regularize group members' behaviors (Feldman, 1984). Group norms are used as social influence mechanisms to move members' behaviors toward the group's preferred standards (Feldman, 1995). Normative beliefs are specified as an individual's perception about a particular behavior, which is influenced by the judgment of significant others (e.g., parents, spouse, friends, teachers) (Ajzen, 1985; Amjad & Wood, 2009). In other words, it is the extent to which individuals take into account social normative pressures. Taking a closer look at normative beliefs is a worthwhile effort, because according to the theory of planned behavior (Ajzen, 1985), normative beliefs are important precursors of behavioral intentions.

Okimoto and Heilman (2012) operationalize the concept of the "bad mother" assumption evaluating judgments of parental performance and interpersonal appeal, based on a comparison of mothers' characteristics and behavior with one's normative beliefs about parenthood; Botsford Morgan and King (2012) conceptualize work–family guilt as an emotion that adversely affects an individual, and that can occur when one's behavior violates the norms of how one believes one should balance the demands of work and family responsibilities. Vinkenburg, Van Engen, Coffeng, and Dikkers (2012) examine employment decisions based on anticipated commitment and competency of mothers and fathers in function of the research participants' normative beliefs of parents' ideal work–home care division; Herman and Lewis (2012) discuss how individuals' sense of entitlement is embedded in belief systems or cultures of the organizations and national cultures they live and work in; Goldberg, Kelly, Matthews, Kang, Li, and Sumaroka (2012) study university students' beliefs about gender roles and the costs and benefits of maternal employment for children across two generations and multiple cultures/ethnicities; Hall, Lee, Kossek, and Las Heras (2012) offer an in-depth study of how individuals who chose to reduce their work schedules conceptualize and enact their criteria of career success, and how discrepancies between individually held beliefs and real life experiences can lead to varying levels of wellbeing; Van Veldhoven and Beijer (2012) propose that the private life context can be expected to affect levels of work-to-family conflict indirectly through descriptive and injunctive norms (Eagly & Karau, 2002) held by individuals themselves or by others in the work environment on what a good parent—and especially a good mother—is or should be like; Kailasapathy and Metz (2012) demonstrate how traditional gender role beliefs in husbands can negatively influence the negotiation of domestic duties in a dual-earner couple. In addition, individuals' own expectations about their probability of success can exclude any attempt to negotiate with managers.

As described by the authors, the lack of submission to—or alignment with norms and beliefs—held by the dominant group or reinforced through the organizational or national culture can have detrimental effects for the individual, above and beyond of the stress of having to combine work and care responsibilities. Examples given by the authors range from guilt (Botsford Morgan & King, 2012), work–family conflict (Van Veldhoven & Beijer, 2012), the lack of spousal support (Kailasapathy & Metz, 2012), unflattering judgments of being a bad mother (Okimoto & Heilman, 2012), a raven mother (Herman & Lewis, 2012), or unsuitable candidate in terms of commitment and competence (Vinkenburg, Van Engen, Coffeng, & Dikkers, 2012). In some cases individuals have little or no choice or control over their situation, as the characteristics used to penalize them are given by birth (e.g., gender, ethnicity, culture), representing a direct violation of the U.N. International Bill of Human Rights. In other cases individuals do have a choice (e.g., marriage, having children, work, have a career), but the discrimination or stereotyping is nonetheless fundamentally unfair, as it concerns basic human motives.

In order to get a better idea of why people discriminate against others based on fundamental, often unchangeable traits or vital choices, we can turn to social identity theory (Tajfel & Turner, 1986). This theory was originally conceptualized as a mega-theory in that it can explain the universal effects of social categorization and group membership regardless of the specific group (Mor Barak, 2011). Social identity theory proposes that people use social categorizations to order their social environment, and attach values to these categories to constitute social identity (Turner & Giles, 1981). Social pressures to positively evaluate one's own groups (e.g., men, managers) through in-group/out-group comparisons lead social groups to attempt to differentiate themselves from others, and maintain or achieve superiority over an out-group (e.g., women, employees). A crucial mechanism to reinforce in-group membership is the adherence to norms and beliefs of the group. Here we use the word "norm" in a first possible meaning according to Encyclopedia Britannica, i.e. *"a principle of right action binding upon the members of a group and serving to guide, control, or regulate proper and acceptable behavior."* Whereas social identity theory gives some insight why we have a basic need for putting people in categories and distancing or judging others to defend our own identity, what is more important for organizational change agents is to know how to deal with stereotypes, unfair attributions, and a lack of support and resources for individuals in the out-group. In the remainder of this manuscript I will formulate a model for changing multilevel normative beliefs about parenting and career success. I will refer to this model as the "Triple-N Model," where "Triple N" stands for (1) Nominating Norms, (2) Navigating Norms, and (3) creating New, No-nonsense Norms.

Phase 1—Intra-Individual Level of Analysis: Norm Nomination—Untangling the Multiple Layers of Socio-Cultural Norms

One of the insights generated by the authors in this volume is that we are all encapsulated in multiple layers of social groups and cultural context that each come along with their own set of norms. The first step in dealing with multiple norms is becoming aware of them. Let's take the hypothetical case of a man called Peter, working in a Spanish university, characterized by strong religious values, who becomes a single parent after a divorce. According to the authors in this volume this may well be the worst case scenario, not only because as a single father he belongs to a high risk group in the population for experiencing work–family conflict (Van Veldhoven & Beijer, 2012). Peter will have to deal with the prejudice of colleagues with a traditional gender role identity (Kailasapathy & Metz, 2012); strong religious values that consider divorce as a "sin"; masculine values and work culture entrenched in SET (science/engineering/technology) professions (Barnard, Powell, Bagilhole, & Dainty, 2010; Herman & Lewis, 2012), conservative values in a country with a familialistic welfare state regime characterized with limited government-enforced work–family policies (Esping-Andersen, 1999), cultural values biased toward masculine oriented standards, and a very low rank on humane orientation (O'Connell, Prieto, & Guttierrez, 2009), part of a larger Latin culture that is more likely to enforce family obligations (Goldberg, Kelly, Matthews, Kang, Li, & Sumaroka, 2012). In the case of Peter, we can see how an already high-level work–family conflict can be exacerbated by social norms that penalize private circumstances. We can also observe how different layers of norms accumulate, and most probably interact, making it very difficult for an individual to confront them. Recognizing or "naming" the norms one is confronting is a first step in untangling them, and deciding how to confront them.

An important distinction that needs to be made in this respect is between norms and normative beliefs. Group norms are inherent to groups to which we may belong or not. They only translate into normative beliefs if the individual adopts the norms or succumbs to the pressure of the representatives of this group. The dilemma of normative beliefs is that on the one hand, adopting normative beliefs is instrumental for adapting to group norms and being accepted. Individuals who violate the group norms are typically sanctioned by other group members. On the other hand, yielding to the norms and normative beliefs may also violate one's true identity.

Phase 2—Inter-Individual and Individual-Group Level of Analysis: Navigation of Norms—Dealing with the Socio-Cultural Norms

Once we know which norms we are dealing with, and where they come from, we can cope with them, one by one, by accepting them, by modifying our perceptions, or by taking them on, with the risk of being sanctioned. Social identity theory has suggested different ways to cope with negative or threatening social identities: (1) individual (inter-group) mobility; (2) group mobility through "social creativity"; and (3) social competition (Mor Barak, 2011; Tajfel & Turner, 1986).

An example of "individual mobility" would be for a woman to adopt "male behavior" such as working hard, competing hard, and sacrificing family to become accepted by male peers and climb the male-dominated corporate ladder. As described by Hall, Lee, Kossek, and Las Heras (2012), some respondents, identified as the "alienated achievers" decide to "play the game," aligning themselves with organizational expectations, despite personal needs or preferences for working part time; only two of the nine (those who were self-employed) were able to sustain a satisfactory reduced-load arrangement in the face of their personal and family life situations and career advancement opportunities. As a consequence they experienced high objective career success but low subjective career success, a high price to pay for obtaining promotions and increasing salaries. In the case of Peter, he may decide to "play the game" and make sure he behaves in the way he is expected to behave. In his case this may imply meeting the male stereotype role behavior and work long hours, sacrifice family time, while maintaining high levels of performance. More than anything, he should make this behavior visible to his colleagues, because he is now a thorn in the eyes of the most fervent defenders of the group norms.

Group mobility through "social creativity" consists in selecting new elements for inter-group comparisons leading to a more favorable evaluation. In their study, Herman and Lewis (2012) point out the importance of showcasing trailblazing, successful working mothers. According to social identity theory this allows individuals in minority groups to compare oneself to an outperforming in-group member and reappraising one's situation. Another example given by Hall et al. (2012) is individuals who redefine or reappraise career success, going against the mainstream, in a way that allows them to be happy with less promotions and salary, and work schedules that allow them to combine career and care demands. For a social identity theorist this would be a case of redefining existing elements for social comparisons so that comparisons become positive. A suggestion of social identity theory is selecting an alternative referent group to which one's in-group is compared instead of the dominant referent. In the case of Peter, he could redefine his own norms of career success, and benchmark himself with female employees instead of male colleagues, and pride himself on juggling work and family responsibilities while meeting standards of performance. He could turn to flexible work arrangements, like working from home. He would take a risk though, because in male-dominated SET industries face time is still the norm, and his colleagues will probably disapprove of his absence of work.

A third, more combative and conflictive strategy is "social competition," or engagement in social action in order to promote change in the status quo and redistribute resources and power in favor of one's in-group. This is the case of several generations of women who fought throughout history for the right to vote, to work, and receive equal pay. A more modest, day-to-day example of this could be found in the women in the Kailasapathy and Metz study (2012), who renegotiate the division of domestic labor and child care with their husbands, and like them, many women in developing countries, trapped between the traditional gender role expectations of their parents and husbands, and the new gender role definitions they observe in developed countries (Poelmans, 2003). Examples may be the foreign students mentioned in the study of Goldberg et al. (2012), who have possibly shifted beliefs about maternal employment thanks to the role model of their mothers and local peers. Upon return to their countries they will no longer take for granted the gender stereotypes that are still pervasive in their home countries, and start a silent revolution. In the contemporary context we can also refer to many male employees who are taking up the parental leave actually allotted to them legally, despite internal and external pressures to return to work earlier. On an organizational level, these are the policy makers, human resource managers and gender experts who actually try to develop new policies and mindsets to counteract discriminative practices. In the case of Peter, he may actually protest against the harassment he is experiencing, and stand up to challenge the normative beliefs of colleagues in his organization that condole this discrimination in order to safeguard their values. His problem may well be that if he dares to voice his concerns this may be seen as a flagrant disloyalty, which might result in losing his job.

Phase 3—Inter-Group Level of Analysis: No-Nonsense—The Development of New "Common Sense" Socio-Cultural Norms of Equity and Leveraging Diversity

It may literally take several generations and centuries of social creativity and competition to reach a stage where we have a critical, organized mass of individuals in our organizations that question dominant mindsets about what is a "good father" or "good mother." In this context we can refer to another meaning of "norm" according to the Encyclopedia Britannica as *"average, a set standard of development or achievement usually derived from the average or median achievement of a large group, a wide-spread or usual practice, procedure, or custom."* An example mentioned in one of the studies in this issue are the Dutch and part-time work (Vinkenburg, Van Engen, Coffeng, & Dikkers, 2012). The fact that these researchers found that participants in their study evaluated men who go against the normative "one-and-a-half model" less favorably, confirms that there is a "one-and-a-half" norm in the first place, something that many other nations around the world look at with envy. The Netherlands is as such a country where a critical mass has been reached—more than 60% of Dutch women work part-time and the number of men in part-time work is above 15%—and where flexible working is no longer associated with garbage contracts but quality part-time jobs with pro-rated pensions and benefits (Vinkenburg et al., 2012). In our hypothetical example, probably a critical, organized group of divorced employees in his organization may weigh up against the dominant norm and silently support him in his endeavor to meet both individual needs and organizational norms. That is, if this group is ever allowed to form. There is a good chance that the dominant group may "neutralize" any shifts in norms by sanctioning, marginalizing, or firing employees that voice their concerns.

Organizations can resist the global movement toward diversity, or lead the way and provide a light at the end of the tunnel of discrimination, prejudice and stereotyping against gender, marital status, parental status, and career preferences. According to Goldberg, Kelly, Matthews, Kang, Li, and Sumaroka (2012), it requires role models (employed mothers), acculturation, direct life experience (own employment) to change mindsets, and the rate of change may be discouraging, but we should not lose out of sight the final purpose—a free and fair society. This allows me to refer to a third connotation of "norm"—"*an authoritative standard or model.*" Individuals, communities, and organizations need clear, unequivocal standards, created by the highest organs of international governments and organizations around the world, that go beyond the International Bill of Human Rights, and cautious concepts like "inclusion." We need the quiet leadership of courageous individuals who swim upstream and challenge the norms around parenting and career success. We need more studies like the ones reported in this special issue to address these pressing issues. What is needed is an effort to divulgate the science and business cases behind the benefits of diversity, and the absolute necessity of full engagement of talent in all social groups, majorities and minorities, to keep up economic growth and productivity despite declining birth rates. As we have seen in the study of Okimoto and Heilman (2012), the judgment of what is a "bad mother" is deeply programmed in our minds, and therefore we need to reboot, and that starts in the earliest years of education. We need to develop mindfulness and cultural intelligence in employees in order to neutralize "attributional rationalizations" and recognize and embrace evidence that is incongruent with gender stereotypes (Heilman & Haynes, 2005).

The "Triple-N" Research Agenda

Given the importance of normative beliefs underlying stereotypes and discrimination, it is important to sophisticate existing theories of how norms translate in normative beliefs, and under which circumstances individuals yield to or challenge normative beliefs. According to French sociologist Moscovici (1976), social norms can only be changed if members of the minority become respected by the majority, become "one of them," and change the system from within. If we thoroughly understand the mechanism underlying the process of changing norms, we can actually develop strategies to develop normative beliefs around respect for diversity. As pointed out above, these norms are deeply embedded in multiple layers of socio-cultural values at the dyadic, functional, organizational, societal, and cultural level and therefore may elude the awareness of the individual and the scrutiny of the researcher. This means we need interdisciplinary scholarship to study the patterns underlying the development of normative beliefs at various levels of analysis. Psychologists, sociologists, cultural anthropologists, and cross-cultural researchers have done tremendous efforts to map the different values and norms that impinge on human behavior, yet less is known how individuals and groups resolve value conflicts in and between multiple levels of analysis. Of special interest are intra-individual conflicts between individually held normative beliefs, in-group and out-group identity, and socio-demographic characteristics; inter-individual conflicts arising from conflicting normative beliefs between majorities and minorities at work or in the family; and inter-group conflict between dominant groups and minorities. If we understand how individuals and groups resolve these conflicts that do not involve the obvious solution of domination and discrimination, we are one step closer to actually tackling them. This calls for research that allows following individuals and groups over time, through different stages of confrontation, adaptation, or conflict resolution. Case studies and ethnographical studies of individuals and organizations resolving discrimination and promoting inclusion are needed to focus on how minorities have managed to emancipate or how majorities have succeeded to integrate minorities.

The studies published in this special issue confirm we need complex models that describe and predict decision-making in both managers and employees so we can unmask and root out cognitive biases, ill-informed decisions, counter-productive assumptions, less-than-optimal solutions, inefficient rationalizations, actions, and negative learning that limit future action. Many of the normative beliefs described in this special issue stay below the threshold of consciousness while influencing decision-making. Therefore we need more research focused on decision-making in the work–family arena (Poelmans, Greenhaus, & Las Heras, in press; Poelmans, & Sahibzada, 2004). In order to study decision-making, we need methods that allow us to observe decision making over time such as ethnographic and diary research, vignette studies or simulations conducted in a laboratory setting, and methods that allow studying decision making in the context of bargaining and communication between parties, across multiple "fault-lines" of diversity, and across nations (Poelmans, Greenhaus, & Las Heras, in press). Given the importance of emotion and the subconscious, social researchers may profit from collaborating with social/cognitive neuroscientists to design studies that can reveal the triggering of stereotypes and automatic adverse perceptions of out-group individuals. This will require collaboration between researchers working across disciplines, time, and geography, pulling together data collected in multiple sources in order to represent different perspectives. As this type of research is cumbersome, it is often at odds with the pressure to publish. The biggest challenge of researchers working in the arena of diversity and sustainability may well be to design studies that match the complexity of the phenomena they want to unveil.

References

Amjad, N., & Wood, A. M. (2009). Identifying and changing the normative beliefs about aggression which lead young Muslim adults to join extremist anti-Semitic groups in Pakistan. *Aggressive Behavior*, *35*, 514–519. doi: 10.1002/ab.20325

Ajzen, I. (1985). From intentions to actions: A theory of planned behavior. In J. Kuhl & J. Beckmann (Eds.), *Action control: From cognition to behavior* (pp. 11–39). Berlin, Heidelberg, New York: Springer-Verlag.

Barnard, S., Powell, A., Bagilhole, B., & Dainty, A. (2010). Researching UK women professionals in SET: A critical review of current approaches. *International Journal of Gender Science and Technology*, *2*, 361–381. Retrieved from: http://genderandset.open.ac.uk

Botsford Morgan, W. M., & King, E. B. (2012). The association between work-family guilt and pro- and anti-social work behavior. *Journal of Social Issues*, *68*(4), 684–703.

Eagly, A. H., & Karau, S. J. (2002). Role congruity theory of prejudice toward female leaders. *Psychological Review*, *109*(3), 573–598. doi: 10.1037/0033–295X.109.3.573

Esping-Andersen, G. (1999). *Social foundations of postindustrial economics*. New York: Oxford University Press.

Feldman, D. C. (1984). The development and enforcement of group norms. *Academy of Management Review*, *9*, 47–53. Stable URL: http://www.jstor.org/stable/258231

Feldman, D. C. (1995). Group norms. In N. Nicholson (Ed.), *The Blackwell encyclopedic dictionary of organizational behavior*. Cambridge: Blackwell.

Goldberg, W. A., Kelly, E., Matthews, N. B., Kang, H., Li, W., & Sumaroka, M. (2012). The more things change, the more they stay the same: Gender, culture, and college students' views about work and family. *Journal of Social Issues*, *68*(4), 814–837.

Hall, D. T., Lee, M. D, Kossek, E. E., & Las Heras, M. (2012). Pursuing career success while sustaining personal and family well being: A study of reduced-load professionals over time. *Journal of Social Issues*, *68*(4), 742–766.

Heilman, M. E., & Haynes, M. C. (2005). No credit where credit is due: Attributional rationalization of women's success in male-female teams. *Journal of Applied Psychology*, *90*, 905–916. doi: 10.1037/0021–9010.90.5.905

Herman, C., & Lewis, S. (2012). Entitled to a sustainable career? Motherhood in science, engineering and technology. *Journal of Social Issues*, *68*(4), 767–789.

Kailasapathy, P., & Metz, I. (2012). Work-family conflict in Sri Lanka: Negotiations of exchange relationships in family and at work. *Journal of Social Issues*, *68*(4), 790–813.

Mor Barak, M. (2011). *Managing diversity: Toward a globally inclusive workplace*. London, UK: Sage Publications.

Moscovici, S. (1976). Social influence and social change. London: Academic Press.

O'Connell, J. J., Prieto, J. M. & Guttierrez, C. (2009). Managerial culture and leadership in Spain. In J. S. Chhokar, F. C. Brodbeck & R. J. House (Eds.), *Culture and leadership around the world. The globe book of in-depth studies of 25 societies* (pp. 623–654). Mahwah, NJ: Lawrence Erlbaum.

Okimoto, T. G., & Heilman, M. E. (2012). The "Bad Parent" assumption: How gender stereotypes affect reactions to working mothers. *Journal of Social Issues*, *68*(4), 704–724.

Poelmans, S. (2003). The multi-level "fit" model of work and family. Editorial to special section: Work/Family issues across cultures. *International Journal of Cross-Cultural Management, 3*(3), 267–274. doi: 10.1177/1470595803003003001

Poelmans, S. (Ed.). (2005). *Work and family: An international research perspective*. Mahwah, NJ: Lawrence Erlbaum Associates.

Poelmans, S., Greenhaus, J., & Las Heras, M. (Eds.) (2012). *Expanding the boundaries of work-family research: A vision for the future*. London: Palgrave.

Poelmans, S., & Sahibzada, K. (2004). A multi-level model for studying the context and impact of work/family policies and culture in organizations. *Human Resource Management Review, 14*(4), 409–431. doi: 10.1016/j.hrmr.2004.10.003

Tajfel, H., & Turner, J. C. (1986). The social identity theory of intergroup behavior. In S. Worchel & W. G. Austin (Eds.), *Psychology of intergroup relations*. (pp. 7–24). Chicago: Nelson-Hall.

Turner, J. C., & Giles, H. (1981). *Intergroup behavior*. New York: Basil Blackwell.

Van Engen, M. L., Dikkers, E. J., Vinkenburg, C. J. (2012). Sustainability in combining career and care: Challenging normative beliefs about parenting. *Journal of Social Issues, 68*(4), 645–664.

Van Veldhoven, M. J. P. M., & Beijer, S. E. (2012). Gender differences in work-to-family conflict: Does private life context matter? *Journal of Social Issues, 68*, xx-xx.

Vinkenburg, C. J., Van Engen, M. L., Coffeng, J., & Dikkers, J. S. E. (2012). Bias in employment decisions about mothers and fathers: The (dis)advantages of sharing care responsibilities. *Journal of Social Issues, 68*(4), 725–741.

STEVEN POELMANS holds a Master in Organizational Psychology and Marketing Management, and a PhD in Management/OB (IESE Business School). He is currently professor and Director of the Coaching Competency Center at EADA Business School, and Partner-Director of WorkItOut (www.wio.es). For 10 years Dr. Steven Poelmans was professor at IESE Business School where he taught leadership, self-leadership, and coaching to MBA students and executives and organized the biannual International Conference of Work & Family. His research, teaching, and consulting mainly focus on employee wellbeing and flexible work arrangements, cultural intelligence, and coaching, mostly with a cross-cultural perspective. His research was nominated twice (2005; 2008) for the prestigious Rosabeth Moss Kanter Award for the best paper in the multidisciplinary field of work and family. He was invited as a professor to Tunis, Peru, Mexico, Iceland, Belgium, Chile, and New Zealand. He published five books and over a dozen peer-reviewed journal articles and chapters in academic volumes, like JOOP, HRM, AMJ, APIR, IJCCM, and PP.

Statement of Ownership, Management, and Circulation
(All Periodicals Publications Except Requester Publications)

1. Publication Title: Journal of Social Issues
2. Publication Number: 001-652
3. Filing Date: 10/1/12
4. Issue Frequency: Quarterly
5. Number of Issues Published Annually: 4
6. Annual Subscription Price: $988.00
7. Complete Mailing Address of Known Office of Publication: Wiley Subscription Services, Inc., 111 River Street, Hoboken, NJ 07030
Contact Person: E. Schmidichen
Telephone: (201) 748-6346
8. Complete Mailing Address of Headquarters or General Business Office of Publisher: Wiley Subscription Services, Inc., 111 River Street, Hoboken, NJ 07030

9. Full Names and Complete Mailing Addresses of Publisher, Editor, and Managing Editor

Publisher: Wiley Subscription Services, Inc., 111 River Street, Hoboken, NJ 07030

Editor: Sheri R. Levy, Department of Psychology, Stony Brook University, 142 Psychology - B Bldg. Stony Brook, NY 11794

Managing Editor: None

10. Owner:

Full Name	Complete Mailing Address
The Society for the Psychological Study of Social Issues	1901 Pennsylvania NW Ste 901, Washington, DC 20006

11. Known Bondholders, Mortgagees, and Other Security Holders Owning or Holding 1 Percent or More of Total Amount of Bonds, Mortgages, or Other Securities. ☒ None

12. Tax Status: Has Not Changed During Preceding 12 Months

13. Publication Title: Journal of Social Issues
14. Issue Date for Circulation Data: September 2012

15. Extent and Nature of Circulation

		Average No. Copies Each Issue During Preceding 12 Months	No. Copies of Single Issue Published Nearest to Filing Date
a. Total Number of Copies (Net press run)		1804	1718
b. Paid Circulation (By Mail and Outside the Mail)	(1) Mailed Outside-County Paid Subscriptions Stated on PS Form 3541	1476	1426
	(2) Mailed In-County Paid Subscriptions Stated on PS Form 3541	0	0
	(3) Paid Distribution Outside the Mails Including Sales Through Dealers and Carriers, Street Vendors, Counter Sales, and Other Paid Distribution Outside USPS®	0	0
	(4) Paid Distribution by Other Classes of Mail Through the USPS (e.g. First-Class Mail®)	0	0
c. Total Paid Distribution (Sum of 15b (1), (2),(3), and (4))		1476	1426
d. Free or Nominal Rate Distribution (By Mail and Outside the Mail)	(1) Free or Nominal Rate Outside-County Copies Included on PS Form 3541	50	41
	(2) Free or Nominal Rate In-County Copies Included on PS Form 3541	0	0
	(3) Free or Nominal Rate Copies Mailed at Other Classes Through the USPS (e.g. First-Class Mail)	0	0
	(4) Free or Nominal Rate Distribution Outside the Mail (Carriers or other means)	0	0
e. Total Free or Nominal Rate Distribution (Sum of 15d (1), (2), (3) and (4))		50	41
f. Total Distribution (Sum of 15c and 15e)		1526	1467
g. Copies not Distributed		278	251
h. Total (Sum of 15f and g)		1804	1718
i. Percent Paid (15c divided by 15f times 100)		96.72	97.21

16. Publication of Statement of Ownership: ☒ If the publication is a general publication, publication of this statement is required. Will be printed in the December 2012 issue of this publication.

17. Signature and Title of Editor, Publisher, Business Manager, or Owner: Elizabeth Konkle, Associate Financial Manager
Date: 10/1/12

PS Form 3526, September 2006